for
Christopher, Scott,
and Katherine

Contents

Preface   ix

Abbreviations   xiii

Introduction   1

1 Ministerial Vocation, 1625–40   27

2 Poetic Vocation, 1628–42   51

3 Prophetic Vocation, 1641–60   77

4 *Paradise Lost*   115

5 *Samson Agonistes*   151

6 *Paradise Regained*   175

Appendix
   Milton Agonistes: The Date of *Samson Agonistes*   195

Notes   205

Index   229

Preface

This book began, now nearly a decade ago, as a doctoral dissertation at the University of Toronto. Believing that Milton's sense of divine calling was central to an understanding of much that he wrote, I set out to explore the growth of his vocational awareness and to demonstrate, if I could, how this conviction of special election might provide a conceptual framework for his entire literary production and a background against which to set his several careers as poet, 'priest', prophet and pamphleteer. The more familiar I became with his works, the more clear it seemed to me that divine vocation was a unifying theme throughout, although its emphasis changes and it acquires a spiritual and psychological complexity in the later works that is absent in the early material. I was struck by the fact that the early poetry up to and including *Lycidas*, despite its technical virtuosity and apparent assurance of tone, was tentative and essentially experimental, for Milton was engaged both in defining his role as poet-priest and in practising flight on his fledgling Pegasus. I sensed, too, that the truly decisive events later in his life were less immediately personal than national, less to be associated with his marriage failure and blindness than with his commitment to what he saw as England's divinely ordained destiny and the (consequently) traumatic experience of the Restoration in 1660. From the early 1640s, when he entered the controversy over episcopacy, Milton believed that his private calling was inextricably linked with and subservient to the national mission, and he came progressively to identify himself within the tradition of Old Testament prophecy. Now, for someone who had served for twenty years as the spokesman of national calling and had expended his divinely entrusted talents in the defence of theocratic republicanism, the Restoration made vocational reassessment inevitable; and this reassessment is reflected, I was convinced, in the poems that Milton published in 1667 and 1671. A concern with vocation is omnipresent in the last three poems, and I felt certain that in some way the protagonists in these works—all of whom undergo vocational trials—provided Milton with correlatives for his own experience and enabled him, especially in the cases of Samson and the postlapsarian Adam, to achieve emotional calm and vocational redefinition as he traced in their spiritual growth his own gradual return to divine favour, rising phoenix-like from the smouldering ashes of the Puritan experiment.

Although my view of Milton's career and the place of divine vocation in his works remains substantially unaltered, the final product bears little resemblance in many ways to the original dissertation. While much of the material which appeared in the thesis reappears here, it has been considerably reworked and reorganised. Further reading has often enabled me to sharpen and extend the argument; and, at the same time, I have benefited greatly from the energies of Milton's critics, whose writings over the past ten years have deepened my appreciation of his achievement. I regret that Christopher Hill's *Milton and the English Revolution* (Faber, 1977) reached me too late to be taken into consideration; it is, I think, an important study, and a knowledge of it would have enabled me to exclude some of the historical material which perhaps makes my third chapter seem now somewhat too digressive.

Like everyone who writes on Milton I am indebted to the Miltonists whose insights form the foundation and much of the superstructure of my own approach. As an alumnus of the University of Toronto, it is, I suppose, inevitable that two such critics should be A. S. P. Woodhouse and Arthur E. Barker; but I owe a great deal, too, to such readers as E. M. W. Tillyard, Joseph H. Summers, Barbara K. Lewalski, Stanley E. Fish, Michael Fixler and others whose names appear in the notes at the end of this volume. Still other debts are of a more immediately personal nature. Professor W. J. Barnes of Queen's University (Canada) prompted my initial interest in Milton and helped to focus my early speculations about the role of vocation in the last poems. Professor H. R. MacCallum of the University of Toronto supervised the project as it took shape in the form of a dissertation; his deep understanding of Milton and his benevolent criticism of my work have saved me, both then and since, from innumerable errors of fact and judgement. I am grateful also to several friends and colleagues at the University of Western Australia who graciously set aside their own work to read the typescript at various stages of its development and to offer their suggestions: Mr D. A. Ormerod, Dr T. H. Gibbons and Dr C. J. Wortham. Special thanks are due to Dr Richard D. Jordan of the University of Melbourne, a friend and fellow Miltonist, who read through much of the final typescript with minute attention; his advice, although I have not always followed it, has been invaluable. My greatest debt, however, is to my family. My wife has experienced the writing of this book along with me and it could never have been completed without her constant sympathy and support; and our children, to whom the work is dedicated, have yielded precedence to Milton with a patience and understanding at which I can only marvel.

Early versions of portions of this book have already appeared in print. Chapters 1 and 2 are based on my paper 'Poet-Priest: Vocational Tension in Milton's Early Development' which was published in *Milton Studies*, ed. James D. Simmonds, VIII (1975), 41–69. Similarly, Chapter 5 is based on an article entitled 'Vocation and Spiritual Renovation in *Samson Agonistes*' which appeared in *Milton Studies*, II (1970), 149–74. Finally, I wish to thank the Yale University Press for permission to quote from *Complete Prose Works of John Milton*, general editor Don M. Wolfe (1953–*), and also Longmans, Green and Co Ltd for permission to quote from *The Poems of John Milton*, edited by John Carey and Alastair Fowler (1968). For the sonnets, however, I have used *Milton's Sonnets*, ed. E. A. J. Honigmann (London: Macmillan, 1966).

Perth, Australia
28 April 1978   J.S.H.

Abbreviations

CV	*A Variorum Commentary on the Poems of John Milton.* Merritt Y. Hughes, general editor. Projected in 5 vols (New York and London, 1970–*).
CW	*The Works of John Milton.* F. A. Patterson, general editor. 18 vols, plus 2 vols Index (New York, 1931–8).
DB	*Dictionary of the Bible.* James Hastings, editor. Revised edition (New York, 1963).
DDC	Milton, *De Doctrina Christiana.*
ELH	*A Journal of English Literary History.*
ES	*English Studies.*
JEGP	*Journal of English and Germanic Philology.*
LM	David Masson. *The Life of John Milton.* 6 vols, plus Index (first published, 1880; reprinted, New York, 1965).
MB	William Riley Parker. *Milton: A Biography.* 2 vols (Oxford, 1968).
MLN	*Modern Language Notes.*
MLQ	*Modern Language Quarterly.*
MLR	*Modern Language Review.*
MQ	*Milton Quarterly.*
ODCC	*The Oxford Dictionary of the Christian Church.* F. L. Cross and E. A. Livingstone, editors. Second edition (London, New York and Toronto, 1974).
OED	*Oxford English Dictionary.*
PL	Milton, *Paradise Lost.*
PM	*The Poems of John Milton.* John Carey and Alastair Fowler, editors (London and Harlow, 1968).
PMLA	*Publications of the Modern Language Association.*
PQ	*Philological Quarterly.*
PR	Milton, *Paradise Regained.*
RES	*Review of English Studies.*
SA	Milton, *Samson Agonistes.*
SEL	*Studies in English Literature.*

SM   *The Student's Milton.* F. A. Patterson, editor. Revised
            edition (New York, 1957).
SOED   *The Shorter Oxford English Dictionary.* Third edition, re-
            vised (Oxford, 1975).
SP   *Studies in Philology.*
TLS   *The Times Literary Supplement.*
UTQ   *University of Toronto Quarterly.*
YP   *Complete Prose Works of John Milton.* Don M. Wolfe,
            general editor. Projected in 8 vols (New Haven and
            London, 1953–*).

Introduction

In the seventeenth century the term *vocation*, like its cognate *calling*, commanded a wide variety of meaning. For present purposes, however, this multiplicity may be reduced to two denotations which are particularly important in terms of Milton's understanding of *vocation*:

1. The action of God in calling persons or mankind to a state of salvation or union with Himself;
2. The action of God in calling a person to exercise some special (especially spiritual) function, or to fill a certain position; the particular function or station to which a person is called by God.[1]

The difference between these meanings is essentially that between a call to faith and a call to works, and the origin of the distinction may be traced to biblical usage. In the Old Testament, where personal election is invariably subordinate to the idea of service, vocation is never an end in itself but is rather seen as a means to a wider end; that is, men are called to extra-personal duties and functions, and their vocations are contingent rather than absolute. Old Testament election is primarily national, and individual calling is meaningful only within the context of Israel's election 'a kingdom of priests and an holy nation' (Exodus 19: 6). The patriarchs, monarchs and prophets of ancient Israel were marked out for active service, for works; the object of their election was not personal salvation but non-personal ministration to a covenanted people, and their function was to serve as divinely motivated instruments of the national mission.[2] In the New Testament, on the other hand, the vocational emphasis is reversed. Election is primarily personal and individual, and attention is focused on personal election to eternal salvation. The noun κλῆσις, 'calling' is reserved almost exclusively for a call to faith and salvation,[3] and the same is true of the verbal adjective κλητός—e.g., 'For many are called (πολλοὶ γάρ εἰσιν κλητοί) but few are chosen'

I

(Matthew 22: 14). Nevertheless, while the aspect of calling as active service in this world falls into the background in the New Testament, it does not in any sense disappear, for the believer is continually reminded of the necessity of performing good works: 'Let your light so shine before men, that they may see your good works, and glorify your Father which is in heaven' (Matthew 5: 16). Yet still, the New Testament emphasis is on election as an end in itself; a man is *called* to faith and salvation, and good works are then enjoined as a seal and pledge of that calling.

Both the Old Testament stress on vocation to extra-personal service and the New Testament emphasis on vocation to personal election are important features of Reformed thought in general and Milton's theology in particular.

(i) VOCATION AND SOTERIOLOGY

> *Be thou partaker of the afflictions of*
> *the gospel according to the power of God;*
> *Who hath saved us, and called us with an*
> *holy calling, not according to our works,*
> *but according to his own purpose and*
> *grace, which was given us in Christ Jesus*
> *before the world began.*
> (2 Timothy 1: 8–9)

In Reformed dogmatics the term *vocation* is used to describe the calling of sinful mankind to salvation. Thus, Leonardus Riissenius in *Compendium Theologiae didactico-elencticae* (1695) asserts that '*Vocatio*, which broadly is derived from *vox*, is the act of God by which through the preaching of the Word and the power of the Holy Spirit He brings man from the state of sin to the state of grace' (xiii, 3); and similarly Samuel Maresius declares in his *Collegium theologicum* (1662) that 'calling' is the divine act 'by which we are transferred from the first Adam to the second, from death, darkness and the state of sin to life, light and the covenant of grace, in order that being planted in Christ the Head and Root we may live and bring forth good fruits' (xi, 2).[4] The definitions given by these two continental theologians are in harmony with Milton's statement in *De Doctrina Christiana*, I, xvii: 'VOCATION is that natural method of renovation by which GOD THE FATHER,

ACCORDING TO HIS PRECONCEIVED PURPOSE IN CHRIST, INVITES FALLEN MEN TO A KNOWLEDGE OF THE WAY TO PLACATE AND WORSHIP HIS GODHEAD AND, OUT OF GRATUITOUS KINDNESS, INVITES BELIEVERS TO SALVATION SO THAT THOSE WHO DO NOT BELIEVE ARE DEPRIVED OF ALL EXCUSE.' (*YP*, VI, pp. 453-4)

This general doctrine of vocation, however, is subdivided in Reformed theology into a *vocatio universalis* and a *vocatio specialis*. Universal or 'natural' calling is held, in the words of the Leiden *Synopsis purioris Theologiae* (1581), to be that 'by which men one and all are invited by the common proofs of nature to the knowledge and worship of God their Creator'. The 'common proofs of nature' are either *internal* since they are 'inscribed on the hearts of all men' or *external* since they are 'graven on the things created by God'; that is, they manifest themselves either through the operation of conscience and *recta ratio*[5] or through God's self-revelation in the *natura naturata*. Special or 'supernatural' calling, on the other hand, is defined (still in the words of the Leiden *Synopsis*) as being that 'by which God calls some out of the entire human race from the defilements of this world to supernatural knowledge of Jesus Christ our Redeemer and to saving participation in his benefits by the ministry of the Gospel and the power of the Holy Spirit'.[6] Milton also makes a distinction between universal and special calling in his chapter on Vocation in *De Doctrina Christiana*:

> Vocation, then, is either general or special. It is by general vocation that God invites all men to a knowledge of his true godhead. He does this in various ways, but all of them are sufficient to his purpose: [cites John 1: 9, Acts 14: 17, Romans 1: 19 and 2: 15] . . . Special vocation means that God, whenever he chooses, invites certain selected individuals, either from the so-called elect[7] or from the reprobate, more clearly and more insistently than is normal. (*YP*, VI, p. 455)

God reiterates the same distinction in *Paradise Lost*, III, 183-90:

> Some I have chosen of peculiar grace
> Elect above the rest; so is my will:
> The rest shall hear me call, and oft be warned
> Their sinful state, and to appease betimes

The incensed Deity, while offered grace
Invites; for I will clear their senses dark,
What may suffice, and soften stony hearts
To pray, repent, and bring obedience due.

Since both general and special calling are closely associated with
renovation,[8] Milton goes on in *De Doctrina Christiana* to discuss the
immediate effects of the call: 'The change in man which follows
his vocation is that whereby the mind and will of the natural man
are partially renewed and are divinely moved towards knowledge
of God, and undergo a change for the better, at any rate for the
time being.' (*YP*, VI, p. 457) This change for the better manifests
itself in penitence and faith.

There is one further point about Milton's understanding of
vocation that requires brief comment—namely, the relationship
between vocation and renovation. Renovation, which is the state
of grace into which fallen and condemned mankind is brought by
God's free mercy (cf. note 8), takes place either naturally or
supernaturally. Vocation is an aspect of natural renovation *only*:
'When I say that [renovation] takes place naturally I mean that it
affects only the natural man. This includes vocation, and the
alteration in the natural man which follows it. VOCATION is [a]
natural method of renovation. . . .' (Ibid., p. 453) On the other
hand, supernatural renovation is the divine operation which
'restores man's natural faculties of faultless understanding and of
free will more completely than before' and, in addition, 'makes the
inner man like new and infuses by divine means new and supernatural faculties into the minds of those who are made new.'
(Ibid., p. 461). The distinction between natural and supernatural
renovation is this: the former depends upon a human response to a
divine call, the latter is the work of God alone. This difference will
be clearer if it is set within the Miltonic concept of salvation.
Depraved as a result of the Fall, man cannot work or even
contribute to the work of his own salvation. Salvation depends on
God alone. The first stage of the work of restoring man to divine
favour is renovation, which is bipartite. On the one hand, by an
act of prevenient grace God calls upon the sinner to repent and to
have faith in the promise of salvation as set out in the Gospel; and
man, who has free will, may respond either positively or negative-
ly to this vocation or calling—or, an initially positive response
may be followed later by rejection.[9] Natural renovation, then,

depends upon the sinner's response to a divine initiative—a vocation and an answer to that vocation. Supernatural renovation, on the other hand, is the work of God alone. Even if a man responds positively to his vocation, he is incapable of effecting his own regeneration, for the weight of original and subsequent sin renders him spiritually impotent. He may indicate his desire for regeneration by accepting his vocation to faith and repentance, but he cannot achieve it for himself. The work of transforming the old Adam into the image of the new Adam is accomplished only because God restores and improves the 'natural faculties' of postlapsarian man by means of supernatural renovation.[10]

So far I have concentrated on the specific terms of Milton's concept of vocation. It remains now to place that doctrine in the context of his theology generally and to show how his formulation restates in its essentials the Arminian position and diverges from Calvinist teaching. This requires a longer perspective, and Milton's position can perhaps best be established by examining his interpretation of Romans 8: 28–30. This difficult text was regarded by Refomed theologians as the central scriptural statement of the mechanics of salvation, although their interpretations of it were various and divergent. The passage reads as follows:

28 And we know that all things work together for good to them that love God, to them who are the called (τοῖς κλητοῖς) according to his purpose.

29 For whom he did foreknow, he also did predestinate to be conformed to the image of his Son, that he might be the firstborn among many brethren.

30 Moreover whom he did predestinate, them he also called (τούτους καὶ ἐκάλεσεν): and whom he called, them he also justified: and whom he justified, them he also glorified.

The stages, then, by which 'the called' are led to salvation are (1) foreknowledge, (2) predestination, (3) calling, (4) justification, and finally (5) glorification.

FOREKNOWLEDGE

In *De Doctrina Christiana* Milton treats the doctrines of foreknowledge and free will together:

By virtue of his wisdom God decreed the creation of angels and men as beings gifted with reason and thus with free will.[11] At the same time he foresaw the direction in which they would tend when they used this absolutely unimpaired freedom. What then? Shall we say that God's providence or foreknowledge imposes any necessity upon them? Certainly not: no more than if some human being possessed the same foresight. . . . Nothing happens because God has foreseen it, but rather he has foreseen each event because each is the result of particular causes which, by his decree, work quite freely and with which he is thoroughly familiar. So the outcome does not rest with God who foresees it, but only with the man whose action God foresees. . . . Divine foreknowledge definitely cannot itself impose any necessity, nor can it be set up as a cause, in any sense, of free actions. . . . A thing which is going to happen quite freely in the course of events is not then produced as a result of God's foreknowledge, but arises from the free action of its own causes, and God knows in what direction these will, of their own accord, tend. In this way he knew that Adam would, of his own accord, fall. Thus it was certain that he would fall, but it was not necessary, because he fell of his own accord and that is irreconcilable with necessity. (*DDC*, I, iii; *YP*, VI, pp. 164–5)

Prescience, then, does not compel occurrence; for, if it did, God would be the author of evil and the cause of the Fall. The link between God's foreknowledge of an event and the event itself is a *necessary* link, since God is omniscient, but it is not a *necessitating* link. This same position is set out in *Paradise Lost*, III, 98–119 in a way that will lead us on naturally to an examination of predestination:

> I made [Man] just and right,
> Sufficient to have stood, though free to fall.
> Such I created all the ethereal powers
> And spirits, both them who stood and them who failed;
> Freely they stood who stood, and fell who fell.
> · · · ·
> They therefore as to right belonged,
> So were created, nor can justly accuse
> Their maker, or their making, or their fate,
> As if predestination overruled

Their will, disposed by absolute decree
Or high foreknowledge: they themselves decreed
Their own revolt, not I: if I foreknew,
Foreknowledge had no influence on their fault,
Which had no less proved certain unforeknown.

PREDESTINATION

The problem of predestination has been a topic of fundamental concern since the earliest centuries of the Christian era. So complex is the subject and its development, indeed, that a casual commentator wishing merely to outline Milton's position on the matter may be excused for trembling inwardly at the prospect of sharing the sad lot of those fallen spirits in Book II of *Paradise Lost* who 'sat on a hill retired' and

> reasoned high
> Of providence, foreknowledge, will and fate,
> Fixed fate, free will, foreknowledge absolute,
> And found no end, in wandering mazes lost.
>
> (558–61)

Although presupposed in the Gospels, the doctrine of predestination is (as we have seen) explicitly set out in the Pauline epistles, especially Romans 8: 28–30 and Ephesians 1: 3–14. The earliest full-scale controversy on the topic erupted in the first quarter of the fifth century in the bitter polemical war waged between Augustine and the Pelagians. Reacting against Pelagian emphasis on free will and denial of the transmission of original sin, Augustine undertook to expound the doctrines of the Fall, original sin, and predestination. As the controversy grew more fierce, he became progressively more uncompromising; and by the time he composed *De Praedestinatione Sanctorum* (428), his position had become inflexibly severe: postlapsarian man, he argues, having inherited liability for Adam's transgression, is a *massa peccati* whose supernatural gifts of liberty and free will have been utterly lost through sin; yet, in His inscrutable wisdom, God has determined by eternal decree to predestinate certain individual sinners to restoration and election, although they have done nothing to merit this free mercy. This Augustinian view of predestination was later adopted by Calvin, who maintained that the saving benefits of Christ's atoning sacrifice apply only to the gratuitously chosen band of the elect. But Calvin went a step beyond Augustine in expressing as dogma a doctrine of 'double predestination'—that is, predestination to reprobation as well as to election:

> By predestination we mean the eternal decree of God, by which he determined with himself whatever he wished to happen with regard to every man. All are not created on equal terms, but some are preordained to eternal life, others to eternal damnation; and, accordingly, as each has been created for one or other of these ends, we say that he has been predestined to life and death.[12]

Although this forbidding doctrine is a corner-stone of his soteriology, Calvin himself did not rashly abstract it from his general theology and insist upon it as the *sine qua non* of his system. His disciples, however, were less moderate. In the works of Theodore Beza, for example, who was Calvin's epigone at Geneva, one comes face to face with the rigid determinism characteristic of derivative Calvinism. For Beza, predestination became virtually an end in itself, and his dogmatic intransigence on the subject asserts itself clearly in *A Booke of Christian Questions and Answers* (translated by Arthur Golding in 1574) where he defines Predestination as

> God's everlasting and unchangeable ordinance, going in order before all the causes of salvation and damnation, whereby God has determined to be glorified, in some by saving them of his own mere grace in Christ, and others by damning them through his rightful justice in Adam and in themselves. And after the custom of scripture we call the former the vessels of glory and the elect or chosen, that is to say, those appointed to salvation from before all worlds through mercy; and the other sort we call reprobates and castaways, and vessels of wrath, that is to say, appointed likewise to rightful damnation from everlasting: both of which God has known severally from time without beginning.[13]

Beza's supralapsarian[14] theology transmitted itself to England in the natural course of things, and there it found such able and influential exponents as the Puritan theologian William Perkins, whose *De Praedestinationis Modo et Ordine* (1598) provoked a reply from Jacobus Arminius with far-reaching implications for predestinarian doctrine.

Before we come to Arminius, however, it may be helpful to summarise the salient features of the Calvinistic doctrine of predestination. First, Calvinist supralapsarianism asserts that the divine decree concerning election and reprobation has priority over all other decrees and that, since it was ordained before the Fall, its establishment was not occasioned by Adam's transgression. Second, God's election and reprobation of individual sinners—demonstrations of unmerited mercy and merited justice, respectively—is wholly gratuitous and is not in any way contingent upon divine foreknowledge of those who would and those who would not respond positively to an offer of saving faith. Third, the gifts of grace and faith are given only to the elect; Christ's atoning sacrifice applies only to those whom God has, from all eternity, marked out for salvation. Fourth, grace is irresistible: the elect cannot decline election and salvation. Fifth, the doctrine of the inamissibility of grace precludes the possibility of human free will.

This harsh doctrine of double predestination found an accomplished opponent in the Dutch theologian Jacobus Arminius, who sought to steer a middle course between Calvinist determinism and Pelagian insistence on human merit and absolute free will. Having studied theology under Beza at Geneva, Arminius returned to his native Holland in 1587 and was called to a pastorate in Amsterdam. In the early 1590s he undertook a close study of Romans, Chapters 7 and 9, and his concentrated investigation of the Pauline doctrines of sin, grace, predestination and free will led him to doubt the necessitarianism of high-Calvinist teaching. He began to see that predestination applies only to believers, that God has predestined to salvation all who believe in Christ. At the same time, however, he kept his soteriology rooted firmly in the Reformed doctrine of solifidianism; and, while Calvinist adversaries repeatedly accused him of Pelagianism, he vigorously and consistently insisted that salvation is by grace alone and that human merit is inadmissible as a cause of salvation.

As an admirer of William Perkins, Arminius acquired a copy of *De Praedestinationis* when it appeared in 1598. Yet he read the work with dismay—for, 'while Perkins wanted to make the doctrine of predestination more "reasonable" than it is in Calvin, his logical rigor drove him to a supralapsarian point of view in which the creation and fall become means for carrying out the prior decree of election or damnation'.[15] Fired by his recent discoveries in the Epistle to the Romans, Arminius set about the task of composing a reply—the *Examination of Perkins' Pamphlet* which is, as Carl Bangs has said, 'the basic document of Arminianism'.[16] On the question of free will Arminius argues for a *via media* between Calvinist denial and Pelagian affirmation, by maintaining that grace (*gratia gratis*) transforms potential free will into actual free will. In other words, divine grace restores the postlapsarian will, which is sufficient only for evil choices, to the position where it is truly and actually free to choose between good and evil. By a further act of grace God has decreed that He will show mercy to those only who believe in the promise that they are saved in Christ, whose merit is imputed to them. The choice confronting the restored free will, then, is that between belief and non-belief. But, since the will is free, grace is defectible: although the gift of salvation in Christ is offered universally, each individual human being uses his free will either to accept or to reject the proffered grace. Carl Bangs summarises Arminius's view of the interrelation of grace and free will in this way: 'The part man plays in salvation is believing. Evangelical belief is the free choice to receive offered grace, which offered grace makes the free choice possible. In all of this man does nothing apart from grace: he earns nothing; he contributes nothing; but he chooses freely, and it is a choice which he can refuse to make, for grace is not an irresistible force.'[17] In asserting the freedom of the will and the amissibility of grace, Arminius diverges fundamentally from the Calvinist teaching he learned under Beza and found again in Perkins' *De Praedestinationis*. On the other hand, however, by denying the efficacy of human merit and attributing salvation to the operation of grace alone, he separates himself from Pelagian doctrine, which declares 'that a man bi his fre wil mai deserue heuen withoute grace'.[18]

With an understanding of the place of grace and free will in Arminius's soteriology one is in a position to consider his view of predestination in the *Examination of Perkins' Pamphlet*. In the first place, he rejects the Calvinist doctrine that the decree concerning predestination has priority over all other divine decrees. He maintains, rather, that predestination is subordinate to the decree appointing Christ as intercessor; and this decretal posteriority is of fundamental importance. Since evangelical grace is extended to man *as sinner* and since the believer is predested *in Christ*, it follows that Christ's establishment as mediator has logical priority over the decree ordaining the election of sinners in Christ.[19] Secondly, he argues that, although sufficient grace is universal, saving grace is given only to believers—that is, all men receive the prevenient grace which permits a sinner to use his free will to accept the divine offer of faith, but subsequent grace which issues in salvation is restricted to those who do, in fact, respond positively to the divine initiative and who persevere in their decision. And finally, Arminius discriminates between absolute and contingent predestination. By absolute predestination—which is without respect to foreknowledge—God decrees that those who believe shall be saved and those who do not believe shall be damned. By contingent or conditional predestination, He ordains that those individuals whom He foresees as believing shall be saved, whereas those whom He foresees as disobedient shall be damned. In other words, 'predestination of classes is absolute or without qualification; predestination of individuals is with respect to foreseen faith'.[20] Six years after his reply to Perkins, Arminius offered the following definitions of election and reprobation in a public disputation (February 1604) with Franciscus Gomarus: 'Predestination . . . is the decree of the good pleasure of God in Christ by which he resolved within himself from all eternity to justify, adopt, and endow with eternal life, to the praise of his own glorious grace, believers on whom he had decreed to bestow faith.' Reprobation, on the other hand, is 'a decree of the wrath, or of the severe will, of God by which he resolved from all eternity to condemn to eternal death unbelievers who, by their own fault and the just judgment of God, would not believe. . . .'[21]

Milton devotes Book I, Chapter iv of *De Doctrina Christiana* to a discussion of predestination. Here is his definition:

The principal SPECIAL DECREE of God which concerns men is called PREDESTINATION: by which GOD, BEFORE THE FOUND-ATIONS OF THE WORLD WERE LAID, HAD MERCY ON THE HUMAN RACE, ALTHOUGH IT WAS GOING TO FALL OF ITS OWN ACCORD, AND, TO SHOW THE GLORY OF HIS MERCY,

GRACE AND WISDOM, PREDESTINED TO ETERNAL SALVA-
TION, ACCORDING TO HIS PURPOSE or plan IN CHRIST, THOSE
WHO WOULD IN THE FUTURE BELIEVE AND CONTINUE IN
THE FAITH. (*YP*, VI, p. 168)

Arminian influence is unmistakeable here. However, before we
look at the similarities between the positions of Arminius and
Milton, there is one point of radical difference that must be
mentioned. Whereas Arminius and his followers retained—albeit
in greatly altered form—the Calvinist doctrine of double predestination, Milton applies the term predestination only to election
and argues that foreordination to damnation, whether as a general decree or in the case of individual men, is unscriptural.
'PREDESTINATION, then,' he declares, 'must always be taken to
refer to election, and it seems often to be used instead of that term';
and later he concludes that 'Reprobation . . . is no part of divine
predestination.' (*YP*, VI, pp. 171, 173)[22] Damnation is the result of
the wilful repudiation of predestination; man damns himself as
the inevitable consequence of refusing to accept the offer of divine
grace. As evil in the Augustinian tradition is seen to be the
absence of good rather than anything positive in itself, so reprobation becomes for Milton the absence of election. The effect of the
Miltonic doctrine of predestination is to stress God's mercy rather
at the expense of His justice and, as well, to give great prominence
to human free will and the defectibility of grace. Since damnation
is the result of a human act rather than a divine decree, the
emphasis—poetically at least—falls clearly on the operation of
free will in response to divine grace. In *Paradise Lost*, for example,
both election and reprobation are the end products of a series of
choices, and the poem may be read as a study in the use of free
will. The education of Adam in the tutorial sessions conducted by
Raphael and Michael is a progressive schooling in the use of
reason, which 'is but choosing'. Conversely, Satan's damnation
results from a series of refusals to accept offered grace and repent:

> Which way I fly is hell; my self am hell;
> And in the lowest deep a lower deep
> Still threatening to devour me opens wide,
> To which the hell I suffer seems a heaven.
> O then at last relent; is there no place
> Left for repentance, none for pardon left?

> None left but by submission; and that word
> Disdain forbids me. . . .
>
> (IV, 75–82)

In short, Satan damns himself. While Adam's free will grows and strengthens as he responds to grace, Satan's will becomes less free as it becomes more and more chained to evil and the self. Satan is a study in the progressive self-abrogation of freedom of the will.

Apart from the question of double predestination, Milton's doctrine is reasonably close to that of Arminius. Both agree that evangelical grace is offered to man as sinner, that it is offered freely to all men and not merely to a preordained group of 'elect' men, that God restores to the individual sufficient free will to respond to the call to salvation, and that He has 'predestined to salvation all who shall believe.' (*YP*, VI, p.183) Commenting on Romans 8: 28–30 (above, p. 5), Milton sets out the order of events in this way: 'God foreknew those who would believe; that is, he decided or approved that it should be those alone upon whom, through Christ, he would look kindly: in fact, then, that it should be all men, if they believed. He predestined these to salvation, and, in various ways, he called all men to believe, that is, truly to acknowledge God. He justified those who believed in this way, and finally glorified those who persevered in their belief.' (Ibid., pp. 181–2) Thus, like Arminius, Milton held that men are predestined *on condition of* belief[23] (rather than being predestined *to* belief, as Calvinists maintained) and that salvation is achieved by the co-operation of restored free will with God's offer of grace.[24]

CALLING

Vocation is inseparably linked with predestination, for it is the means by which the decree of election is accomplished. As we have seen (pp. 4–5), Milton considers the doctrine of vocation within the context of a bipartite tenet of renovation. By 'natural renovation' or vocation, God invites all men to use their free will to accept salvation, which is promised on condition of faith and repentance. By 'supernatural renovation', God restores fallen man's faculties of reason and free will so that he may respond to this invitation, and on those who respond He bestows increasing powers. Thus, supernatural renovation depends upon grace alone, but natural renovation depends on co-operation between grace and restored free will. Like Arminius, Milton eschews Pelagian self-sufficiency by insisting that salvation is *sola gratia* and modifies Augustinian and Calvinistic determinism by insisting on the collaboration of human free will and divine grace.

Milton also aligns himself with Arminius in his view of the nature and extent of grace. First, in contradistinction to the Calvinist doctrines that saving grace is available only to those foreordained to election and that such grace is inamissible, Milton adopts the Arminian position that grace is initially offered to all men but that it is defectible and may fail of its purpose since it depends on human co-operation.[25] Second, while Milton's distinction between general and special vocation echoes the usual Reformed division of *vocatio universalis* and *vocatio specialis*, the resemblance is verbal rather than substantive—for again his debt is to Arminius and not to Calvin. In the Leiden *Synopsis* (above, p. 3), which represents the Calvinist point of view, the phrase *vocatio universalis* refers simply to a general call to recognise and worship God; it is a call which comes alike to elect and reprobate, but it does not and cannot lead to salvation. *Vocatio specialis*, on the other hand, is that imposition on the elect of irresistible saving grace, by which means 'God calls some out of the entire human race . . . to supernatural knowledge of Jesus Christ our Redeemer and to saving participation in his benefits'. For Milton, however, both general and special vocation lead to salvation if a man perseveres in his calling by co-operating with proffered grace. His distinction is between *degrees* of grace rather than *kinds* of grace, and the division seems to originate in Arminius's doctrine of 'unequal' grace.[26] In his chapter on predestination (*DDC*, I, iv) Milton declares that 'sufficient grace' is universally extended but that God, in His inscrutable wisdom, retains the right to give more grace to some than to others:

> If, then, God rejects none except the disobedient and the unbeliever, he undoubtedly bestows grace on all, and if not equally upon each, at least sufficient to enable everyone to attain knowledge of the truth and salvation. I say not equally upon each, because he has not distributed grace equally, even among the reprobate, as they are called. . . . For like anyone else, where his own possessions are concerned, God claims for himself the right of making decrees about them as he thinks

fit, without being obliged to give a reason for his decree, though
he could give a very good one if he wished. . . . So God does not
consider everyone worthy of equal grace, and the cause of this is
his supreme will. But he considers all worthy of sufficient grace,
and the cause is his justice. (*YP*, VI, pp. 192–3)

Out of this distinction between sufficient and unequal grace grows
the distinction between general and special vocation. All men are
called to faith and repentance by a general vocation, but 'certain
selected individuals' are called 'more clearly and more insistently
than is normal.' (Ibid., p. 455)

As Milton's examples testify, special vocation embraces not
only the New Testament emphasis on personal election to salvation but also the Old Testament emphasis on service. In clarifying
the phrase 'certain selected individuals', Milton cites the examples of Abraham, whose vocation to sire the Chosen People was
national as much as personal, and of the Israelites themselves,
whom God called 'for the sake of his name and of the promises he
had made to their forbears.' (Ibid., p. 456) Special vocation, then,
seems also to involve special responsibility, a calling to divine
service as well as to individual election—although, of course, the
person called is free to decline even the clear and insistent
prompting of a *vocatio specialis*, as many Hebrews had refused the
convenantal obligation to serve Yahweh as 'a kingdom of priests,
and an holy nation'.

It is with special vocation in its aspect of extra-personal service
that I am primarily concerned in the present study. Perhaps
Milton's firmest conviction was that he had been called to serve as
an instrument of the divine will. Like the Nazarite Samson, into
whose characterisation he poured a good deal of his own spiritual
and intellectual biography, Milton thought of himself as 'a person
separate to God,/Designed for great exploits' (*SA*, 31–2), and his
sense of special vocation provides a firm conceptual framework
which unifies the whole of his literary production. The early years
are devoted largely to preparation and vocational definition:
called to serve God from the pulpit and through his poetry, he
concentrates on the improvement of his divinely implanted talents and on defining the requirements expected of him as God's
poet-priest. In the prose works of 1641–60 the vocational emphasis shifts from his role as poet-priest to his role as poet-
prophet: all the signs declare that England has been marked out

as the new Israel, and Milton's divinely appointed role, his special vocation, is to serve both in poetry and prose as the prophet of national rebirth and the providential instrument called to exhort his countrymen to fulfil their divine mission of carrying reformation to the world. The failure of the Puritan experiment, however, necessitated a period of vocational reassessment—a theme which is central in the last poems of 1667 and 1671. Each of Milton's protagonists—Adam, Samson and Christ—is educated in the limits of power and the vocational expectations imposed on him by divine service; each learns, as Milton himself had learned, what is involved in serving as the special instrument of God. Adam is instructed in his responsibilities as the father of mankind, first in a state of prelapsarian perfection and later in a fallen world of his own making; Samson, fallen from favour and close to despair, redefines his special status and with divine aid resolves the vocational tension between prophecy and fact in his promised role as Israel's deliverer; and in *Paradise Regained* Christ is led through temptation to a precise understanding of his messianic vocation. Each of these poems, I believe, performed a cathartic function for Milton; in *Samson Agonistes* and *Paradise Regained*, and in the case of the postlapsarian Adam in *Paradise Lost* as well, I find below the narrative surface an extrapoetic source of imaginative power in Milton's own attempt to redefine his role as God's servant after the collapse of the Puritan New Jerusalem in 1660. By imposing an aesthetic pattern on private experience in these last poems, he was enabled to achieve both emotional calm and vocational redefinition.

I shall return in a moment to the question of special calling by examining another tradition in Reformation thought, in which the idea of vocation is seen as a divine call to specific secular occupations. Before doing so, however, a brief word is needed about the ultimate purpose of theological vocation in Milton's soteriology.

JUSTIFICATION AND GLORIFICATION

The *terminus a quo* of vocation is fallen man in a state of guilt and condemnation; the *terminus ad quem* is regenerate man in a state of grace, that is, justified and glorified. The object of vocation, then, is regeneration, which Milton defines as the process by which 'THE OLD MAN IS DESTROYED AND... THE INNER MAN IS REGEN-

ERATED BY GOD THROUGH THE WORD AND THE SPIRIT SO THAT HIS WHOLE MIND IS RESTORED TO THE IMAGE OF GOD, AS IF HE WERE A NEW CREATURE. MOREOVER THE WHOLE MAN, BOTH SOUL AND BODY, IS SANCTIFIED TO GOD'S SERVICE AND TO GOOD WORKS.' (*YP*, VI, p. 461) For Milton as for all other Reformed theologians, however, the work of transforming the old man of sin into the new man of faith belongs to God alone: 'The condition of man after the fall of Adam is such that he cannot turn and prepare himself, by his own natural strength and good works, to faith and calling upon God: wherefore we have no power to do good works pleasant and acceptable to God without the grace of God by Christ preventing us, that we may have a good will, and working with us, when we have that good will.'[27] By prevenient grace God calls the sinner to faith and repentance, and by subsequent grace He makes it possible for him to persist in his calling to faith and repentance. Man's only part in his regeneration is to use his free will to co-operate with divine grace in this task of spiritual reconstruction.

The proximate ends of regeneration are justification and sanctification.[28] The Reformed doctrine of justification by faith alone (solifidianism), which originates with Luther,[29] holds that the believer is accounted righteous in God's sight by virtue of his faith in Christ; where salvation is concerned, there is no room for human merit or righteousness—sinful man remains guilty *in fact*, but by a legal fiction God graciously agrees to treat him as though he were innocent, because, through his faith, Christ's righteousness and merit are imputed to him.[30] The doctrine is proclaimed by God (speaking to the Son) in *Paradise Lost*, III, 285–94.[31]

> be thou in Adam's room
> The head of all mankind, though Adam's son.
> As in him perish all men, so in thee
> As from a second root shall be restored,
> As many as are restored, without thee none.
> His crime makes guilty all his sons, thy merit
> Imputed shall absolve them who renounce
> Their own both righteous and unrighteous deeds,
> And live in thee transplanted, and from thee
> Receive new life.

Vocation and justification are followed by sanctification or holiness. Although good deeds and holy living do not contribute to salvation, they are enjoined as the pledge and seal of a man's election—a good tree must bring forth good fruit. Heinrich Heppe summarises the Reformed doctrine of sanctification in this way: 'sanctification is to be distinguished as well from justification as from vocation; for vocation is the beginning of regeneration, whereas sanctification is the continuation of it to gradual completion. . . . [Justification] rests directly upon the sacrificial death and merit of Christ; [sanctification] on the contrary is an effect which the death and life of Christ produce in the person called. The former is a once-for-all act of God imparted in the same way; the latter is a gradual process variously completed according to the varying measure of the Spirit which the individual receives. In the former man's relation to the grace that sanctifies him is purely passive; in the latter he co-operates with it.'[32] An even better definition is provided in a sermon of Archbishop Edwin Sandys:

> Holiness is the end of our election. . . . Unto holiness we are not only constrained by His commandment, but allured also by His example: 'Be holy, because I am holy.' [1 Peter 1: 1] Unto this we are called: 'For God did not call us unto uncleanness, but unto holiness' [I Thess. 4: 7] So that, unless we esteem vilely of our own election, unless we refuse to satisfy the will, to obey the commandment, to follow the example, and to answer the vocation in which God hath called us, we must be holy.[33]

Finally, if justification and sanctification may be said to be the proximate ends of regeneration, then glorification may be said to be its ultimate end. 'Since the glorification of God is the purpose of all things, and since as the original source of all blessedness God wills to be glorified in the faithful, the latter are called by the Father not only to the enjoyment of Christ's grace but also to Christ's glory, which however, is not imparted to the elect in its entire perfection until after death.'[34] In *De Doctrina Christiana* Milton follows the lead of other Reformed theologians by distinguishing between incomplete and complete glorification. Incomplete glorification is the adumbration of eternal bliss vouchsafed to the elect while they are still alive: 'WE . . . ARE FILLED WITH A CERTAIN AWARENESS BOTH OF PRESENT GRACE AND DIGNITY AND OF FUTURE GLORY, SO THAT WE HAVE ALREADY BEGUN TO BE BLESSED.' (*YP*, VI, p. 502) Complete glorification, on the other hand, is achieved by believers only after death and 'consists in eternal and utterly happy life, arising chiefly from the sight of God.' (Ibid., p. 630) Glorification, then, is applied salvation; and the relationship between vocation and glorification is happily and succinctly expressed by William Ames in his *Medulla Theologica* (1627) when he describes glorification as the moment when 'the end of their calling will be present to all the called; for we are called to the eternal glory of God.' (I, xli, 2)[35]

(ii) VOCATION AND SECULAR OBLIGATION

> *Let every man abide in the same*
> *calling wherein he was called.*
> (1 Corinthians 7: 20)

When Richard Steele wrote in 1684 that 'God doth call every man and woman . . . to serve him in some peculiar employment in this world, both for their own and the common good',[36] his words had behind them the authority of a long and important tradition in Reformation thought. Over a century earlier Calvin had put his imprimatur on the doctrine in *Institutes of the Christian Religion*:

> . . . the Lord enjoins every one of us, in all the actions of life, to have respect to our own calling. He knows the boiling restlessness of the human mind, the fickleness with which it is borne hither and thither, its eagerness to hold opposites at one time in its grasp, its ambition. Therefore, lest all things should be thrown into confusion by our folly and rashness, he has assigned distinct duties to each in the different modes of life. And that no one may presume to overstep his proper limits, he has distinguished the different modes of life by the name of callings. Every man's mode of life, therefore, is a kind of station assigned him by the Lord, that he may not be always driven about at random.[37]

The conviction that secular obligations were imposed on individuals by divine will was a staple of English Puritanism from its earliest days;[38] and it became even more prominent in Puritan thought during the seventeenth century because of its connection with covenant theology. The idea, however, was popular with

Anglicans as well, although they were generally more restrained in their expression of it. So popular, indeed, was the doctrine in England by the 1590s that Falstaff in *1 Henry IV* could use it in waggish defence of his addiction to larceny:

> *Prince*   I see a good amendment of life in thee—from praying to purse-taking.
> *Falstaff*   Why, Hal, 'tis my vocation, Hal. 'Tis no sin for a man to labour in his vocation. (I, ii, 103–6)

In addition to the spiritual vocation examined in the preceding section, then, there is a temporal vocation as well. Yet these two sorts of calling are intimately connected. As we have seen, spiritual vocation leads to justification and sanctification, that is, to adoption through Christ's imputed merit and to good works performed with the aid of the Holy Spirit as the pledge of that election. Temporal calling is an aspect of sanctification: a man is called not simply to good works but to good works performed within the context of the specific office assigned to him by the government of heaven. In the sixteenth and seventeenth centuries, doing the work that lay nearest one was not, as it became later for Thomas Carlyle, merely a matter of therapy for religious despair; it was enjoined as a religious duty, for God expected contentment and obedience of those whom He had appointed to their particular trade or profession—*laborare est orare*. The sociological and economic implications of this concept have been much discussed by historians and theologians.[39] However, since a good deal of this scholarly debate is devoted to historical and economic issues, its relevance to this present study of Milton is tangential and there is no need to rehearse it here. In order to understand Milton's relation to the doctrine of secular vocation as divine calling it will be enough to glance briefly at the source of the idea in Luther and then to consider in somewhat greater detail its exposition in an important English tractate, William Perkins' *Treatise of Vocations*.

For medieval Christianity 'vocation' meant 'religious vocation'. An individual was called out of the world to exercise a special function as priest, nun, friar, monk, or anchorite. The religious life conferred a special status on those who submitted themselves to it and was regarded as the highest form of Christian obedience; the performance of secular duties and one's daily work, on the other hand, were occupations rather than 'callings', pursuits occasioned by the penalty of Adam rather than responses to an inner summons to the rigours of the *imitatio Christi*. The medieval barriers between religious and secular service, however, were broken down by Luther who, in refuting the spiritual pretensions of the monastic ideal, taught that all lawful vocations were divine callings. The Christian body comprises many members, and although the work of each is different, they are all members of the same body; and so Luther 'presents man's vocation as something positive, saying that man, by labor and prayer, can serve as a mask for God, a coworker with him, through which God effects his will in external affairs'.[40] The essence of vocation is extra-personal service; a man is called to obedience in his secular vocation, not for personal gains (either temporal or spiritual), but so that he may serve as the vehicle of God's continuing care for mankind. Secular vocations may vary greatly in importance and glory, but each is nevertheless a medium for transmitting God's love to man. By conscientiously discharging the duties of the office to which he has been appointed, an individual demonstrates his obedience to God and at the same time becomes a useful member of the Christian community. But it must be added that the good works which a man performs in the pursuit of his vocation do not in any way contribute to his election. Salvation is *sola gratia* and *sola fide*; and therefore, in his *Kirchenpostille* (1522) and elsewhere, Luther firmly separates vocation from any notion of merit: 'In heaven, before God, vocation has as little to contribute as do good works. Good works and vocation (love) exist for the earth and one's neighbour, not for eternity and God. God does not need our good works, but our neighbour does. It is faith that God wants. Faith ascends to heaven.'[41] Vocation, then, expresses itself in terms of selfless service; it is, as I said a moment ago, an aspect of sanctification.

The Reformed attitude to secular vocation is fully and clearly set out in William Perkins' *A Treatise of Vocations, or Callings of men* (1603).[42] Not surprisingly, the tract's major premise is that all lawful[43] callings, however menial, are ordained by God and that one must acquiesce humbly and obediently in His determinations:

> . . . *a vocation or calling, is a certaine kind of life, ordained and imposed on man by God, for the common good.* . . . For example, the life of a

king is to spend his time in the gouerning of his subiects, and
that is his calling: and the life of a subiect is to liue in obedience
to the Magistrate, and that is his calling. The state and
condition of a Minister is, to leade his life in preaching of the
Gospell and word of God, and that is his calling. A master of a
family is to leade his life in the gouernment of his family, and
that is his calling. In a word, that particular and honest manner
of conuersation, whereunto euery man is called and set apart,
that is (I say) his calling. . . . The author of euery calling, is God
himselfe: and therefore Paul saith; *As God hath called euery man, let
him walke,* [1 Cor. 7,] vers. 17. And for this cause, the order and
maner of liuing in this world, is called a *Vocation*; because euery
man is to liue as he is called of God. For looke as in the campe,
the Generall appointeth to euery man his place and standing;
one place for the horseman, & another for the footman, and to
euery particular souldier likewise, his office and standing, in
which he is able to abide against the enemie, and therein to liue
and die: euen so is it in humane societies: God is the Generall,
appointing euery man his particular calling, and as it were his
standing: and in that calling, he assigns vnto him his particular
office; of performance whereof he is to liue and die. And as in a
campe, no souldier can depart his standing, without the leaue of
the Generall; no more may any man leaue his calling, except he
receiue liberty from God. (p. 727)

Committed to the view that disorders in the temporal world were
the result of a general failure on the part of men to obey the divine
ordinance of vocation, Perkins insists that a man 'must keepe
himselfe within the compasse, limits, or precincts' of his own
proper calling:

when any man is without the cōpasse of his calling, he is out of
the way, and by this means he bereaues himself of the protection of the Almighty; and lies open and naked to all the
punishments and plagues of God. And if we marke it well, the
word of God shews euidently to what dangers they are subiect,
that do any thing either without or against their callings.
Sampsons strength lay not in his haire (as men commonly
think) but because he went out of his calling, by breaking the
vow of a Nazarite, when he gaue occasion to Dalilah to cut off
his haire, therefore he lost his strength; for God promised

strength but with a commandement that he should be a Nazarite to the end, Iud. 13.5 (pp. 728–9)

If this account of Samson's fall lacks the psychological sophistication of *Samson Agonistes*, it is nevertheless true—as I shall argue in
Chapter 5—that Milton follows Perkins in treating Samson's
failure to keep within the limits of his appointed vocation as the
theological and thematic centre of the story. In the Miltonic
version, however, Samson's vocation as the saviour of Israel takes
precedence over his calling as a Nazarite.

Perkins goes on to say that vocation must be divided into
general calling and particular calling. 'The generall calling', he
explains, is common to all Christians and is that 'whereby a man
is called out of the world to be a child of God, a member of Christ,
and heire of the kingdom of heauen. This Calling belongs to euery
one within the compasse of the Church, not any one excepted'
(p. 729). Particular or personal calling, on the other hand, 'is that
speciall calling that belongs to some particular men: as the calling
of a Magistrate, the calling of a Minister, the calling of a Master,
of a father, of a child, of a seruant, of a subiect, or any other calling
that is common to all' (ibid.). By general calling, then, he refers to
that *vocatio universalis* described in the preceding section of this
Introduction; but, since his subject is primarily secular walks of
life in *A Treatise of Vocations*, he reserves the term 'particular
calling' to describe, not a theological *vocatio specialis*, but rather
'the execution of some particular office, arising out of that distinction which God makes between man and man in euery societie'
(p. 731). Yet, while he distinguishes between general and particular calling, Perkins would not divorce them; on the contrary, he
insists that the latter must be firmly rooted in the former: 'Euery
man', he declares, 'must ioyne the practise of his personall calling,
with the practise of the generall calling of Christianitie. . . . More
plainely: Euery particular calling must be practised in, and with
the generall calling of a Christian. It is not sufficient for a man in
the congregation, and in common conuersation, to be a Christian,
but in his very personall calling, he must shew himselfe to be so'.
(p. 733) These two vocations must be joined with an indivisible
bond, as body and soul are joined—and, he continues, 'if thou
wouldest haue signs and tokens of thy election and saluation, thou
must fetch them from the constant practise of thy two callings
jointlie togither' (ibid.). This statement brings us to the very heart

of Perkins' argument, for it is clear that he is concerned to have vocation serve as a bridge between justification (faith) and sanctification (works). The Christian receives a general calling to embrace the faith by which he is justified, and he is called also to a specific secular occupation or vocation in which he is to serve God by serving man and by performing works that symbolise his regenerate status. However, since faith has precedence over works, 'a particular calling must giue place to the generall calling of a Christian, when they cannot both stand togither' (p. 734).

Having established the theological basis of his doctrine of vocation, Perkins passes on to the more pragmatic aspects of the concept. One of the first problems to which he addresses himself is the question of how a man may know for certain that he has been called by God into his particular station and function in life:

> Now, that euery man may certenly know himselfe to be called of God, to this or that calling, he must haue two things: Gifts for the calling of God, and Allowance from men. For the first, whom God calleth, to them he giueth competent and conuenient gifts, as knowledge, understanding, dexterity to this or that, and such like; and thereby makes them able for the performance of the duties of their callings. Contrariwise, they that enter into any calling, beeing vtterly vnable to performe the duties thereof, were neuer called of God. For the second, men are to be set apart to their particular callings by the appointment of men, whom God hath left on earth as his instruments, for the ordering and disposing of vocations. For God has his deputies to allot men their offices in euery society: . . . for ecclesiasticall callings, the *Gouernours* of the Church; for ciuill, the Magistrate, and men of authoritie in the Common-wealth. (p. 737)

No one, then, may lawfully enter a vocation unless he knows himself to possess the necessary aptitude and skills (which are the gifts of God) and, as well, unless he has the approval of those men whom God has set in authority to judge the fitness of aspirants for their callings. This notion of a dual proof of vocational qualification goes far toward explaining Milton's early desire to have his inner conviction of poetic ability corroborated by external authority. It helps to account, for instance, for the abrupt self-revelations offered in *Prolusion 6* (see below, pp. 52–4) or, more significantly, for the great emphasis that he placed on the enthusiastic reception accorded his nascent Muse by the intellectual elite of Italy: 'perceiving that some trifles which I had in memory', he wrote in *The Reason of Church-Government*, 'met with acceptance above what was lookt for ... [and] were receiv'd with written Encomiums, which the Italian is not forward to bestow on men of this side the *Alps*, I began thus farre to assent both to them and divers of my friends here at home, and not lesse to an inward prompting which now grew daily upon me, that by labour and intent study ... I might perhaps leave something so written to aftertimes, as they should not willingly let it die.' (*YP*, I, pp. 809–10; see below, pp. 69–70).

Perkins devotes much of the remainder of his *Treatise of Vocations* to such topics as the virtues requisite for a vocation and a closely argued inquiry into the lawful occasions and means of changing one's vocation, and these matters need not detain us here. The central points have been made: all lawful vocations are divine callings; in performing the duties of his vocation a man serves his neighbour and demonstrates his obedience to God; a man must keep himself within the limits of his appointed office and must be sanctioned in his calling both by internal authority and external approval; and finally, a man must recognise that vocation binds together justification and sanctification, that is, that his secular calling functions as an adjunct to the work of grace renovating the inner man of faith.

Milton seldom deals in a direct and discursive way with the doctrine of secular vocation. Indeed, the only clear statement of the concept that I have been able to discover in his writings occurs in a brief comment (Milton's own) in his *Commonplace Book*: 'The nature of each person should be especially observed and not bent in another direction; for God does not intend all people for one thing, but for each one his own work.' (*YP*, I, p. 405) Nevertheless, as the chapters which follow will show, a firm belief in divine imminence and providential direction underpins all of his thinking about vocation. Both as poet and polemicist he believed that he was called and sustained in his calling by God. As a poet he would heartily have assented to Boccaccio's declaration in Book 15 of the *Genealogia Deorum Gentilium*: 'Whatever the vocation of others, mine, as experience from my mother's womb has shown, is clearly the study of poetry. For this, I believe, I was born. . . . Wherefore, since I believe that I am called to this profession by

God's will, it is my purpose to stand fast in the same.'[44] As a polemicist, having 'the use, as I may account it, but of my left hand', he showed initial reluctance; but an inward prompting convinced him that obedience was required of those whom God has appointed to serve Him as special instruments and, by 1654, as he told Leonard Philaras, God 'himself looks out for me . . . and takes me as if by the hand and leads me throughout life' (*YP*, IV, ii, p. 870). Milton believed, then, that his own secular careers were divine vocations,[45] and he knew also that, while 'God doth not need/ Either man's work or his own gifts' (*Sonnet 19*), it is death to hide those talents divinely implanted for the service of God and man.

1 Ministerial Vocation, 1625–40

Milton's decision to become a poet is frequently assumed to have been connected with his resolve to abandon a career in the church. According to H. F. Fletcher, it was sometime in 1627–8 when 'Milton decided not to become the priest that his parents and friends had intended him to become by going to Cambridge, but to turn toward letters, polite letters, as a definite career'. A. S. P. Woodhouse puts the moment of choice in 1632 on the threshold of Milton's retirement to Hammersmith and locates the central statement of his resolve in *Sonnet 7*; and John T. Shawcross believes the decision between the pulpit and poetry to have been deferred until the autumn of 1637.[1] Despite their differences, each of these readers would agree that the determination to serve God through poetry either involved or was fixed by his decision to relinquish holy orders. According to this view, Milton is seen as standing at a fork in the vocational road where the choice of one career implies the rejection of the other. However, although evidence is meagre, there are compelling reasons for thinking that there is no significant connection between Milton's decision to become a poet and his decision to abandon a career in the church. Indeed, once the notion of vocational tension and its corollary of an enforced choice is discarded, a revaluation of the evidence leads to important conclusions about Milton's early development.

It was to the service of the English church, Milton declared in 1642, that 'by the intentions of my parents and friends I was destin'd of a child, and in mine own resolutions' (*YP*, I, p. 822). There can be no doubt that he went up to Cambridge in 1625 expressly for the purpose of preparing himself for orders in the Church of England; but there is no necessary reason to suppose (as Haller does)[2] that he intended to join the spiritual brotherhood of Puritan divines working for further reform within the ecclesiastical establishment. It is equally clear from *At a Vacation Exercise* (1628), however, that at about this same time or shortly thereafter he began to harbour serious poetic aspirations. There is, of course,

27

no conflict here. Numerous contemporary clerics wrote poetry and gained reputations in both employments: Giles and Phineas Fletcher, John Donne and George Herbert, to mention only four of the more prominent figures. Moreover, although an allegiance to Ovid and the classical elegists influenced much of his early verse, Milton knew that literature could serve as an extension of the ministerial office; as he was to put it later, poetic ability is 'of power beside the office of a pulpit, to imbreed and cherish in a great people the seeds of vertu, and publick cavility' (*YP*, I, p. 816). The decision to become a poet, like that to become a minister of the Word, was taken early; and the vocational streams issuing from these twin resolves run parallel and are of equal strength until at least 1637 when he composed *Lycidas*. I shall reserve discussion of Milton's sense of poetic vocation for the following chapter and turn now to a closer examination of his proposed career in the church.

Normal procedure for intending ordinands in the Jacobean and Caroline church, and the necessary qualifications for church careers, were established in Articles 34 and 35 of the 1604 canons. Article 34 reads, in part: 'No bishop shall henceforth admit any person into sacred orders, which is not of his own diocese, except he be . . . of one of the universities of this realm . . . ; and desiring to be a deacon is three and twenty years old, and to be a priest four and twenty years complete; and hath taken some degree of school in either of the said universities . . . .'3 Oxford and Cambridge in the early seventeenth century functioned pre-eminently as seminaries of the Church of England; indeed, F. W. B. Bullock notes that between 1617 and 1637 'the average annual number of those proceeding to the B.A. degree at Cambridge was 266 and the average number of Cambridge graduates ordained about 207 per annum, so that roughly 78 per cent were ordained'.4 Destined for the priesthood, then, Milton went up to the university to obtain those formal qualifications which would constitute an essential part of his preparation for holy orders. Admitted to Christ's College, Cambridge, in February 1625 (barely two months after his sixteenth birthday) and matriculating on 9 April, he faced seven years of study before he could be admitted to the diaconate and eight before he could become a priest. Under Article 34 he was ineligible for the priesthood until he had reached his twenty-fourth birthday on 9 December 1632. Both Milton and his family no doubt planned, therefore, that he should take the four-year programme of studies leading to the B.A. degree, and then, since he would still be too young in 1629 for the priesthood, that he should undertake a further three years of study culminating in the M.A. degree. Since he could expect to proceed to the M.A. in mid-1632, he would have only a few months after graduation to wait until he was old enough, in December, to enter the priesthood. But he might also, either with or without ordination, elect to remain at the university after graduation and read for the Bachelor of Divinity or one of the higher degrees.[5]

Neither in 1632 nor later, however, did Milton enter holy orders. And, while there is unanimous agreement among later commentators that Milton's initial plan was to become a minister, there is no consensus as to when or why this plan was abandoned. Milton himself, it must be said, is far from helpful in providing a solution. Apart from a letter of 1633 (the meaning and intention of which are widely disputed) and some brief remarks in the preface to Book Two of *The Reason of Church-Government*, he has nothing to say in a direct and personal way about his plans for a career in the church. The passage in *The Reason of Church-Government* is certainly the most important piece of evidence we possess on this question, for it is the only place in his writings where Milton states directly his reasons for rejecting a clerical vocation. For this reason, it will be well to have the passage (*YP*, I, pp. 822–3) before us from the beginning:

> But were it the meanest under-service, if God by his Secretary conscience injoin it, it were sad for me if I should draw back, for me especially, now when all men offer their aid to help ease and lighten the difficult labours of the Church, to whose service by the intentions of my parents and friends I was destin'd of a child, and in mine own resolutions, till coming to some maturity of yeers and perceaving what tyranny had invaded the Church, that he who would take Orders must subscribe slave, and take an oath withall, which unlesse he took with a conscience that would retch, he must either strait perjure, or split his faith, I thought it better to preferre a blamelesse silence before the sacred office of speaking bought, and begun with servitude and forswearing. Howsoever thus Church-outed by the Prelats, hence may appear the right I have to meddle in these matters, as before, the necessity and constraint appear'd.

From a vocational viewpoint this passage is of paramount importance for two reasons. First, it provides a clear and straightforward explanation of Milton's decision to forgo holy orders. He did not leave the church willingly; indeed, he asserts with some acerbity that he was 'Church-outed'. The decision was forced upon him by prelatical tyranny, and especially by an oath in which that tyranny manifested itself most oppressively. There is no hint of vocational tension between poetry and the pulpit, nothing to suggest that his decision to renounce a career in the church was in any way prompted by or connected with a preference for poetry. It is true that the passage raises important questions and that its terms are less precise than one might wish. What is the oath to which Milton refers? What does the phrase 'till coming to some maturity of yeers' mean? I shall return to these questions later; for the moment, it is enough to notice that Milton states categorically that he was forced to abandon a church career as a result of ecclesiastical tyranny and an unspecified oath.

Second, the evidence of this passage lays claim to special consideration because it is unique. Nowhere else, in verse or in prose, did Milton think it necessary either to retract or qualify the vocational statement in *The Reason of Church-Government*. It seems clear, then, that we should take him at his word. There is no alternative but to accept the explanation given in *The Reason of Church-Government* for his decision to reject a career in the church. But this has not been the case. On the contrary, later readers have largely ignored the passage or attempted to explain it away; and they have usually done so because its vocational statement does not accord with the critical preconception (which can be supported only circumstantially) that Milton gave up a church career because he wished to devote himself to poetry.

H. F. Fletcher, for example, who assumes a choice between poetry and the pulpit to have been made in 1627–8, argues that 'after this junior year at Cambridge with its large amount of much admired verse, shown to Diodati, colleagues, parents, friends, and probably many others, it would scarcely have been possible for Milton to think seriously any longer of entering the Anglican priesthood'.[6] The only internal authorities to which Fletcher appeals are *Prolusion 7* and a passage in *Elegy 6* (lines 55 ff) which, if taken together, 'supplement each other in pointing to a decision made about 1627 or 1628'.[7] The argument is not convincing. The careers of men like Donne, Herbert and Herrick make it clear that there is no necessary vocational tension between poetry and the priesthood, and there is no evidence to show that Milton ever

considered them to be incompatible; indeed both *Prolusion 7* and
Elegy 6 indicate that the highest sorts of poetry function ideally as
adjuncts to the ministerial office. Moreover, because *Prolusion 7*
and *Elegy 6* treat literature as a vehicle of continuing revelation
and do so without reference to any plans for a church career can
provide no basis for arguing (as Fletcher does) that Milton has
abandoned the priesthood in favour of poetry. The simple truth is
that these two works are concerned with literature, not with the
ministry; and that a prospective clergyman should decide to
consecrate his creative talents to God's service is surely an action
so straightforward as to preclude the necessity of ingenious
explanation. Furthermore, while Fletcher rests his case on the
supposedly enthusiastic reception of Milton's early verse by
parents and friends, there is no record whatsoever of the accolades
which he imagines; and Milton himself disparaged his early
poetry, dismissing the verses composed in the years 1628–9 as
'some trifles' (*YP*, I, p. 809) and describing the early poems in
general as *tenues sonos*, 'trivial songs' (*Ad Patrem*, 4). Finally,
Fletcher points out that in 1627–8 there were no 'vital differences
between Milton's ecclesiastical position and what he found in the
Anglican Church. Such differences did not bother him much
before the middle 1630s and even later'.[8] But Milton explicitly
declares in *The Reason of Church-Government* that he was 'Church-
outed', that the decision to abandon orders was occasioned by a
serious rift between his views and those of the hierarchy of the
established church.

While I firmly endorse Fletcher's view of Milton's Anglican
orthodoxy in the years before 1630, not all recent commentators
are willing to do so. Some readers—notably E. M. W.
Tillyard—believe that Milton's Puritan sympathies were militant enough to force a rupture with the established church before
he left Cambridge, for on 2 July 1628 Milton wrote to his friend
Alexander Gill in these terms (*YP*, I, p. 314):

There is really hardly anyone among us, as far as I know, who,
almost completely unskilled and unlearned in Philology and
Philosophy alike, does not flutter off to Theology unfledged,
quite content to touch that also most lightly, learning barely
enough for sticking together a short harangue by any method
whatever and patching it with worn-out pieces from various
sources—a practice carried far enough to make one fear that

the priestly Ignorance of a former age may gradually attack our Clergy.

On the basis of these remarks Tillyard thinks it probable that 'Milton had already abandoned the idea of taking Orders'.[9] But surely there is nothing in the passage itself to indicate that he has given up a church career or even that he has contemplated it. That the letter voices disillusionment is beyond dispute; but precisely what is the source of discontent? Not the church—unless Milton is being disingenuous, and there is no reason to suppose that he is. His dissatisfaction is with the university and, as in *Prolusion 3*, he is deploring the sterile scholastic methodology on which the educational system at Cambridge was grounded. If there were to remain any truth in the phrase *stupor mundi clerus Anglicanus*, then intending priests would have to be more thoroughly and conscientiously prepared for their sacred calling.

William Haller favours 1632 as the year in which Milton renounced his plan to enter the church. As support for this date Haller appeals to the well-known passage (*YP*, I, p. 884) in the *Apology for Smectymnuus* where Milton, speaking of his departure from Cambridge, takes the occasion

> to acknowledge publickly with all gratefull minde, that more than ordinary favour and respect which I found above any of my equals at the hands of those curteous and learned men, the Fellowes of that Colledge wherein I spent some yeares: who at my parting, after I had taken two degrees, as the manner is, signifi'd many wayes, how much better it would content them that I would stay; as by many Letters full of kindnesse and loving respect both before that time, and long after I was assur'd of their singular good affection towards me.

Haller concludes: 'Milton's abandonment of the career in the church for which he had been so carefully educated was definitely signified by his declining the invitation which, he says, was offered him by the fellows to remain at Christ's.'[10] Four brief points may be made in reply. First, Milton says nothing in the *Apology* about abandoning a career in the church; indeed, in the passage in question he says nothing about the church at all. Second, there is no connection, either necessary or implied, between the decision to leave the university and that to leave the church. As a Master of

Arts Milton was more than adequately qualified as a candidate for orders. Moreover, it was only in exceptional circumstances—as, for example, when a fellowship was vacant—that a student would remain at the university after taking the M.A. degree. Third, Haller's word 'invitation' is misleading: there is no suggestion in the *Apology* that Milton was formally invited to stay on at Christ's; rather, he was 'encourag'd' to continue his studies (doubtless at his own expense), and his tutors expressed understandable regret at losing the company of so able a student and friend.[11] Fourth, if by the word 'invitation' Haller is implying that Milton may have been offered a fellowship, that possibility is erased both by the college statutes and by the fact that in 1632 there were no vacant fellowships at Christ's.[12]

A more convincing argument for assigning to 1632 Milton's decision to abandon holy orders is advanced by A. S. P. Woodhouse:

> Exactly when Milton's resolve was taken to forgo holy orders and devote himself to poetry alone, we cannot with certainty determine. But three convincing factors, it is reasonable to suppose, entered into it—his sense that in the circumstances service in the church was ineligible, the realization that his talents warranted his devoting of himself to poetry, and a religious experience whose ultimate result was to transfer to the chosen medium all the sense of 'calling' that had attached to the ministry, and more. Nor are we without strong indication of the probable date. His quitting Cambridge, in the summer of 1632, would precipitate a decision. This was followed by five months given, it would seem, to silent self-examination, whose outcome was the sonnet, *How soon hath Time* (December 1632). . . .[13]

In December 1629, some eight months after the composition of the delightfully 'pagan' *Elegy 5*, Milton brought the first stage of his literary apprenticeship to an end and, for the first time, he imposed a firm sense of direction on his poetic career. Henceforth, he asserted in *Elegy 6*, he would dedicate his poetic talent to the service of God, and he offered the *Nativity Ode* as the first pledge of that resolve. As Woodhouse has demonstrated, however, Milton more than once relapsed in 1630–1 into the secular and erotic veins that he had determined in December of 1629 to eschew.[14] And therefore, 'vastly important as is the experience recorded in the *Nativity*, it is not final' but 'requires for its completion another experience'.[15] Woodhouse locates the record of that completing experience in *Sonnet 7*:

> On the threshold of the [Hammersmith] period Milton's act of self-dedication required to be renewed, as it was in *Sonnet 7*. From the determination there taken, to live and write hereafter 'As ever in my great Taskmaster's eye', there is no retreat: it leaves its mark on the whole of Milton's subsequent career. . . . [Thus,] if the December of 1629 sees a first decision and resolve, that of 1632 sees its final and irrevocable confirmation.[16]

From the evidence of *Sonnet 7* and Milton's 'Letter to a Friend' (1633), Woodhouse draws two conclusions: (1) shortly after his arrival at Hammersmith in late 1632 Milton rededicated his poetic talents to God's service and resolved to become a religious poet, and (2) his decision to become a poet implied his abandonment of a clerical vocation. Compelling as this argument is at first sight, it can, I believe, on closer examination be shown to be mistaken, for neither the sonnet nor the letter will bear the weight of Woodhouse's assertions.

Sonnet 7, which antedates the letter by some months, may be quoted in full (Honigmann's text):

> How soon hath Time the suttle theef of youth,
> Stoln on his wing my three and twentith yeer!
> My hasting dayes flie on with full career,
> But my late spring no bud or blossom shew'th.
> Perhaps my semblance might deceive the truth,
> That I to manhood am arriv'd so near,
> And inward ripenes doth much less appear,
> That som more timely-happy spirits indu'th.
> Yet be it less or more, or soon or slow,
> It shall be still in strictest measure eev'n,
> To that same lot, however, mean, or high,
> Toward which Time leads me, and the will of Heav'n;
>   All is, if I have grace to use it so,
>   As ever in my great task-Masters eye.

That these lines enshrine an act of conscious self-dedication to God's service is clear enough. But to what service does the dedication apply? Milton does not say. He merely laments that, unlike many young men of comparable age, he has not yet attained 'inward ripenes' that is, the intellectual and spiritual maturity necessary for the career he proposes to follow. (Notice the pun on 'career' in line 3.) However, the uncertainty and insecurity of the octave give way in the sestet to assurance and security: he is in God's hand. But the poem provides no indication of where the divine hand is directing him; indeed, there is no clear vocational statement in the lines at all. Rather, Milton senses himself led toward an unspecified 'lot' which, 'however mean, or high' (again inconclusive and vague), has been determined for him by Providence. If God will grant him grace to conform to his destiny, then (he recognises) he will eventually be confirmed in this unnamed vocation by Time—the 'suttle theef of youth' is now the precondition of vocational preparedness.

Since the sonnet itself specifies no particular career, any interpretation of it which sees the inward promptings as directing Milton exclusively towards a poetical vocation must be seen to have imposed that meaning on the lines. And might not 'the will of Heav'n' sanction both poetry and preaching? Since Milton had long planned to be both a poet and a priest, this is surely the logical inference; and it is also a conclusion supported by Milton's conviction, articulated as early as *Elegy 6* and *Prolusion 7*, that the ethical and spiritual functions and aims of the two offices overlap. Moreover, there is nothing in *Sonnet 7* to suggest that Milton has decided against a church career. Unlike *Elegy 6*, with its determination to eschew 'light elegy', *Sonnet 7* rejects nothing; the only decision made in the sonnet is the positive one to follow the promptings of God's will, *wherever* they may lead him.

Although the vocational frame of reference in *Sonnet 7* could encompass both the priesthood and poetry, there is one consideration which strongly suggests that the main subject of the poem is the calling to the ministry. Milton's spiritual stock-taking and the rededication of himself to God's service in *Sonnet 7* were occasioned by a particular circumstance, for the poem commemorates his twenty-fourth birthday, which fell on 9 December 1632.[17] No doubt it was composed within a few days of this date. Poetically, this event would seem to have no significance whatever; but in terms of the church career for which his university education has been a long and expensive preparation, this birthday was of great importance. Under the provisions of Article 34 in the 1604 canons, Milton was finally eligible to enter the priesthood. But he did not proceed to orders. Instead, he wrote a sonnet explaining to himself and perhaps to his parents as well his reason for postponing ordination. Despite his physical maturity, he asserted, there was still wanting the full spiritual and intellectual maturity that must precede the commitment of one's life to the formal service of God. Time and Providence direct him still toward 'that same lot' (namely, the ministry) to which his talents have been consecrated from childhood; and, until such time as 'inward ripenes' is fully and finally achieved, he prays for the sustaining grace to live and work 'As ever in my great taskMasters eye'.

How, then, should we interpret the experience recorded in *Sonnet 7*? There are, I think, two separate answers. *Poetically*, Milton is dedicating himself and his creative gifts to God's service as he had done in 1629; here, however, on the threshold of his retirement at Hammersmith, he vows that there will be no backsliding (as there had been after the resolve of 1629) into purely secular and amatory verse. *Vocationally*, the poem enshrines an act of submission and obedience rather than an act of rejection; as such, it argues the postponement but not the abandonment of the plan to take holy orders. Time—now more a source of hope than of apprehension—promises increases of knowledge and spiritual accomplishments; and so with the assurance of divine guidance Milton settled in at Hammersmith to prepare himself, both intellectually and spiritually, to serve God from the pulpit and through poetry.

This reading of *Sonnet 7* is supported by the 'Letter to a Friend'[18] which Milton composed in 1633 for an unknown correspondent, in order to give account 'of this my tardie moving; according to the praecept of my conscience, wch I firmly trust is not wthout god' (*YP*, I, p. 319). As in *Sonnet 7*, he justifies his study-retirement to Hammersmith and his decision to delay ordination on the grounds that he is not yet prepared, either in learning or spiritual accomplishments, to take this final step:

it is more probable therefore that not the endlesse delight of speculation but this very consideration of that great com̄andment* does not presse forward as soone as may be to

---

* The 'great com̄andment' is that 'set out by the terrible seasing of him that hid the talent' in Matthew 25: 24–30.)

underg[o] but keeps off wth a sacred reverence & religious advisement how best to undergoe[,] not taking thought of beeing late so it give advantage to be more fit, for those that were latest lost nothing when the maister of the vinyard came to give each one his hire. (*YP*, I, p. 320)

In the next sentence he excuses the length of this justification of his 'tardie moving' with the witty observation, 'heere I am come to a streame head copious enough to disburden it selfe like Nilus at seven mouthes into an ocean, but then I should also run into a reciprocall contradiction of ebbing & flowing at once & doe that wch I excuse myselfe for not doing[,] preach & not preach.' And then at the conclusion of the letter he makes the quality of this 'preaching' to his friend a further reason for his retirement to Hammersmith for continued study and preparation:

this therfore alone may be a sufficient reason for me to keepe me as I am least having thus tired you singly, I should deale worse wth a whole congregation, & spoyle all the patience of a Parish. for I my selfe doe not only see my owne tediousnesse but now grow offended wth it that has hinderd [me] thus long from coming to the last & best period of my letter . . . . (*YP*, I, pp. 320–1)

On the strength of this letter a number of scholars[19] have argued that Milton had, by 1633, determined against a church career and instead decided to devote his talents to poetry. The letter itself, however, makes no reference to a poetic career, and this fact has led Woodhouse to claim that it is 'a somewhat disingenuous document'.[20] But what possible reason is there to assume that Milton is being insincere? Deceit is not a Miltonic trait and, in any case, the vocational statement in the letter is clear and straightforward, 'the plain implication of the language being', as J. H. Hanford has observed, 'that he intends, when he is ready, to labour in the vineyard as a minister'.[21] The circumstances surrounding the letter's composition are not difficult to reconstruct: a friend (perhaps Thomas Young) has inquired why, being now fully qualified for the ministry, Milton is delaying ordination, and Milton replies with complete candour that the postponement of holy orders has been occasioned by his need of further study and spiritual preparation, 'not taking thought of beeing late so it

give advantage to be more fit'. As Parker rightly points out, the
letter 'implies throughout that the writer will eventually become a
clergyman' — it 'is not an apology for giving up the ministry; it is
an apology for what has seemed to a good friend procrastination'
(*MB*, I, p. 122).

Without some solid evidence (which neither *Sonnet 7* nor the
'Letter to a Friend' will provide) there is no basis from which to
argue that Milton had rejected a clerical vocation before 1633.
Indeed, all of the evidence we possess and all of the logical
inferences which the problem would seem to admit point clearly
to the conclusion that the decision was not finally taken until
much later. In the first place, although it was customary for a
young man to enter the church as soon as he was qualified by age
and education to do so, it was not unusual for some to delay
ordination, often for a number of years. George Herbert, for
example, was in his mid-thirties when he formally committed his
life to the church; similarly, Edward King delayed holy orders,
presumably in order to prepare himself for a more effective
ministry (*MB*, I, p. 156). Moreover, while many of his contemporaries were driven by financial considerations to embark on
their careers as soon as possible, Milton was not bound by such
constraints; his father, a well-to-do scrivener, was both able and
willing to subsidise the further period preparation that Milton
believed necessary. In the second place, the intensive programme
of reading undertaken at Hammersmith and Horton from 1632 to
early 1638 argues that Milton was training himself more
thoroughly for the priesthood. With the aid of the *Commonplace
Book* (begun in 1634–5),[22] it is possible to establish with some
accuracy the nature and scope of these private studies; and
perhaps the lost 'Index Theologicus',[23] if it were begun about this
time, would have allowed us to supplement the outline further.
From the evidence we do possess, however, one important fact
about Milton's private studies emerges clearly: the reading programme, whatever its implications for a poetic preparation, was
admirably suited to someone preparing himself for the ministry.
Although he read Dante and Ariosto, Milton devoted most of his
energies during these years to historical and patristic works.[24] In a
1554 edition of *Ecclesiasticae Historiae Autores* he worked his way
systematically through the prolix church histories of Eusebius,
Socrates Scholasticus, Theodoret, and many others; at the same
time he was immersed in the works of the Greek and Latin Fathers

and, in 1636, he purchased a copy of John Chrysostom's *Orationes*.
The obvious pertinence of such a programme to one preparing for
the ministry, coupled with the diligence and singlemindedness
with which the studies were pursued, makes it seem certain that
Milton was still planning a career in the church. In the third
place, until the mid-1630s there is not the slightest indication of
any dissatisfaction on Milton's part with the established church.
The fact that he later became strident in dissent provides no basis
for arguing, *a posteriori*, that his Puritanism was always uncompromising and militant; indeed, there is not even any solid
evidence to confirm the usual assumption that he was a Puritan
before 1637. Certainly, prior to William Laud's translation to
Canterbury in 1633, there was little in the English church and
nothing in Milton's writings to account for the declaration in *The
Reason of Church-Government* that he was 'Church-outed' by prelatical tyranny. The ecclesiastical climate of 1632–3 is well summarised by Parker (*MB*, I, pp. 151–2):

> . . . it was still possible to enter the Church of England without
> being a Laudian. A person of vaguely Calvinistic sentiments
> like [Milton] could easily have obtained a living and contrived,
> somehow, to avoid compliance with many of the required forms
> and ceremonies. He had observed his own former tutor,
> Thomas Young, doing just that in his ministry at Stowmarket
> . . . Better still, he might have become a 'lecturer', confining
> himself to religious teaching and performing no church rites at
> all. This device had been originated by Puritans, and was a
> congenial solution for a young man educated for the ministry
> but unwilling to conform to episcopal discipline.

Although Parker believes Milton's Puritan convictions in 1632 to
be more deeply rooted than I would concede, we agree that
'Milton left Cambridge quite amenable to the old idea of becoming a minister' (*MB*, I, p.153). Whether orthodox Anglican or
moderate Puritan, he settled in his father's house at Hammersmith to prepare himself for a more effective ministry, without any
hint of the future rupture between his views and those of the
prelatical hierarchy.

The earliest record of Milton's disapproval of the national
church comes in 1637 in the passionate indictment of clerical
corruption in lines 108–31 of *Lycidas*:

Last came, and last did go,
The pilot of the Galilean lake,
Two massy keys he bore of metals twain,
(The golden opes, the iron shuts amain)
He shook his mitred locks, and stern bespake,
How well could I have spared for thee, young swain,
Enow of such as for their bellies' sake,
Creep and intrude, and climb into the fold?
Of other care they little reckoning make,
Than how to scramble at the shearers' feast,
And shove away the worthy bidden guest;
Blind mouths! that scarce themselves know how to hold
A sheep-hook, or have learned aught else the least
That to the faithful herdman's art belongs!
What recks it them? What need they? They are sped;
And when they list, their lean and flashy songs
Grate on their scrannel pipes of wretched straw,
The hungry sheep look up, and are not fed,
But swoll'n with wind, and the rank mist they draw,
Rot inwardly, and foul contagion spread:
Besides what the grim wolf with privy paw
Daily devours apace, and nothing said,
But that two-handed engine at the door,
Stands ready to smite once, and smite no more.

That Milton was seriously dissatisfied with the clergy when he wrote these lines cannot be disputed. There is no more biting and heartfelt arraignment of them in English literature. But do the lines imply a disillusionment so complete, a resentment so deep-rooted, that he determined to abandon the vocation to which he had been dedicated from childhood? Did the unsettling political and ecclesiastical events of 1637[25] result in so forceful an alienation from the church that further thought of the ministry was inconceivable? It is possible that they did; and John T. Shawcross argues persuasively that 'sometime during the summer of 1637 Milton decided against a church career and, by the beginning of autumn, in favour of a poetic one'.[26] There are compelling reasons, however, for believing that such was not the case and that, on the contrary, *Lycidas* contains a positive statement of ministerial calling.

The *assumptions* that Milton had rejected the ministry by the end

of 1637 and that his Puritanism was as militant in 1637 as it was in
1642 have led, I believe, to a general misinterpretation of the lines
denouncing clerical corruption in *Lycidas*. It is significant that the
poem as a whole is concerned with both poetry and the priesthood, for Milton (like Edward King) planned to be a poet as well
as a priest. Arthur Barker has argued convincingly that the
structure of *Lycidas* is tripartite, composed of three movements
which are 'practically equal in length and precisely parallel in
pattern'. The first movement (lines 15–84), concerned with
Lycidas as poet-shepherd, examines the problem of 'the possible
frustration of disciplined poetic ambition by early death'; the
second (lines 85–131), treating his role as priest-shepherd, examines the problem of 'the frustration of a sincere shepherd in a
corrupt church'; and the third (lines 132–85) is an apotheosis
which resolves these problems and 'unites the themes of the
preceding movements in the ultimate reward of the true poet-
priest'.[27] There is no indication in the poem that Milton has
decided to substitute poetry for the priesthood; indeed, the
apotheosis of lines 132–85 transforms both poet and priest:
Lycidas fulfills his poetic hopes by joining the celestial diapason
and he fulfills his pastoral vocation by becoming a protective
deity, a 'genius of the shore' to guard all those 'that wander in that
perilous flood' (183–5). The logical inference is that Milton still
plans to be both priest and poet—and that the poem's structure
and thematic emphases reflect this dual ambition.

In the light of these general comments on *Lycidas* we can return
now to St Peter's speech in lines 113–31. Three points may be
made about this section. First, the passage is not (as is sometimes
argued)[28] a frontal attack on the prelate-ridden hierarchy of a
church that has forced Milton out of holy orders. The arraignment is not particularised; it is directed at clerical depravity in
general and not that of the bishops especially. In fact, the
Anglican hierarchy is never mentioned in the poem, although that
of Rome does not escape so easily.[29] The lines quite simply show
that Milton, an intending ordinand, is revolted by the rampant
abuse and self-interest at all levels in the church in which he
proposes to serve. They are the sentiments of a young ethical
idealist deploring depravation and corruption in his chosen profession. Second, the imminence of purgation, of divine retribution
in the form of a 'two-handed engine' (whatever that may be),
makes it clear that Milton expected the church shortly to become

a reformed and regenerate institution. Certainly, this image has
more of hope than of despair in it, more to suggest a reason for
embracing than for abandoning the church. Third, the fact that
Milton put the speech denouncing the clergy into the mouth of St
Peter, himself the first bishop and the traditional paradigm of
episcopal perfection, argues strongly that in 1637 he had not yet
come to that fundamental opposition to prelature that character-
ises the anti-prelatical tracts of 1641–2.

There is no reason to doubt that Milton was well informed
concerning the religious and political divisions among his countrymen; doubtless, he was also aware of the emotional contagion
bred by those issues which was sweeping London at the time.[30]
Except in *Lycidas*, however, he never mentions them; and his
silence is not difficult to explain. Diligently pursuing his private
studies at Horton, Milton ventured forth only on rare occasions to
London or Oxford, and on those few occasions when he was lured
away from the 'obscurity and cramped quarters' (*YP*, I, p. 327) of
his father's country house he was motivated only by the desire
'either to purchase books or to become acquainted with some new
discovery in mathematics or music' (*YP*, IV, i, p. 614). The
Horton years (1635–8) are marked by relentless study. Apart
from the revision of *Comus* and the composition of *Lycidas*, he
apparently wrote no poetry; and in two letters of 1637 to Diodati
he speaks only of his studies, from which he permits 'scarcely
anything to distract me' (*YP*, I, p. 323). Horton was sufficiently
isolated and Milton sufficiently occupied with studies and his own
plans that he remained relatively untouched, in a way that
residence in the heart of London would hardly have allowed, by
events that few could have foreseen would erupt in the convul-
sions later to rend church and state. While by no means ignorant
of contemporary affairs, Milton was not sufficiently aroused by
the events of 1637 to commit himself to the Puritan cause by any
decisive personal action. There is no indication in *Lycidas* or any
other of his works in this period that he felt the tension between
Puritan and Anglican in so deep and personal a way that he was
forced to abandon his plan for holy orders; indeed, there is
nothing in his writings or biography before 1639, when news of the
first Bishops' War cut short his Italian trip, to suggest that his
Puritanism was militant enough to cause him to become actively
involved in political or ecclesiastical controversy, and even then
he waited a further two years before he finally decided (or was

induced) to raise his left hand against the bishops.

If what we know or can infer about Milton's religious convictions in 1637 argues that he had not yet decided against a church career, it may be added that the same conclusion is confirmed by all that we know of his character. It seems certain that the rejection of life-long plan to take holy orders was not a step which Milton took either lightly or hastily; the decision, when it was finally and irrevocably made, was the climax of a long process of self-examination. Milton was never one to abandon any of his plans or hopes easily. Through all the vicissitudes of civil war and the Interregnum, right up to the eve of the Restoration when all hope was lost, he was to give most of his energy and all of his eyesight to the cause of liberty and the establishment of the English New Jerusalem. It is inconceivable that such a man would relinquish his plans to enter the priesthood until he were certain that there remained no possibility, from a position within the church itself, of redressing prelatical evils and effecting ecclesiastical reformation. Milton was not, by nature, a Satanic rebel seeking to overthrow a cause from without by proclaiming his *non serviam* and resorting to subversion and insurrection to achieve his ends. Rather, he sought always, as long as it remained possible to do so, to work for change and reformation within the framework of constituted authority. On more than one occasion over the course of his career, he had just cause to view himself in the role of an Abdiel, that faithful seraph whose steadfastness in the face of rebellion the blind poet was to have the Almighty praise in the words:

> Servant of God, well done, well hast thou fought
> The better fight, who single hast maintained
> Against revolted multitudes the cause
> Of truth, in word mightier than they in arms;
> And for the testimony of truth hast borne
> Universal reproach, far worse to bear
> Than violence: for this was all thy care
> To stand approved in sight of God, though worlds
> Judged thee perverse. (*PL*, VI, 29–37)

Given Milton's firmness of character, his immersion in his studies, and even *Lycidas* itself, there is no evidence to suggest that he had abandoned a calling within the church in 1637.

The significance of the condemnation of the church in *Lycidas* is that for the first time Milton aligns himself with the Puritan faction. It is often thought that such and allegiance has been implicit from the beginning of Milton's career—as, for example, in his choice of 'Puritan' Cambridge over 'Anglican' Oxford—but claims like this will not bear examination.[31] He *may* have had Puritan leanings for some years, but these required time to mature. Nevertheless, *Lycidas* is the first statement, public or private, of Puritan sympathies; and this declaration of religious allegiance would not have precluded a plan to work for reform, as many moderate Puritans were still doing in 1637, from a position within the Church of England. The anticlerical passage in *Lycidas*, then, should be regarded more as a 'position paper' than a religious manifesto whose claims were intended to issue in immediate action. Like the experience which led, in 1629, to an act of poetic self-dedication in *Elegy 6* and the *Nativity Ode*, the dedication to the Puritan cause needed time to develop. And, as the decision of 1629 was reaffirmed three years later in *Sonnet 7* and the original resolve made firm and final, so also the determination of 1637 (toward which he may have been moving for some time but did not articulate until *Lycidas*) was not completed until it was reconfirmed in the early 1640s, when a pledge to the Presbyterian cause achieved fruition in the antiprelatical tracts of 1641–2.

In April or May 1638, some six months after composing *Lycidas*, Milton set off on a trip to the Continent. The experience of fifteen months abroad, months spent almost entirely in Catholic Italy, was to prove crucial, for it deepened Milton's Puritanism and, in proportion, doubtless increased any uneasiness he may have had about a career in the English church. Although he had determined while in Italy not to 'begin a conversation about religion, but if questioned about my faith [to] hide nothing, whatever the consequences' (*YP*, IV, i. p. 619), he did not hesitate to express his beliefs freely—so freely, in fact, that he seems to have been somewhat of an embarrassment to his Italian hosts. At Naples, for example, the affable Giovanni Battista Manso 'gravely apologized' that, 'even though he had especially wished to show me many more attractions, he could not do so in that city, since I was unwilling to be more circumspect in relation to religion' (*YP*, IV, i, p. 618); and Manso presented his outspoken English friend with a complimentary, but pointed, Latin distich:

Ut mens, forma, decor, mos, si pietas sic,
Non Anglus, verum herculè Angelus ipse fores.[32]

Milton's unwelcome harangues earned him a certain notoriety among the Italians, and his reputation followed him down the peninsula. While still at Naples he learned from merchants 'of plots laid against me by the English Jesuits, should I return to Rome' (*YP*, IV, i, p. 619). But the rumours did not prevent his going back—nor did they silence him once he had arrived, for he later wrote of his return trip to the Eternal City: 'For almost two more months, in the very stronghold of the Pope, if anyone attacked the orthodox religion, I openly, as before, defended it.' (*YP*, IV, i, p. 619) Such head-on confrontations over theology no doubt taught Milton much about himself and his faith, giving his Puritan sentiments ample opportunity for pointed development and entrenchment. In Italy he would quickly have been made aware, in a way scarcely possible from the books at Horton, of the ideological gulf between Protestant and Catholic, and he must at the same time have come to appreciate, both doctrinally and emotionally, the charge that Laud was moving the English church toward Papism. Any doubts he may have entertained about a career in the Laudian church can only have been heightened by his contact with Catholicism in Italy.

It was probably the first Bishops' War (March 1639) which caused Milton to cancel a visit to Sicily and Greece, and to return to England: '. . . the sad tidings of civil war from England summoned me back. For I thought it base that I should travel abroad at my ease for the cultivation of my mind, while my fellow-citizens at home were fighting for their liberty.' (*YP*, IV, i, p. 619) But he did not hurry home. Returning to England by land through Switzerland, he stopped to visit Giovanni Diodati, the eminent professor of theology at Geneva and the uncle of Milton's friend Charles Diodati,[33] and did not finally reach London until August or September 1639. Although he has more than once been criticised for the leisurely pace at which he answered the summons of his countrymen fighting for their liberty, his account in the *Defensio Secunda* needs little justification. The statement quoted above occurs in a passage where Milton is defending his personal integrity against trumped-up charges; and this fact, combined with the fifteen years of polemical warfare in defence of

Christian liberty which separate the events themselves from their description in the *Defensio Secunda*, have doubtless led him to overstate the cause as it then affected him. The Bishops' Wars were the unhappy result of Laud's effort to impose episcopacy and a Prayer Book discipline on Presbyterian Scotland. The conflict must have seemed remote to Milton, who up to that time had shown little interest in politics; moreover, although Italy intensified his Puritanism, there is no evidence to indicate that he was a committed Presbyterian in 1639. Probably feeling that he had little to contribute, and perhaps himself undecided between the rival claims of Anglican and Presbyterian, he nonetheless thought it best to return home, in case he could be of help.

Once back in England he took quarters in St Bride's Churchyard near Fleet Street, 'and there, blissfully enough, devoted myself to my interrupted studies, willingly leaving the outcome of these events [the second Bishops' War of August-September 1640], first of all to God, and then to those whom the people had entrusted with this office' (*YP*, IV, i, p. 621). In other words, he kept out of the political arena and resumed the programme of studies begun at Hammersmith in 1632; he also, although he does not mention it in the *Defensio Secunda*, undertook at this time the education of his nephews John and Edward Phillips. There is nothing inexplicable or surprising in this behaviour—unless one clings to the assumption that Milton had been a firmly committed Puritan from 1637 or even earlier.

When Milton returned from his continental tour in the late summer of 1639, many things had changed. He had left England as a moderate Puritan, perhaps with some doubts about his proposed church career; he returned with both his Puritan sympathies and his vocational doubts intensified by experience abroad. At home, meanwhile, the political and ecclesiastical climate had altered dramatically during his fifteen months' absence. Tensions between Puritan and Anglican, serious enough in 1637–8, were nearing the breaking-point by the end of 1639. But it was to be the year 1640 that was decisive—the year in which the fates of Laud, Strafford, and ultimately Charles himself were sealed. In April 1640 Charles was constrained to call Parliament in order to raise money to subdue the rebellious Scots. The Short Parliament, assembled with the Convocation of Canterbury, met on 13 April, but in the hope of obtaining a peace with Scotland refused to vote the king taxes and so was promptly dissolved on 5

May. Under Laud's supervision, however, Convocation continued in session after the dissolution. As well as voting Charles
the taxes he wanted, Convocation took the opportunity provided
by this illegal session to pass the *Constitutions and Canons Ecclesias-
ticall,* an elaborate defence of the doctrine and discipline of the
Laudian church. While the *Canons* contained much that was
controversial, nothing aroused Puritan ire so much as the notori-
ous 'Et Cetera' oath in Article VI—an oath to be imposed on the
entire English clergy whereby each priest would swear never to
consent to the alteration of 'the Government of this Church, by
Arch-bishops, Bishops, Deanes, and Arch-deacons, &c. as it
stands now established, and as by right it ought to stand'.³⁴

After the promulgation of Laud's *Canons* in June 1640, events
moved forward swiftly. In September the second Bishops' War
ended in defeat and the humiliating Treaty of Ripon by which
Charles was obliged to pay the Scots in excess of £20,000 a month
until their claims were settled by further negotiation. The succes-
ses in arms of their Scottish co-religionists, coupled with the
passion aroused by the Laudian *Canons,* made English Presbyterians more hopeful and more vocal. The king's chronic
insolvency forced him to recall parliament later that autumn, and
the members of the Long Parliament that assembled on 3
November lost no time in discomfiting Charles by attacking his
counsellors and bishops. Strafford was impeached and high
treason proceedings against him, initiated by Pym in the Commons on 11 November, passed to the Lords on 24 November. On
11 December the celebrated London Petition demanding the
abolition of episcopal government 'with all its dependances,
rootes and branches' was delivered to the Commons on behalf
of the 15,000 Londoners who had signed it. Four days later
Laud's *Canons* were declared void and on 18 December Laud
himself was charged with treason and imprisoned in the Tower.
For Charles and his ministers the beginning of the end had
passed swiftly.

During these exciting months of 1640 Milton was living in the
heart of London. No longer sequestered with his books in the
peaceful house. at Horton, he was caught in the tumultuous
current sweeping the nation toward civil war. In such circumstances it was impossible to remain neutral for long, and not much
time can have passed after he settled in St Bride's Churchyard
until he dedicated himself without reservation to the Puritan and

Parliamentary cause. Finally, with the publication of the Laudian *Canons* in June 1640, he took the decisive step that he had seriously meditated for at least several months: he gave up all thought of a career in the English church.

There seems little reason to doubt that this is essentially what happened. Indeed, it is the account that Milton himself has left us in *The Reason of Church-Government*: 'comming to some maturity of yeers and perceaving what tyranny had invaded the Church, that he who would take Orders must subscribe slave, and take an oath withall, which unlesse he took with a conscience that would retch, he must either strait perjure, or split his faith, I thought it better to preferre a blamelesse silence before the sacred office of speaking bought, and begun with servitude and forswearing.' (*YP*, I, pp. 822–3) There can be no real doubt that the oath here referred to is the 'Et Cetera' oath of the 1640 canons. The only other oath to which the passage might be alluding is that in the 1604 canons, and there is no indication that Milton ever held it in any disesteem or ever thought it a symbol of episcopal despotism. On the contrary, he had already twice subscribed to the oath of 1604 without perjuring himself or splitting his faith—first, on proceeding to the B.A. in 1629 and, again, on taking the M.A. in 1632.[35] Moreover, when he wrote *The Reason of Church-Government* Milton thought it unnecessary to specify a particular oath because he assumed that his readers would not mistake his meaning; in 1642 such an assumption could only be true of the hated 'Et Cetera' oath which had been a burning issue among English Puritans. The Laudian tyranny which Milton witnessed in the church after his return from Italy in late 1639 turned him finally against the idea of taking holy orders and, in terms of a vocation in the church, the *Canons* of 1640 was the straw that broke the camel's back. It was clear that he could not be both a Puritan and a priest in the Church of England.

It is not known what prompted Milton to enter the controversy over episcopacy; however, whether on his own initiative or at the invitation of the Smectymnuans (one of whom was Thomas Young), he first exercised his left hand against the bishops in *A Postscript*, bound as an appendix to the Smectymnuan *Answer to a Booke Entituled, An Humble Remonstrance* (March 1641). In the five pamphlets against prelacy which Milton published in rapid succession between May 1641 and April 1642, references to the priesthood are relatively frequent. His break with the Anglican establishment is complete. He argues vigorously for a Pres-

byterian settlement in the church and, like Puritans throughout
the century, he asserts that it is the inward call from God and not
the episcopal rite of ordination that marks a man as a chosen
vessel of the word.[36] Coupled with the fact that, apart from *Lycidas*,
Milton had not spoken of ministerial calling since the 'Letter to a
Friend' of 1633 and that after 1642 the subject is not mentioned
again until the discussion of clerical vocation in *De Doctrina
Christiana* and the attack on the clergy in *The Likeliest Means to
Remove Hirelings* (1659), the repeated allusions to ministerial
calling in the antiprelatical tracts of 1641–2 argue that the topic
was then much in his thoughts and that his decision to reject a
church career had been a recent one.

To summarise the chronology I have been suggesting: Milton,
who had been dedicated to the ministry from childhood, went up
to Cambridge in 1625 to prepare himself for a career in the
English church. However, feeling himself neither academically
nor spiritually ready for orders when he reached the canonical age
of twenty-four in December 1632 (see *Sonnet 7*), he deferred
ordination and retired to his father's country house—first at
Hammersmith and later at Horton in Buckinghamshire—in
order to devote himself in solitude to a programme of private
studies. During the Horton years (1635–8) an uneasiness with the
Laudian church and his appreciation of a rift between his religious views and the practice of the Anglican establishment became
sufficiently acute for him to deplore priestly corruption and
self-interest in the anticlerical passage in *Lycidas*. But like the
choice between divine and secular poetry in 1629 (see *Elegy 6*), the
determination of 1637 was not final and required time to mature;
he therefore continued his private studies and in the spring of 1638
left for Italy, perhaps thinking that the issues at home, from which
he had been largely isolated at Horton, would resolve themselves
in time. His Puritan sympathies and his doubts about a church
career, intensified by the experience of Catholic Italy, resulted in
a dedication to the Presbyterian cause probably not long after his
return to England in the late summer of 1639. Finally, with the
promulgation of the Laudian *Canons* in June 1640, he decided
irrevocably against a formal vocation in the church. It was
perhaps this long delayed decision against a church career which
prompted him to take a larger house in Aldersgate Street and to
increase the number of his students. If he were not to be a
preacher, then he would become a schoolmaster.

2 Poetic Vocation, 1628–42

'My father', Milton wrote in 1654, 'destined me in early childhood for the study of literature, for which I had so keen an appetite that from my twelfth year scarcely ever did I leave my studies for my bed before the hour of midnight.' (*YP*, IV, i, p. 612) Twelve years earlier he had expressed his filial gratitude and described his dedication to literature in similar though more precise terms: 'I must say therefore that after I had from my first yeeres by the ceaselesse diligence and care of my father, whom God recompence, bin exercis'd to the tongues, and some sciences, as my age would suffer, by sundry masters both at home and at the schools, it was found that whether ought was impos'd me by them that had the overlooking, or betak'n to of mine own choise in English, or other tongue, prosing or versing, but chiefly this latter, the stile by certain vital signes it had, was likely to live.' (*YP*, I, pp. 808–9) This assessment, so vigorously reconfirmed by posterity, is best seen as a rare instance of Miltonic understatement.

Exactly when Milton decided to become a poet cannot with certainty be determined, but there is no reason to doubt that the decision was taken early. He was born into a cultured and accomplished family where the fine arts were given a respected place in domestic life and where, as he tells us in *Ad Patrem* and elsewhere, his own literary interests and talents were encouraged and applauded. His father, a scrivener by trade, earned an enviable reputation in the world of music,[1] and during Milton's formative years the house in Bread Street must often have welcomed such talented visitors as the composer William Byrd; perhaps it was also at this time that the future author of *Arcades* and *Comus* was first introduced to another musician, the precocious and affable Henry Lawes. But the younger Milton's genius was to fulfil itself in poetry rather than music. Although he did not lisp in numbers from his mother's knee, his aptitude for poetry nevertheless declared itself very early according to Aubrey: 'Anno Domini 1619, he was ten years old, as by his picture: &

was then a Poet.'² None of this early verse, however, has survived.
The earliest pieces that have come down to us from his pen—the
verse paraphrases of Psalms 114 and 136—date from 1624, his
last year at St Paul's School.³ Apart from these two English
paraphrases, and four epigrams (three Latin and one Greek)⁴
which have tentatively been assigned to 1624, no other samples of
his pre-Cambridge verse have survived.

During his four undergraduate years (February 1625–March
1629) Milton wrote a considerable amount of poetry, most of it in
Latin and much of it either topical or occasional. Only two
English poems (both belonging to 1628) have been preserved
from these years: *On the Death of a Fair Infant*, occasioned by the
death of his little niece in January 1628,⁵ and *At a Vacation Exercise*,
composed in July or August of the same year. From a vocational
point of view the *Vacation Exercise* is by far the most illuminating of
all the poems, Latin or English, belonging to his undergraduate
days at Cambridge.

Sometime shortly before the conclusion of the summer term in
1628, Milton was unexpectedly called upon to preside as 'Dictator' over the festive assembly marking the end of the college
year. In the Latin oration (*Prolusion 6*) which he composed—not
without apology⁶—for this occasion, he rose valiantly if somewhat awkwardly to the heights of ribaldry and coarse humour
expected of him as 'Dictator'. However, having sustained this
foreign mood for some time, he abruptly terminated the *prolusio* by
declaring that he would 'overleap the University Statutes as if
they were the wall of Romulus and run off from Latin into
English' (*YP*, I, p. 286),⁷ and the announcement of this innova-
tion was followed by a hundred lines of English decasyllabic coup-
lets—the *Vacation Exercise*–in which he confided to the assembly
his private poetic aspirations. Eschewing 'those new-fangled
toys, and trimming slight/Which takes our late fantastics with
delight' (lines 19–20),⁸ he told his fellow-students how he
would prefer to employ the vernacular:

> Yet I had rather, if I were to choose,
> Thy service in some graver subject use,
> Such as may make thee search thy coffers round,
> Before thou clothe my fancy in fit sound:
> Such where the deep transported mind may soar
> Above the wheeling poles, and at heaven's door

Look in, and see each blissful deity
How he before the thunderous throne doth lie,
Listening to what unshorn Apollo sings
To the touch of golden wires, while Hebe brings
Immortal nectar to her kingly sire:
Then passing through the spheres of watchful fire,
And misty regions of wide air next under,
And hills of snow and lofts of piled thunder,
May tell at length how green-eyed Neptune raves,
In heaven's defiance mustering all his waves;
Then sing of secret things that came to pass
When beldame Nature in her cradle was;
And last of kings and queens and heroes old,
Such as the wise Demodocus once told
In solemn songs at king Alcinous' feast,
While sad Ulysses' soul and all the rest
Are held with his melodious harmony
In willing chains and sweet captivity.

                                                    (29–52)

This is the first but by no means the last time that Milton
interrupts a public statement in order 'to covnant with any
knowing reader' on the topic of his poetic aspirations.

As Hanford has noted, the *Vacation Exercise* constitutes a 'mature and serious meditation on his vocation as a poet'.[9] And the
lines do tell us a good deal, not only about Milton's poetic
ambitions in 1628, but also about his understanding of the poet's
role. It is clear that he has decided to become a serious poet. The
anomalous occasion—a festive college assembly—which he
chose to announce his decision argues that he attached great
importance to his advertisement of poetic calling, that he thought
the decision in some sense momentous and that it was, perhaps, a
recent one which he was simply unable to keep to himself. He had,
of course, written a considerable amount of verse already, much of
it very fine from one so young; but there is nothing in this earlier
poetry to indicate a sense of mission and commitment. However,
that is precisely the sense imparted by the *Vacation Exercise*: it is a
manifesto, a public declaration of poetic calling. Moreover, the
patriotic announcement that he will write in the vernacular
is significant. Not only does this declaration oppose the humanist emphasis on composition in Latin or at least in

imitation of Latin models (both of which he rejects), but it also marks an important change in Milton's poetic career, for in 1628 he had written only three English poems (the two Psalm paraphrases and *Fair Infant*), as compared with well over a dozen in Latin. Nevertheless, the decision was taken in earnest. To the decade following 1628 only three Latin poems (*Elegy 5*, *Elegy 6*, *Ad Patrem*) may be assigned with any certainty; the remainder, apart from the Italian sonnets, are in English. Clearly Milton did have an important announcement to make in the *Vacation Exercise*: he had determined to become a serious poet and he had elected to follow Spenser and Sidney rather than Virgil and Buchanan.

If it is clear from the *Vacation Exercise* that Milton is firmly resolved to become an English poet, it is equally clear that he is not certain of how to fulfil that resolve. He will not, he says, write in empty phrases or with conceit-ridden artificiality; rather, he proposes to clothe decorous thoughts in inspired imagery, using his native language to adorn 'some graver subject'. But the precise nature of the 'graver subject' remains as yet unsettled and so too does the poetic form in which to cast it. He does, however, offer some suggestions: perhaps he will compose inspired odes like Pindar; perhaps, like Hesiod or Du Bartas, he will sing the mysteries of the foundation of the universe; or perhaps he will choose, as Homer and Spenser had done, to embroider a heroic theme 'of kings and queens and heroes old'. These are all possibilities, but it is too soon yet to commit himself.[10]

There is one further point that needs to be made here about the *Vacation Exercise*: it shows Milton already moving toward that lofty view of the poetic function set out in the autobiographical sections of the 1641–2 pamphlets and the later poetry. The true poet is an inspired creature; his 'deep transported mind' soars aloft beyond the 'wheeling poles' of the Ptolemaic universe to the courts of celestial Apollo. As well as penetrating the inmost sanctuaries of deity, he can also disclose the mysteries of the *natura naturata*, revealing those 'secret things that come to pass/ When beldame Nature in her cradle was'. But the true poet is more even than this, more than an exalted visionary; he is also a persuasive teacher whose words, like the 'melodious harmony' of the Phaeacian bard, hold his auditors rapt in 'willing chains and sweet captivity'. Here in a rudimentary form, perhaps more implicit than explicit, is the foundation of the elevated Miltonic conception of the poet's role: he is the spokesman of the gods, the interpreter of divine mysteries and of the secrets of the created universe, whose inspired utterance serves as a mode of continuing revelation. This outline of the poetic function, although sharpened in detail in later statements, remains conceptually unaltered from the *Vacation Exercise* of 1628 all the way to *Paradise Lost* where the 'celestial patroness' of God's blind poet-priest 'deigns Her nightly visitation unimplored' (IX, 21–2) to sing into his slumbering ear the story of heaven and earth and deeds more than heroic.

Nine months after the *Vacation Exercise*, when he returned momentarily to Latin verse in *Elegy 5* (April–May 1629), Milton did not forget the promises made the previous summer. *Elegy 5* is a poem about poetry and poetic insight.[11] With the return of spring has come also a renewal of inspiration and a restoration of the power of song; and the mysterious impulse of vernal and imaginative rebirth has given the poet a theme to celebrate—namely, Spring herself:

> Concitaque arcano fervent mihi pectora motu,
> Et furor, et sonitus me sacer intus agit.
> Delius ipse venit, video Peneide lauro
> Implicitos crines, Delius ipse venit.
> Iam mihi mens liquidi raptatur in ardua coeli,
> Perque vagas nubes corpore liber eo.
> Perque umbras, perque antra feror penetralia vatum,
> Et mihi fana patent interiora Deum.
> Intuiturque animus toto quid agatur Olympo,
> Nec fugiunt oculos Tartara caeca meos.
> Quid tam grande sonat distento spiritus ore?
> Quid parit haec rabies, quid sacer iste furor?
> Ver mihi, quod dedit ingenium, cantabitur illo;
> Profuerint isto reddita dona modo.
>
> (11–24)

My soul is deeply stirred and glows with its mysterious impulse, and I am driven on by poetic frenzy and the sacred sound which fills my brain. Apollo himself is coming—I can see his hair wreathed in Penean laurel—Apollo himself is coming. Now my mind is whirled up to the heights of the bright, clear sky: freed from my body, I move among the wandering clouds. I am carried through shadows and caves, the secret haunts of the poets, and the innermost sanctuaries of the gods are open to me. I see in my mind's eye what is going on all over Olympus, and the unseen depths of Tartarus do not escape my eyes. What song is my spirit singing so loudly with wide-open mouth? What is being born of this madness, this sacred frenzy? The spring, which gave me inspiration, shall be the theme of the song it inspires: in this way her gifts will be repaid with interest.

(*PM*, p. 86)

This description of poetic afflatus, except that it is presented as actual (a conventional fiction) rather than simply imagined, is not fundamentally different from that in lines 33–44 of the *Vacation Exercise*. Both are couched in pagan imagery and both imply more a yearning after than an attainment of visionary experience: *Quid parit haec rabies, quid sacer iste furor?* Taken together, however, these two poems mark the first definite stage in Milton's gradually maturing awareness of poetic destiny and form a prelude to the deepened sense of calling shortly to come.

The composition of the *Nativity Ode* and *Elegy 6* in December 1629 marks the second stage of Milton's sense of poetic vocation, and here for the first time he imposes a firm direction on his literary career. The vague ambitions of the earlier poems become sharply focused and the adumbrations of a poetic destiny are made explicit and precise. *Elegy 6*, which was apparently composed at the same time as the *Nativity Ode*,[12] is an answer to a letter from Diodati who had sent Milton some verses but apologised for their quality since Christmas festivities had left him little time for poetry. In his reply Milton contrasts his friend's intemperance with his own self-discipline and outlines the types of verse best suited to their separate temperaments and activities. For Diodati, there is 'light elegy' (*elegia levis*) whose patron deities are Bacchus, Erato, Ceres, Venus and Cupid; and it is not surprising with advocates such as these that Diodati should be led to indulge in feasting and immoderate drinking. But for the poet who has dedicated himself to more serious pursuits and who, as Jove's priest, aspires to sing of wars and heroes half-divine, life must be both abstemious and chaste:

> Ille quidem parce Samii pro more magistri
>   Vivat, et innocuos praebeat herba cibos;
> Stet prope fagineo pellucida lympha catillo,

Sobriaque e puro pocula fonte bibat.
Additur huic scelerisque vacans, et casta iuventus,
    Et rigidi mores, et sine labe manus.
Qualis veste nitens sacra, et lustralibus undis
    Surgis ad infensos augur iture deos.
. . . .

Diis etenim sacer est vates, divumque sacerdos,
    Spirat et occultum pectus, et ora Iovem.

(59–66, 77–8)

Let this poet live frugally, like the philosopher from Samos, and
let herbs provide his harmless diet. Let a bowl of beech-wood,
filled with clear water, stand by him, and may he drink soberly
from a pure spring. In addition his youth must be chaste and
free from crime, his morals strict and his hand unstained. He
must be like you, priest, when, bathed in holy water and
gleaming in your sacred vestment, you rise to go and face the
angry gods. . . . For the poet is sacred to the gods: he is their
priest: his innermost heart and his mouth are both full of Jove.

(*PM*, pp. 118–19)

These lines tell us much about Milton's poetic self-dedication of
1629. Here for the first time he articulates his conviction of the
necessary correlation between a poet's moral nature and the
quality of his poetic achievements. For the religious poet, poetry is
a form of priesthood and inner purity is the precondition of divine
inspiration.[13] The poet whose heart and lips breathe Jove must
himself conform inwardly to the purity of the deity whom he
invokes to inspire his song. Abstemiousness alone is inadequate:
'In addition his youth must be chaste and free from crime, his
morals strict and his hand unstained.' Henceforward Milton's
commitment to the correlatives of personal rectitude and inspired
creativity is an unshakeable tenet of his poetic creed: 'how he
should be truly eloquent who is not withall a good man, I see not.'
(*YP*, I, p. 874) It leads to the doctrine of chastity in *Comus* and also
to the famous statement in the *Apology for Smectymnuus* that 'he who
would not be frustrate of his hope to write well hereafter in
laudable things, ought him selfe to bee a true Poem, that is, a
composition, and patterne of the best and honourablest things;
not presuming to sing high praises of heroick men, or famous
Cities, unlesse he have in himselfe the experience and practice of

all that which is praiseworthy.' (*YP*, I, p. 890) And the conviction
that noble poetry springs only from 'the upright heart and pure'
leads him in *Paradise Lost* to follow his invocation for inspiration
with a prayer for inner purity:

> what in me is dark
> Illumine, what is low raise and support;
> That to the highth of this great argument
> I may assert eternal providence,
> And justify the ways of God to men.
>
> (I, 22–6)

There is another aspect of Milton's poetic self-dedication
which, although it is not specifically mentioned in *Elegy 6*, requires brief notice here. Very early in life Milton came not only to
the belief that poetic ability was 'the inspired guift of God rarely
bestow'd (*YP*, I, p. 816) but also to the belief that this divine gift
had to be developed by human industry, for 'God even to a
strictnesse requires the improvement of these his entrusted gifts'
(*YP*, I, p. 801). The old adage *orator fit, poeta nascitur* is only a
partial truth. 'For who', he asks in *Prolusion 7*, 'can worthily gaze
upon and contemplate the Ideas of things human or divine, unless
he possesses a mind trained and ennobled by Learning and study,
without which he can know practically nothing of them?' (*YP*, I,
p. 291) Indeed, there have been few men who have laboured as
earnestly as John Milton to fulfil that command in the twenty-fifth
chapter of Matthew's Gospel 'set out by the terrible seasing of him
that hid the talent' (*YP*, I, p. 320). When he speaks in *The Reason
of Church-Government* of that 'labour and intent study which I take
to be my portion in this life' (*YP*, I, p. 810), he is describing a
lifelong habit of disciplined preparation which can be
documented from Diodati's early reproof that he did not know
'the proper limit of labour' (*YP*, I, p. 377), to the rigorous
programme of study pursued at Hammersmith and Horton, to
Aubrey's description of him in old age.[14]

It is no accident that immediately after the statement of poetic
priesthood in *Elegy 6* Milton announces that he is writing a poem
to celebrate the Nativity; it is (he says) his gift to the Christ-
child—a theme inspired by the first rays of the sun on Christmas
morning. The sudden transition to the *Nativity Ode* at the end of
Elegy 6 teaches us, as Woodhouse suggests, 'to read the contrast

between the elegiac vein and the heroic [in *Elegy 6*] as a repudiation of the former, [and] to transliterate the description of the
heroic poet into Christian terms as the account of a dedicated
spirit divinely inspired'.[15] Thus, the *Nativity Ode* is Milton's formal
dedication of his poetic talent to God's service and the first-fruits
of his pledge to become a specifically Christian poet. The newly
acquired sense of mission and purpose is clearly stated in the
prelude to the ode where, having fixed the season and the
occasion, the poet addresses his Muse:

> Say heavenly Muse, shall not thy sacred vein
> Afford a present to the infant God?
> Hast thou no verse, no hymn, or solemn strain,
> To welcome him to this his new abode,
> Now while the heaven by the sun's team untrod,
>   Hath took no print of the approaching light,
> And all the spangled host keep watch in squadrons bright?
>
> See how from far upon the eastern road
> The star-led wizards haste with odours sweet,
> O run, prevent them with thy humble ode,
> And lay it lowly at his blessed feet;
> Have thou the honour first, thy Lord to greet,
>   And join thy voice unto the angel quire,
> From out his secret altar touched with hallowed fire.
>
>   (15–28)

Beneath the fiction of a competition in gift-giving between the
Muse with her 'humble ode' and the Magi hasting toward
Bethlehem with their more sumptuous offerings runs a deeper
current of great vocational importance. The prelude describes the
hymn which follows it as the work of the 'heavenly Muse'. The
inspiration, that is, is declared to be both actual and productive,
rather than fictive and merely conventional as it had been in the
Vacation Exercise and *Elegy 5*. In the *Nativity Ode* Milton thinks of
himself as a *stylus Dei*, an amanuensis of deity. And while it is true
that this stance, like the pagan afflatus of the earlier pieces, is
sanctioned by a long tradition, the sincere and confident tone of
the *Nativity Ode* makes it plain that the inspiration to which it lays
claim is far from being a conventional literary *topos*.

The implications of this view of inspiration in terms of Milton's

awareness of poetic calling are revealed in the image which
concludes the prelude: 'And join thy voice unto the angel quire/
From out his secret altar touched with hallowed fire'. The allusion
here is to Isaiah 6: 5–8 where the prophet receives his divine
commission:

> Then said I, Woe is me! for I am undone; because I am a man of
> unclean lips, and I dwell in the midst of a people of unclean lips:
> for mine eyes have seen the King, the Lord of hosts. Then flew
> one of the seraphims [*sic*] unto me, having a live coal in his
> hand, which he had taken with the tongs from off the altar: And
> he laid it upon my mouth, and said, Lo, this hath touched thy
> lips; and thine iniquity is taken away, and thy sin purged. Also I
> heard the voice of the Lord, saying, Whom shall I send, and
> who will go for us? Then said I, Here am I; send me. And he
> said, Go . . . .

In connecting his poetic calling with the election of Isaiah, Milton
is declaring that he, too, has been marked out for special service,
that he has been summoned to a poetic as well as a literal
priesthood. Significantly, the same image recurs over a decade
later in *The Reason of Church-Government* where Milton informs his
reader that the great poem he is meditating will be accomplished
'by devout prayer to that eternall Spirit who can enrich with all
utterance and knowledge, and sends out his Seraphim with the
hallow'd fire of his Altar to touch and purify the lips of whom he
pleases' (*YP*, I, pp. 820–1). And when that great poem finally
came to be written, the anonymous 'heavenly Muse' of the *Nativity
Ode* had been identified as Urania, the blind poet's

> celestial patroness, who deigns
> Her nightly visitation unimplored,
> And dictates to me slumbering, or inspires
> Easy my unpremeditated verse.
>
> (IX, 21–4)

For Milton, *inspiration* is neither the anti-rational afflatus of the
Corybantic priests in Plato's *Ion* 534a nor (at the other extreme) is
it merely an empty rhetorical trope; it is rather, as it was for
Isaiah, the operation of a sanctifying grace that continuously
nourishes and sustains those whom God has marked as His

special servants. And, while Milton's sense of poetic calling deepens and sharpens considerably in the years separating the *Nativity Ode* from *Paradise Lost*, the image of the live coal laid by the seraph on Isaiah's lips remains the constant symbol (in a Coleridgean sense)[16] of his poetic vocation.

For his poetic as for his ministerial calling Milton envisaged a long period of training. No doubt he had himself in mind when in 1630 he distinguished between 'slow-endeavouring art' on the one hand and Shakespeare's 'easy numbers' and animated 'Delphic lines' on the other hand (*On Shakespeare*, lines 9–12). And given Milton's belief in the necessity of intellectual and spiritual preparation, it is significant that the *Nativity Ode*, which opens with a declaration of divine inspiration and then ranges through all time and space from the Creation to the Last Judgment in inspired vision, should close with the hushed, motionless image of a traditional Nativity scene:

> But see the virgin blest,
> Hath laid her babe to rest.
>> Time is our tedious song should here have ending:
> Heaven's youngest teemed star,
> Hath fixed her polished car,
>> Her sleeping Lord with handmaid lamp attending:
> And all about the courtly stable,
> Bright-harnessed angels sit in order serviceable.
>> (237–44)

The mission described in the prelude, that of presenting his 'humble ode' to the new-born Christ, is here completed; and the poet ends his song and withdraws to join the angelic host sitting 'in order serviceable' about the stable. Like the angels, he is a dedicated spirit; like them, he is framed for active service. But the time for active service has not yet come, either for Milton in an actual sense or for the Christ child in a retrospective sense:

> But wisest fate says no,
> This must not yet be so,
>> The babe lies yet in smiling infancy,
> That on the bitter cross
> Must redeem our loss. . . .
>> (149–53)

As a poet Milton must first prepare and render himself more fit to serve, for only then can his 'tedious song' be fully and finally transformed into the earthly counterpart of that harmony of spheres and the angelic diapason described in lines 93–140. The *Nativity Ode*, then, is both his announcement of election as a religious poet and, at the same time, his admission that much preparation and growth are necessary before that calling can be fully achieved. His first-fruits are 'humble' and 'tedious', but the *Nativity Ode* is merely a beginning. The emblematic stasis of the final stanza implies an active purpose and contains the promise of future achievement. As B. Rajan succinctly expresses it: 'the bright-harnessed angels are the energy of light, mobilized and held ready for a creative purpose. . . . For Milton, too, a serviceable order has been created and the instruments are at hand for the greater work ahead.'[17]

From a vocational standpoint, the most striking feature of Milton's early poetry is its reiterated protestation of unpreparedness, coupled with its firm belief in a future of promise and achievement. In a very real sense the vocational emphasis of every serious poem Milton wrote from 1629 to 1637 may be said to have been summed up in the relaxed and picturesque conclusion of *Il Penseroso*:

> But let my due feet never fail,
> To walk the studious cloister's pale,
> And love the high embowed roof,
> With antique pillars' massy proof,
> And storied windows richly dight,
> Casting a dim religious light.
> There let the pealing organ blow,
> To the full-voiced choir below,
> In service high, and anthems clear,
> As may with sweetness, through mine ear,
> Dissolve me into ecstasies,
> And bring all heaven before mine eyes.
> And may at last my weary age
> Find out the peaceful hermitage,
> The hairy gown and mossy cell,
> Where I may sit and rightly spell
> Of every star that heaven doth shew,

And every herb that sips the dew;
Till old experience do attain
To something like prophetic strain.

(155–74)

As a poet, Milton has a very clear idea of where he is going; but he knows also that he has a long way to go before he arrives. Like Bunyan's pilgrim, he sees his goal in the distance but is aware that the road leading to it is winding and arduous. The passage is composed of three sentences, each beginning with a verb in the subjunctive mood; and these verbs control the tone of the lines. The search for the 'prophetic strain' (the poet's goal) is conditioned by 'old experience' which is the end result of an educative process where common, intellectual, and poetic experience are met and re-experienced over and over again.[18] In other words, it is vision felt as process or as evolving insight. And for this reason the poetic aspirations in *Il Penseroso* are tempered by the recognition that experience, of which Milton has little, is the precondition of achievement.

The vocational antithesis of a sense of present unreadiness set against an assurance of future accomplishment is reasserted at the end of 1632 in the quest for 'inward ripenes' in *Sonnet 7* (above pp. 34–6), and the same antithesis is carried into *At a Solemn Music* which was probably written in January or February 1633. Developing the musical analogies so prominent in the early poetry, *At a Solemn Music* enlarges on the prophetic and visionary nature of the poetry that Milton aspires to write:

Blest pair of sirens, pledges of heaven's joy,
Sphere-born harmonious sisters, Voice, and Verse,
Wed your divine sounds,
. . . .
And to our high-raised phantasy present,
That undisturbed song of pure concent,
Ay sung before the sapphire-coloured throne
To him that sits thereon
. . . .
That we on earth with undiscording voice
May rightly answer that melodious noise;
As once we did, till disproportioned sin

Jarred against nature's chime, and with harsh din
Broke the fair music that all creatures made
To their great Lord . . . .

(1–3, 5–8, 17–22)

These lines contain the clearest early statement of Milton's elevated conception of the nature and role of the religious poet. Like the musician, he imitates and interprets for fallen man the celestial harmony that sin has rendered inaudible; he is a priestly intermediary between God and men, whose function and aim is the spiritual re-education of postlapsarian mankind. But the poet who aspires to become such an inspired teacher must be fitted to his task; he requires both visionary experience (grace) and, as well, all the experience with which life and learning (nature) can provide him. It is therefore significant that the statement of poetic function in *At a Solemn Music* is followed by a prayer for enlightenment:

O may we soon again renew that song,
And keep in tune with heaven, till God ere long
To his celestial consort us unite,
To live with him, and sing in endless morn of light.

(25–8)

But this all lies in the future. And, while there is little doubt that Milton imagines himself the prospective scribe of that renewed 'song of pure concent', it is equally clear that he recognises himself to be still unfit to serve as the sacred instrument through whom these prophetic strains will find utterance.

In the years 1634–8 Milton wrote little poetry. Indeed, only three poems may be assigned with confidence to this period: *Comus*, *Lycidas*, and a Greek translation of Psalm 114. To this list I would add *Ad Patrem*, dating it late 1637 or early 1638. In none of these poems is there any indication that Milton has come to think of himself as a mature poet. On the contrary, the same combination of unreadiness and expectation characteristic of the pre-1634 verse reappears in these later poems. It is explicit in *Lycidas* and implied in the bibliographical history of *Comus*.

Comus, composed and performed in 1634, was not finally published until 1637. Even then it was Henry Lawes, not Milton, who arranged for the printing: 'Although not openly acknowledg'd by the Author, yet it is a legitimate off-spring, so lovely, and so much desired, that the often Copying of it hath tir'd my Pen to give my severall friends satisfaction, and brought me to a necessity of producing it to the publike view.' (*SM*, p. 44)[19] Moreover, it appeared to the public view without Milton's name; and the title-page bears, as a motto, lines 58–9 of Virgil's second eclogue: *Eheu quid volui misero mihi! floribus austrum Perditus* ('Alas! what harm did I wish upon my wretched self by allowing the south wind to blow upon my flowers?'). There is no reason to think that Milton did not supply this motto and, while its significance has been variously interpreted, one aspect of its meaning is beyond doubt: even after submitting the masque to extensive revision, Milton was still reluctant to see it published.

It is not known why, despite his hesitation and doubts, Milton allowed Lawes to publish *Comus*. I suspect, however, that his reasons were similar to those of Keats, who in sending *Endymion* to press asked his reader to judge more the attempt than the result and to expect more in the future than the present had succeeded in producing: 'It is just that this youngster should die away: a sad thought for me, if I had not some hope that while it is dwindling I may be plotting and fitting myself for verses fit to live.'[20] As Keats in 1818 was fitting himself for 'verses fit to live', so Milton in 1637 was contemplating 'an immortality of fame' and preparing himself for works that later generations would not willingly let die: 'You ask', he wrote to Diodati in November 1637, 'what I am thinking of? So help me God, an immortality of fame. What am I doing? Growing my wings and practising flight. But my Pegasus still raises himself on very tender wings.' (*YP*, I, p. 327)[21] Despite the bantering good-humour of this letter Milton undoubtedly meant what he said. *Practising flight* is the dominant vocational note of the early poetry—poetry which reveals a young man learning his craft, experimenting with various subjects, poetic forms and metres, and growing more self-assured with every effort. Since the *Vacation Exercise* he has known himself to have a poetic calling, and in the *Nativity Ode* he announced his election as a Christian poet; moreover, in both the *Nativity Ode* and *At a Solemn Music* he set out his lofty conception of the religious poet he was destined to become: not only a divinely-inspired teacher, but also an instrument of regeneration whose mimetic re-creations of celestial harmony constitute a mode of continuing revelation, a means by which God continues to speak and to manifest His will to men in this world. Paraphrasing Plato's *Republic* x 616–17, he had delineated his role as interpreter and mediator between God and man in lines 62–73 of *Arcades* (1633?):

> then listen I
> To the celestial sirens' harmony,
> That sit upon the nine enfolded spheres,
> And sing to those that hold the vital shears,
> And turn the adamantine spindle round,
> On which the fate of gods and men is wound.
> Such sweet compulsion doth in music lie,
> To lull the daughters of Necessity,
> And keep unsteady Nature to her law,
> And the low world in measured motion draw
> After the heavenly tune, which none can hear
> Of human mould with gross unpurged ear.

Nevertheless, while his poetic achievements and his conviction of calling give him every reason to believe that 'an immortality of fame' will indeed be his in the course of time, it is equally clear from *Il Penseroso, Sonnet 7* and *Comus* that there is still much to learn both about himself and about poetry. But his assurance is well-founded; he has been called to serve as God's poet-priest and, with personal application and the aid of grace, all is as ever in his great Taskmaster's eye.

The protestation of unreadiness and the reluctance to commit himself to print before due season implied in the publishing history of *Comus* is made explicit in the opening lines of *Lycidas* (where the first words, 'Yet once more', perhaps refer to the recently published masque):

> Yet once more, O ye laurels, and once more
> Ye myrtles brown, with ivy never sere,
> I come to pluck your berries harsh and crude,
> And with forced fingers rude,
> Shatter your leaves before the mellowing year.
> Bitter constraint, and sad occasion dear,
> Compels me to disturb your season due:
> For Lycidas is dead, dead ere his prime,
> Young Lycidas, and hath not left his peer:
> Who would not sing for Lycidas? he knew

> Himself to sing, and build the lofty rhyme.
> He must not float upon his watery bier
> Unwept, and welter to the parching wind,
> Without the meed of some melodious tear.
>
> (1–14)

These lines are a forceful assertion of artistic unripeness. The 'sad occasion' of Edward King's death has constrained him to gather prematurely the plants symbolic of the poet's garland. His reluctance is not mere posturing. It is perfectly consonant with all that we know of his early literary activity: before *Lycidas* he published only two poems — *On Shakespeare* (1632) and *Comus* (1637) — and both appeared anonymously; *Lycidas* itself in the *Justa Eduardo King naufrago* (1638) is signed simply 'J.M.', although many of the other contributors to the volume signed their names in full. Moreover, *Lycidas* is an occasional poem which Milton was invited to compose; there is no reason to assume that it would have been written or that Milton would have sought to publish it had there not been an invitation to contribute to the Cambridge volume in memory of Edward King.[22] Indeed, given his reluctance to hurry into print, it may well be (as Rinehart suggests)[23] that the fourteen-line prelude in *Lycidas* is a 'broken sonnet' designed as a technical illustration of the fact that premature song has caused Milton to force his Muse.

At the end of *Lycidas* the note of artistic unreadiness is sounded again; but it is here coupled, in a union familiar from the poetry of 1629–33, with the promise of future achievement. In line 185 the poet re-enters his poem as an 'uncouth swain', rude but full of promise, who

> touched the tender stops of various quills,
> With eager thought warbling his Doric lay:
> And now the sun had stretched out all the hills,
> And now was dropped into the western bay;
> At last he rose, and twitched his mantle blue:
> Tomorrow to fresh woods, and pastures new.
>
> (188–93)

In striking contrast to the hesitancy and reluctance of the fourteen-line prelude, it is now with 'eager thought' that he fingers the responsive, yet still frail, stops of his pastoral pipe. The composition of the monody has given him additional confidence and experience. Like the day dying in the western bay, the long period of experimentation and preparation is drawing also to a close. Pulling around his shoulders the bardic mantle of blue—the colour symbolic of his hope and his election[24]—he rises confidently to greet the new dawn of poetic promise. But the 'fresh woods, and pastures new' of poetic achievement lie still in the future, albeit the proximate future. Rather than the first product of the long-anticipated new day, *Lycidas* is but its harbinger.

The rousing motions of *Lycidas*, however, the premonition of a new and exciting period in his poetic development gave rise, not to an immediate increase in poetic activity, but to a voyage—in a sense a literary pilgrimage—to Italy, with the further intention of visiting Sicily and Greece, the homelands of Theocritus and of Homer, Euripides and Plato. In terms of Milton's poetic vocation the importance of this journey abroad can scarcely be overstressed, for it strongly confirmed his belief in his abilities and calling and, as well, it opened new dimensions and imposed new directions on his aspirations. His own account in *The Reason of Church-Government* is central to an understanding of the vocational significance of his Italian experience:

I must say therefore that after I had from my first yeeres by the ceaselesse diligence and care of my father, whom God recompence, bin exercis'd to the tongues, and some sciences, as my age would suffer, by sundry masters and teachers both at home and at the schools, it was found that whether ought was impos'd me by them that had the overlooking, or betak'n to of mine own choise in English, or other tongue, prosing or versing, but chiefly this latter, the stile by certain vital signes it had, was likely to live. But much latelier in the privat Academies of *Italy*, whither I was favor'd to resort, perceiving that some trifles which I had in memory, compos'd at under twenty or thereabout (for the manner is that every one must give some proof of his wit and reading there) met with acceptance above what was lookt for, and other things which I had shifted in scarsity of books and conveniences to patch up amongst them, were receiv'd with written Encomiums, which the Italian is not forward to bestow on men of this side the *Alps*, I began thus farre to assent both to them and divers of my friends here at home, and not lesse to an inward prompting which now grew daily upon me, that by labour and intent study (which I take to be my portion in this life) joyn'd with the strong propensity of nature, I might perhaps leave something so written to aftertimes, as they should not willingly let it die. These thoughts at once possest me, and these other. That if I were certain to write as men buy Leases, for three lives and downward, there ought no regard be sooner had, then to Gods glory by the honour and instruction of my country. For which cause, and not only for that I knew it would be hard to arrive at the second rank among the Latines, I apply'd my selfe to that resolution which *Ariosto* follow'd against the perswasions of *Bembo*, to fix all the industry and art I could unite to the adorning of my native tongue; not to make verbal curiosities the end, that were a toylsom vanity, but to be an interpreter & relater of the best and sagest things among mine own Citizens throughout this Iland in the mother dialect. That what the greatest and choycest wits of *Athens*, *Rome*, or modern *Italy*, and those Hebrews of old did for their country, I in my proportion with this over and above of being a Christian, might doe for mine: not caring to be once nam'd abroad, though perhaps I could attaine to that, but content with these British Ilands as my world, whose fortune hath hitherto bin [to have had] ... her noble atchievments made small by the unskilful handling of monks and mechanicks. (*YP*, I, pp. 808–12)

Much that Milton says here about his poetic calling is already familiar from earlier statements; but there is in this passage a greater sense of control and a more precise sense of direction. Although he has by no means forgotten his long apprenticeship or the poetic aspirations he has harboured since the *Vacation Exercise* of 1628, he makes it very clear that he believes his Italian experience to have been the catalyst which confirmed him in the knowledge of his aptitude and ability, and which gave him as well at least a possible subject for the great poem for which he had been preparing himself. He remembers with gratitude, of course, his debt to his father, and he remembers his early training at the hands of tutors like Thomas Young and also at St Paul's School and Christ's College. But it was pre-eminently, he says, the warm reception of his poetic gifts by the intellectual and artistic elite of Italy—corroborated by the 'inward prompting' of God which increased almost daily after his return to England—that led him to acknowledge and act upon the praise of friends at home and upon his own natural inclination for poetry. It was Italy that finally convinced him that he 'might perhaps leave something so written to aftertimes, as they should not willingly let it die'.

As his Italian visit confirmed him in the belief that he was 'certain to write' and that his poetry would survive him and live in future ages ('as men buy Leases, for three lives and downward'), it also ratified his early determination to employ his native language in the adornment and elaboration of 'some graver subject'. England might be honoured in Latin, but she could be instructed only in English; and for this reason he resolved to be 'an interpreter & relater of the best and sagest things among mine own Citizens throughout this Iland in the mother dialect'. The importance which Milton placed on the decision to be 'content with these British Ilands as my world' is indicated again by his declaration in lines 171–8 of *Epitaphium Damonis* (a poem composed within a few months of his return from Italy) that he was resolved to abandon international in favour of domestic fame:

> omnia non licet uni
> Non sperasse uni licet omnia, mi satis ampla
> Merces, et mihi grande decus (sim ignotus in aevum
> Tum licet, externo penitusque inglorius orbi)
> Si me flava comas legat Usa, et potor Alauni,
> Vorticibusque frequens Abra, et nemus omne Treantae,
> Et Thamesis meus ante omnes, et fusca metallis
> Tamara, et extremis me discant Orcades undis.

But after all, one man cannot do everything, or even hope to do everything. I shall have ample reward, and shall think it great glory, although I be forever unknown and utterly without fame in the world outside, if only yellow-haired Usa reads my poems, and he who drinks from the Alan, and Humber, full of whirling eddies, and every grove of Trent, and above all my native Thames and the Tamar, stained with metals, and if the Orkneys among their distant waves will learn my song. (*PM*, p. 282)

From the determination taken here to write only in English he did not waver or retreat until over a decade later Salmasius forced him to defend his nation, in Latin, in the international forum.

In order to achieve the end of instructing his countrymen in

virtue and righteousness in the vernacular, Milton again
renewed his 'interrupted studies' shortly after returning from
Italy in August or September 1639. The programme of private
reading, as demanding as that of the Hammersmith and Horton
years, was now centred, however, not on ecclesiastical history or
the Church Fathers, but on English history. As we know from
the *Commonplace Book*, he spent 1639–41 studiously immersed in
the works of such writers as Bede, Malmesbury, Gildas, Stow,
and Holinshed. The primary aim of this reading was to gather
materials for his *magnum opus*. At first, he planned that this work
should be an 'Arthuriad', a subject perhaps suggested by his
Italian friends, for he mentions it in the two Latin poems which
express his gratitude for their kindness and hospitality to him.
In *Mansus*, he writes:

> O mihi si mea sors talem concedat amicum
> Phoebaeos decorasse viros qui tam bene norit,
> Si quando indigenas revocabo in carmina reges,
> Arturumque etiam sub terris bella moventem;
> Aut dicam invictae sociali foedere mensae,
> Magnanimos heroas, et (O modo spiritus ad sit)
> Frangam Saxonicas Britonum sub Marte phalanges.
>
> (78–84)

O may it be my good luck to find such a friend [as you, Manso],
who knows so well how to honour Phoebus' followers, if ever I
bring back to life in my songs the kings of my native land and
Arthur, who set wars raging even under the earth, or tell of the
great-hearted heroes of the round table, which their fellowship
made invincible, and—if only the inspiration would
come—smash the Saxon phalanxes beneath the impact of the
British charge. (*PM*, p. 266)

And the same heroic subject recurs in the *Epitaphium Damonis:*

> Tum gravidam Arturo fatali fraude Iogernen
> Mendaces vultus, assumptaque Gorlois arma,
> Merlini dolus.
>
> (166–8)

Then I shall tell of Igraine, pregnant with Arthur as a result of
fatal deception: I shall tell of the lying features which misled

her, and of the borrowing of Gorlois's armour, Merlin's trick.
(*PM*, p.282)

After the *Epitaphium Damonis* nothing more is heard of an
Arthuriad, and Milton seems to have turned his attention from
mythic to historical figures, combing the chronicles for 'what
K[ing] or Knight before the conquest might be chosen in whom to
lay the pattern of a Christian *Heroe*' (*YP*, I, pp. 813–4). Between
1640 and 1642 he recorded in the *Trinity Manuscript* about a
hundred possible dramatic subjects from British history and the
Bible. Of particular interest among these subjects, in view of what
he was later to do, are the four drafts or outlines for a play on the
Fall, and the brief suggestion for a drama on 'Samson marriing or
in Ramath Lechi', along with another simply called 'Dagonalia'.
The length and detail of many of the biblical outlines makes it
highly probable that in 1640–2 he had virtually settled on a
scriptural theme, although he continued to canvass historical
subjects as well. The quite fully developed outlines entitled
'Paradise Lost' and 'Adam unparadiz'd' suggest the further
possibility that his interest was even then centring on the story of
the Fall; and this possibility is supported by Edward Phillips'
claim that about this time he was shown ten lines which were later
incorporated into Satan's address to the sun in Book IV of *Paradise
Lost*.[25]

In terms of Milton's poetic vocation, the significant point is that
it was only *after* the Italian experience that his expectation of a
poetic destiny in the form of a great work issued in concrete
planning in the subjects for plays recorded in the *Trinity Manuscript*. Moreover, in pointed contrast to his reluctance in *Comus*
and *Lycidas* to appear in print, he arranged after he returned from
Italy for a private printing of the *Epitaphium Damonis* (probably in 1640),[26] copies of which were sent to friends at home and in
Italy; and in this same year his tribute *On Shakespeare* was reprinted, this time with his initials. Milton, then, returned from
the Continent in late 1639 assured of his poetic ability and im-
bued with a firm sense of artistic direction. Much study was
still necessary, of course, but with promulgation of the Laudian
Canons in June 1640 and the consequent determination to abandon a career in the church, he was left free to devote all of his
energies to a continued poetic preparation. And while he prepared his Pegasus for flight he solved the immediate economic problem, that of earning a living, by opening a private

school and taking in pupils, beginning with his two young nephews, John and Edward Phillips.

The plans for a prolonged period of artistic preparation were interrupted by Milton's entry into the controversy then raging over episcopacy. The pamphlets of 1641–2, however, far from constituting an unfortunate setback for the poetic plans, are in actuality the fulfilment, in prose rather than in poetry, of his decision to serve God and work for His glory 'by the honour and instruction of my country'. Important as Italy and all that preceded it were to his artistic development, it was only the experience of ecclesiastical controversy that finally formed Milton into the religious poet whom we know in the later poems. In the six antiprelatical pamphlets (including *A Postscript*), he learned what it meant to be God's spokesman, the prophet of the divine will; and these pamphlets are, in fact, the school in which he first was taught to justify God's ways to men. Political events aside, *Paradise Lost* and the last poems of 1671 might have been composed anytime after 1642; before that date, no such poetry would have been possible.

The decision to fight for the establishment of the English New Jerusalem and the experience of active service in God's cause are the final stages in Milton's maturing awareness of a poetic vocation. Although for many years he was to serve as a prophet in prose of national liberty and reformation, it is clear from the first of the antiprelatical pamphlets that once God's Presbyterian will for England has been fully achieved in the destruction of the bishops, Milton aspires to be the poet of that new and pacific age:

> Then amidst the *Hymns*, and *Halleluiahs* of *Saints* some one may perhaps bee heard offering at high *strains* in new and lofty *Measures* to sing and celebrate thy *divine Mercies*, and *marvelous Judgements* in this Land throughout all Ages; whereby this great and Warlike Nation instructed and inur'd to the fervent and continuall practice of *Truth* and *Righteousnesse*, and casting farre from her the *rags* of her old *vices* may presse on hard to that *high* and *happy* emulation to be found the *soberest, wisest,* and *most Christian People* at that day when thou the Eternall and shortly-expected King shalt open the Clouds to judge the severall Kingdomes of the World.... (*YP*, I, p. 616)

The 'prophetic strain' for which he had longed ten years before in *Il Penseroso* is here, in contrast to the unspecified and vague hopes of the early poem, centred on a definite theme: the praise of divine mercy for the special favour bestowed on the English nation and the exhortation to his countrymen to live in virtue and righteousness in preparation for the imminent Parousia. What is most interesting about this passage from *Of Reformation*, however, is that Milton treats his private poetic vocation as but an extension of his public role as the prose prophet of reformation; his poetic calling is both defined by and subsumed into the national mission of self-regeneration and carrying reformation to the world.

Two months later in *Animadversions upon the Remonstrant's Defence* (July 1641) he reasserts his function and calling as God's English poet in almost identical terms:

> When thou hast settl'd peace in the Church, and righteous judgement in the Kingdome, then shall all thy Saints addresse their voyces of joy, and triumph to thee, standing on the shoare of that Red Sea into which our enemies had almost driven us. And he that now for haste snatches up a plain ungarnish't present as a thanke-offering to thee, which could not bee deferr'd in regard of thy so many late deliverances wrought for us one upon another, may then perhaps take up a Harp, and sing thee an elaborate Song to Generations. (*YP*, I, p. 706)

Here again Milton's poetic aspirations are tied to the rebirth of his country. Nevertheless, he has every expectation that in the near future the ungarnished offering of his left hand will be fulfilled more perfectly in the 'elaborate Song to Generations' that will mark him as the bard of the coming reign of God's victorious English saints.

Some seven months after the *Animadversions*, he returned once more to the subject of his poetic calling in *The Reason of Church-Government*. In the famous preface to the second section of this pamphlet he publicly declares himself to be a serious national poet and he sets down in considerable detail both his poetic creed and the types and nature of the poetry he is planning to write. As in *Elegy 6* and *At a Solemn Music*, he stresses the didactic function of all high poetry and emphasises the sacerdotal role of the religious poet. The ability to compose the epic, tragedy and lyric, he asserts (*YP*, I, pp. 816–18), is

the inspired guift of God rarely bestow'd but yet to some

(though most abuse) in every Nation: and [is] of power beside the office of a pulpit, to imbreed and cherish in a great people the seeds of vertu, and publick civility, to allay the perturbations of the mind, and set the affections in right tune, to celebrate in glorious and lofty Hymns the throne and equipage of Gods Almightinesse, and what he works, and what he suffers to be wrought with high providence in his Church, . . . teaching over the whole book of sanctity and vertu through all the instances of example with such delight to those especially of soft and delicious temper who will not so much as look upon Truth herselfe, unlesse they see her elegantly drest.

Almost immediately after this general assessment of the poetic function Milton covenants with his 'knowing reader' about the nature of the great poem which he is meditating, which indeed he has already begun, as being 'a work not to be rays'd from the heat of youth, or the vapours of wine, like that which flows at wast from the pen of some vulgar Amorist, or the trencher fury of a riming parasite, nor to be obtain'd by the invocation of Dame Memory and her Siren daughters, but by devout prayer to that eternall Spirit who can enrich with all utterance and knowledge, and sends out his Seraphim with the hallow'd fire of his Altar to touch and purify the lips of whom he pleases' (*YP*, I, pp. 820–1). Here, again drawing on the image of purification and dedication from Isaiah 6 that he had used twelve years earlier in the *Nativity Ode* to announce his calling as a religious poet, Milton proclaims that the divinely-inspired hymn of personal and public thanksgiving is but 'some few yeers' from completion. And although those few years were to be protracted by political events far beyond anything he anticipated in 1642, the great poem was destined nevertheless to procure for him that 'immortality of fame' which he had confided to Diodati was his ultimate goal.

It is no accident that, having defined at length the sacredness of the poetic office and set before the reader his own literary plans, Milton concludes the preface in *The Reason of Church-Government* by declaring that he has been 'Church-outed by the Prelats'. The man who now aspires to be the poet-priest of his nation has not so much rejected a calling into the church—except as the bishops would define such a calling—as he has extended the notion of ministerial vocation to embrace a call to serve as God's spokesman and interpreter through poetry. As early as *Prolusion 7* and

Elegy 6 Milton had articulated his belief that the functions and aims of the two offices—poetry and the ministry—overlap; but this conviction was not actively confirmed until participation in ecclesiastical dispute led him to embrace a literary vocation, at first in prose, but always looking forward to that time when he would write a great poem that would be 'doctrinal and exemplary' to his nation.

3 Prophetic Vocation, 1641–60

Nearly half a century has elapsed since Tillyard complained that Milton's prose works have 'far too often ... been treated as a static, an alien mass, a kind of obstructing rock in the stream; which can be commented on as a whole and without reference to dates or developments'.[1] The intervening decades have done much to correct this situation. A number of scholars have demonstrated that important relationships exist between the products of the left and right hands, and they have stressed the continuity of purpose and outlook which underpins Milton's activities both as poet and pamphleteer. An even greater scholarly energy has been devoted to examining the artistry and rhetorical technique in individual pamphlets and has shown that many of them are works of considerable technical accomplishment. And yet, apart from studies like Arthur Barker's *Milton and the Puritan Dilemma* or Michael Fixler's *Milton and the Kingdoms of God*, little attention has been paid to the evolving self-awareness and deepening vocational tone in the prose works.

Milton's prose marks a crucial phase in his development because, as I suggested in the preceding chapter, his involvement in political and ecclesiastical controversy provided the school in which he was first taught to justify the ways of God to men. In the years 1641–60 Milton's relationship with his God grew closer than it had ever been, and through the prose there reigns the deepening conviction that he has been marked for special service as God's spokesman to the nation—like Isaiah and Jeremiah he has been called as a prophet of the Lord. As William Kerrigan observes, 'Milton believed himself a prophet. The traditional idea became inseparable from the self who had received that tradition. He spoke as a prophet, rarely of the prophet, and this belief in intimate impulse and divine favor sustained him through most of his life.'[2] It must be emphasised, however, that this conviction of prophetic vocation did not come all at once and in a blinding flash. It evolved gradually over a considerable period of time. A longing for the 'prophetic strain' in the early poetry and the carefully nurtured belief in the immortality of fame to be achieved through his poetic priesthood are the convictions of a largely unfocused idealism. He had been called to serve God, but he was still uncertain as to how precisely he was to fulfil this high calling. The solution of this problem—or at least the first stage of it—came in 1641 when Milton was prompted to join the controversy over episcopacy.

Convinced that England was a covenanted nation and that the prelates were wilfully thwarting the divinely ordained national mission, Milton took up his pen to defend the cause of continuing reformation. In *Of Reformation* and the pamphlets which followed he became a spokesman pleading God's own cause and, for the first time in his career, his visionary idealism found a firm centre of focus. More significantly still, his sense of a personal calling was both directed and defined by its conjunction with the calling of the nation at large; and this concurrence of vocations carried with it important implications for Milton's poetic destiny, for it gave him a theme (if not a precise subject) for the great poem which he hoped to write. Believing that the bishops would be disposed of quickly and that their fall would usher in the reign of the saints and ultimately the Parousia itself, he took occasion throughout the antiprelatical tracts to promise his readers that polemics were but the prelude to poetry. The jarring blast of prophecy would shortly give place to a fitting poetic tribute for God's great mercies to His English nation—an elaborate song of thanksgiving to grace the lips of generations yet unborn. Whether based on scriptural or on English history, the poem was intended to glorify the establishment of the English New Jerusalem, a paradise far more tangible and immediate than that which Michael is able to offer Adam in the closing book of *Paradise Lost*. In the first flush of his reforming ardour, when the consummation seemed perhaps only months away, it was natural for Milton to construe his poetic calling as an extension of his prophetic vocation.

The visionary optimism of 1642, however, was qualified by a more sober realism in the years which followed. Domestic and civil strife, coupled with the slackening zeal and finally the defection of his Presbyterian allies, forced upon Milton the recognition that the national regeneration which God had willed for England might well be frustrated. The ship of reformation found herself in heavy seas battling cross-winds and contrary currents; if she were not to founder, then strong and able voices must be heard above the tempest guiding her to her appointed haven. Milton believed that he was one of these voices and that God had called him to this task. In the pamphlets of 1644–60 he proclaimed again and again the essential truth as he perceived it; however, as the barbarous dissonance of the recalcitrants and backsliders grew louder and greater with the passage of time, there were fewer and fewer of his countrymen willing to heed his words.

Milton's divergence from the religious and political mood of the majority in the nation, his gradual isolation as he continued to meditate the divine will to a progressively dwindling band of the elect, manifested itself in an increasing self-identification with the Old Testament prophets. The nature and extent of this deepening identification from 1642 to 1660 may be quickly and accurately gauged in his use of two passages from Jeremiah. In *The Reason of Church-Government* (1642), the first of the antiprelatical tracts to which he signed his name, Milton opens the preface to the second book by discussing at some length the onerous responsibilities of the prophetic office:

> though they cannot but testify of Truth and the excellence of that heavenly traffick which they bring against what opposition, or danger soever, yet needs must it sit heavily upon their spirits, that being in Gods prime intention and their own, select heralds of peace, and dispensers of treasure inestimable without price to them that have no pence, they finde in the discharge of their commission that they are made the greatest variance and offence, a very sword and fire in house and City over the whole earth. This is that which the sad Prophet *Jeremiah* laments, *Wo is me my mother, that thou hast born me a man of strife, and contention* [Jer. 15: 10]. And although divine inspiration must certainly have been sweet to those ancient profets, yet the irksomnesse of that truth which they brought was so unpleasant to them, that every where they call it a burden. (*YP*, I, pp. 802–3)

This anatomy of the prophet's duty, which is extended well beyond the canonical prophets to include the figure of Tiresias from Sophocles' *Oedipus Tyrannus*, serves as much more than an abstract analysis of the unhappy burden imposed on the humanity of those called to labour as God's spokesmen. It is, in fact, intended as an affirmation of Milton's own calling and a justifica-

tion of his speaking out against the bishops. His conviction that he
has been entrusted with a divine commission is sincere if somewhat self-conscious. Nevertheless, it is important to see that he
does not align himself directly with Jeremiah; rather, the parallel
is established by implication and he treats the prophet's vocation
as a distant analogue of his own experience. He is also careful to
distinguish the plenary inspiration of the Old Testament prophet
from the indirect prompting by which he has been summoned:
'neither envy nor gall hath enterd me upon this controversy, but
the enforcement of conscience only.' (*YP*, I, p. 806)[3] By the spring
of 1660, however, when Milton sent forth the second edition of *The
Readie and Easie Way to Establish a Free Commonwealth*, his identification with the prophetic tradition is complete. He speaks as a
prophet rather than of the prophets. Secure in his calling, he
makes no attempt to explain or defend his stance; and drawing on
Jeremiah 22: 29, he addresses 'the last words of our expiring
libertie' to a nation rushing headlong into the betrayal of her holy
mission: 'What I have spoken, is the language of that which is not
call'd amiss *the good Old Cause*: if it seem strange to any, it will not
seem more strange, I hope, then convincing to backsliders. Thus
much I should perhaps have said though I were sure I should
have spoken only to trees and stones; and had none to cry to, but
with the Prophet, *O earth, earth, earth!* to tell the very soil it self,
what her perverse inhabitants are deaf to.' (*YP*, VII, pp. 462–3)
The language and cadence of this moving peroration, the tone
combining exhortation with resignation, echo the prophetic tradition within which Milton locates himself. Like Jeremiah before
him, God's English prophet stands alone, unmoved and undis-
mayed by the howling and the fury round about him. Careless of
personal safety and wrapped in the mantle of divine authority, he
proclaims God's will with a just and timely fear of that 'precipice
of destruction' toward which the covenanted nation is being
propelled 'through the general defection of a misguided and
abus'd multitude' (ibid., p. 463). The Restoration was by then
inevitable, and it is a measure of the depth of Milton's vocational
conviction that he continued to speak out when all purely rational
hope was lost.

It may be added that the twenty years of polemics and the sad
course of political events greatly affected Milton's view of his
poetic calling. The plan for a great poem to celebrate the founding
of the English New Jerusalem had to be abandoned, and after the

unfettered idealism of 1642 the conjunction between poetry and prophecy began to erode. He wrote little poetry during these years and the few allusions to his poetic destiny in the later prose works are veiled and cautious. The Restoration necessitated a time of revaluation and reassessment, and this is reflected in the later poetry. Indeed, as I shall argue in the remaining chapters, the last poems are very largely concerned with the theme of divine vocation. Poetry for Milton often served a cathartic function. In the *Nativity Ode*, *Sonnet 7* and *Lycidas*, for example, he turned to verse at critical moments in his intellectual or religious life; and in each case the imposition of an aesthetic pattern on his own experience enabled him either to resolve a personal crisis or to transcend a private difficulty by transposing its solution from the realm of nature to that of grace.[4] I have elsewhere argued that this same principle may be applied to *Sonnet 23*, where art imposes form and control on biography while at the same time biography imparts emotional force to the patterns of art.[5] It seems to me equally true that biographical considerations play an important role in the last poems as well. After the Restoration Milton found it necessary to reassess his prophetic vocation and to reaffirm his personal covenant with God within the altered context of a society that had wilfully rejected its divinely ordained mission of civil, ecclesiastic and domestic reformation. I believe that *Samson Agonistes*, which I would place in 1660–1 (see Appendix), records the crucial phase of this vocational revaluation. Not only does Samson's physical plight in a Philistian prison recall that of God's blind poet-prophet in enforced concealment in Bartholomew Close, but the Hebrew warrior's vocational concerns—his fear that God had perhaps finished with him and withdrawn His favour, his anxiety that he had acted presumptuously in executing what he supposed to be the promptings of the divine will, and so on—parallel the misgivings which Milton must have experienced in 1660. Since the composition of *Paradise Lost* straddles the Restoration, it may also be the case that Adam's bipartite education under the tutelage of Raphael (prelapsarian) and Michael (postlapsarian) reflects Milton's own preoccupation with a contrast between the life that would have been possible in the theocracy which he had fought so hard to establish and the life now necessary in a fallen and monarchical England where the kingdom of God is a promise and Eden a state of mind. Such speculation—and I claim no more for it—may well not be convincing to readers of *Paradise Lost*, since we know little for certain about the composition of the epic; and I have no desire to push it beyond decorous limits. The case for *Samson Agonistes* is much stronger, but I shall defer the detailed study of the poem's vocational implications to its appropriate place in later chapters.

It is impossible in a single chapter to do anything like justice to the range and complexity of Milton's view of his prophetic vocation in the prose works. There are, however, two points which merit special consideration. The most important aspect of Milton's prophetic vocation is his conviction that his own calling is only meaningful within the context of the national mission, and this belief places him firmly in the tradition of Old Testament prophecy. It will be useful, therefore, to clarify his relation to this tradition by sketching its development in the Bible and its later naturalisation in Milton's England. The second point which requires some elaboration is Milton's view of prophetic inspiration and the significance of his attitude in terms both of the prose and the later poetry.

(i) A COVENANTED NATION

> *Blessed is the nation whose God is the Lord; and the people whom he hath chosen for his own inheritance.*
> (Psalm 33: 12)

The traditional origin of the Hebrew conviction of racial destiny is found in Genesis 12: 1–3 where Abraham is promised that in his seed all the nations of earth will be blessed. Maturing during the time of the later patriarchs Isaac and Jacob, this original *berîth* or covenant leads ultimately to the central event in Jewish history, the Sinai covenant mediated by Moses between Yahweh and His chosen people. The precise terms of the Sinai covenant are important and bear repetition: 'if ye will obey my voice indeed, and keep my covenant, then ye shall be a peculiar treasure unto me above all people: for all the earth is mine: And ye shall be unto me a kingdom of priests, and an holy nation.' (Exodus 19: 5–6) The significant fact is that the Hebrews are not chosen for their own sake, for God's favour carries with it a heavy load of responsibility. Israel is not simply a chosen nation, but is a holy people—'*am kādhôsh*–charged with the priestly mission of spreading the knowledge and worship of Yahweh to the Gentiles.

By the time of the rhapsodist prophets in the eighth century B.C.—Amos and Hosea in Northern Israel, and Isaiah in Judah—the Hebrews had come to appreciate how far short of their calling as a 'kingdom of priests' they had fallen. Not only had they failed to promote Yahwism among the Gentiles, but more grievously they had, by a process of religious syncretism, permitted Canaanite ritual and belief to defile the purity of the Law handed down on Sinai. In the most stirring terms the prophets warned that nothing short of complete reformation could save the nation from condign punishment. Since these prophets, like their successors over the next two centuries, saw their individual calling as meaningful only in the context of Israel's election, it is not surprising that their pleas and comminations as well as their eschatology should be based firmly on the centrality of covenant theology in the Hebrew consciousness. As the spokesmen of national destiny, their voice was that of Israel and her God. They pandered to the special interests neither of class nor dynasty, and indeed, were often driven to speak against their own wills in a way that endangered personal safety.

The prophetic interpretation of history is enunciated with great clarity and power in the writings of Deutero-Isaiah, the last of the major Hebrew prophets. This anonymous poet, who arose among the Judaean exiles in Babylon in the middle of the sixth century B.C., composed chapters 40–55 of the Book of Isaiah, and, apart from the covenants made with Abraham and Moses, his writings constitute the most important statement of national vocation in the Old Testament. According to Deutero-Isaiah, Israel remains an elect nation despite her apostasy and despite the Lord's present anger with her: 'Remember these, O Jacob and Israel; for thou art my servant: I have formed thee; thou art my servant: O Israel, thou shalt not be forgotten of me. I have blotted out, as a thick cloud, thy transgressions, and, as a thick cloud, thy sins: return unto me; for I have redeemed thee.' (Isaiah 44: 21–2) The prophet then goes on to tell his fellow-exiles that Yahweh has appointed Cyrus the Great, king of Persia, to redeem Israel by freeing the captives and restoring the temple in Jerusalem; once reunified, the nation can resume her priestly mission, her ordained role of serving as 'a light to the Gentiles'. Again and again he reminds the Hebrews of their special status, in accents of

ringing triumph and exultation; his voice is the voice of Israel
herself: 'Listen, O isles, unto me; and hearken, ye people, from far;
The Lord hath called me from the womb; from the bowels of my
mother hath he made mention of my name. And he hath made my
mouth like a sharp sword; in the shadow of his hand hath he hid
me, and made me a polished shaft; in his quiver hath he hid me;
And said unto me, Thou art my servant, O Israel, in whom I will
be glorified.' (49: 1–3) After surveying the election-covenant faith
of Israel from the time of Abraham, the eschatological vision
reaches its climax in an intensely imagined promise of imminent
deliverance, coupled with an urgent call for regeneration and
sanctification.

Deutero-Isaiah is pre-eminently the prophet of redemption.
His constant theme is the national covenant with Yahweh and his
abiding concern is that Israel should cleanse and prepare herself
spiritually to fulfil her divine mission. With variations of emphasis, the other prophets share this theme. Thus, although Amos
and Micah with their stern theologies of doom stress divine justice
rather than mercy, their prophecies are nevertheless grounded in
a conviction of covenant solidarity; it is because Israel has
violated the covenant that they pronounce her doom: 'Hear this
word that the Lord hath spoken against you, O children of Israel,
against the whole family which I brought up from the land of
Egypt, saying, You only have I known of all the families of the
earth: therefore I will punish you for all your iniquities. Can two
walk together, except they be agreed?' (Amos 3: 1–3) While he
called for repentance and extended hope on that condition, Amos
saw too deeply into the hearts of his countrymen to believe that his
pleas and warnings would have much effect: 'Seek good, and not
evil, that ye may live: and so the Lord, the God of hosts, shall be
with you, as ye have spoken. Hate the evil, and love the good, and
establish judgment in the gate: it may be that the Lord God of
hosts will be gracious unto the remnant of Joseph.' (5: 14–15)
Amos's pessimism, although more pronounced than that of other
prophets, leads to an important qualification of national election
which is shared by all the prophets—namely, the realisation that
there is an election within the election. Since even the more san-
guine prophets perceived clearly that only a handful of the
'chosen people' would heed the call to repentance, the duty of fulfilling the covenant passed from the nation at large into the hands
of a godly and regenerate kernel within it, a 'holy seed' represen-

ting the true Israel.[6] Although the doctrine of the remnant is found throughout the Old Testament, it is particularly prominent in the prophetic books where it becomes, for the first time, a definite and coherent doctrine closely allied with the covenant theology that we have been examining. Israel has failed in her response to election and has been punished accordingly, but still God's redemptive purpose will not be frustrated, for the inheritance is to be preserved in a divinely chosen remnant. Without the merciful intervention of grace, however, the covenant would have been abrogated, with disatrous results for the Hebrew people: 'Except the Lord of hosts had left unto us a very small remnant, we should have been as Sodom, and we should have been like unto Gomorrah.' (Isaiah 1: 9) The doctrine of the remnant, largely developed by Isaiah, is a theme taken up by other prophets (e.g., Jeremiah 44: 14 and Micah 7: 18) and functions as a bridge between the threat of punishment and the promise of restoration. Zephaniah sums up the hope of the remnant with a truly pastoral simplicity: 'The remnant of Israel shall not do iniquity, nor speak lies; neither shall a deceitful tongue be found in their mouth: for they shall feed and lie down, and none shall make them afraid.' (Zeph. 3: 13) They are the new flock, regenerate and pure, in whom the inheritance promised to Abraham and Moses shall be brought to perfection.

In conclusion, then, it may be said that the essential feature of Old Testament election is that it is primarily national.[7] Personal calling is invariably contingent on the national mission. As individuals, Abraham and Moses are the special servants of Yahweh, but their importance as providential agents is subsumed under the broader object of their election, namely, that they should bring Israel to an understanding of her vocational role in the divine scheme of things and that they should mediate the terms of the national covenant with the Lord. In a similar way the personal charisma of military leaders like Saul and David is second in importance to their function as warrior-princes consolidating the strength and extending the boundaries of God's chosen nation. The prophets of the divided monarchy and the Babylonian captivity likewise demonstrate the dependence of private calling upon the national vocation. The prophetic office requires a devaluing of individual personality, and its function is the didactic one of bringing errant Israel to strict observance of the Mosaic covenant. It is for this reason, as W. F. Albright notes, that 'from David's time on, the prophetic mission was closely associated with moral and political as well as purely religious revival'.[8] In the Old Testament, then, individual election is subordinated to national election and is meaningful only within that wider context.

In later centuries the concept of a covenanted people with a divine mission passed into European consciousness and was vigorously adopted (and adapted) by various groups as a sure foundation for emergent nationalism. Frequently the idea is pressed into the service of a radical millenarianism and is symptomatic of frenzied, deflected spirituality;[9] but this is not always the case. In Tudor and Stuart England, for example, while the Puritan left provides ample evidence that the theme of national vocation was a common fantasy in the tradition of popular eschatology, it is important to see that the idea is prominent in the thinking of conservative reformers as well—indeed, even Matthew Parker, the scholarly Archbishop of Canterbury (1559–75), felt strongly enough on the subject of national and ecclesiastical election to counsel Lord Burghley in these terms: 'The comfort that these puritans have, and their continuance, is marvellous; and therefore if her Highness with her council (I mean some of them) step not to it, I see the likelihood of a pitiful commonwealth to follow; *Deus misereatur nostri*. Where Almighty God is so much English as he is, should not we requite his mercy with some earnesty to prefer his honour and true religion?'[10] During the sixteenth and seventeenth centuries it was widely believed that England was a covenanted nation and that God had special plans for His English church. The accession of Elizabeth, the defeat of the Spanish Armada, the discovery and foiling of the Gunpowder Treason, the parliamentary victory in the civil wars, and the establishment of the Protectorate were all interpreted—though for different reasons and by different groups—as manifest evidence of divine care and favour shown to an elect nation.

The early years of Elizabeth's reign were fraught with dangers, both real and imagined, from the powerful Catholic nations to the south; and the Protestant exiles, returning to England after the bloody interlude of Marian repression, were well aware that the success—indeed the very existence—of their cause depended on the religious and political solidarity of the nation. It was clear to the reformers that the Babylonian captivity of the church[11] had come to an end and that Elizabeth had been appointed to restore the true church and bring to perfection the reformation that God had ordained. All the signs indicated unequivocally that England was the new Israel; and for this reason, as William Haller points out, the English people had to be made 'to understand the whole pattern of events from the beginning to the present in order that they should realise their own place as a nation in that process, their immediate responsibility, the destiny to which they were called. Only thus could they rightly grasp the meaning of the current struggle with alien powers threatening their destruction and the necessity of supporting the queen and her government.'[12]

The English reformers, therefore, undertook to educate both sovereign and people in their duties and responsibilities. As interpreters of the divine will the prophet-reformers drew the parallels between England and Israel, exhorting the nation to consummate her destiny. With an eye on the frailty of human nature and the subtlety of the Roman Antichrist, William Whittingham and his fellow-translators reminded the queen of her divine vocation in the epistle prefixed to the Geneva Bible and likened her task to that of Zerubbabel whom the prophet Zechariah had admonished on divine command to rebuild the Temple after the return from Babylon (Zech. 4: 6–10):

> Which thing when we weigh aright, and consider earnestly how muche greater charge God hath laid vpon you in making you a builder of his spiritual Temple, we can not but partely feare, knowing the crafte and force of Satan our spiritual enemie, and the weakness and vnabilitie of this our nature: and partely be feruent in our prayers toward God that he wolde bring to perfection this noble worke which he hath begon by you: and therefore we indeuour our selues by all means to ayde, & to bestowe our whole force vnder your graces standard, whome God hath made as our Zerubbabel for the erecting of this most excellent Temple. . . .[13]

The prophetic stance of the Geneva translators is no rhetorical feint; their conviction of inner prompting is as sincere as is Zechariah's belief in the angel who declares that 'the Lord of hosts hath sent me unto you' (4: 9). Although their inspiration is indirect, it is nonetheless actual. They are impelled to speak because they, too, are God's instruments in the work of rebuilding the English temple.

Undoubtedly the most important assertion of national vocation in Elizabethan England is John Foxe's *Acts and Monuments of the Church* (1563), which was written expressly to proclaim 'the acts and proceedings of the whole Church of Christ, namely the Church of England'.[14] According to Foxe, scripture and history alike declared that the divine purpose was about to be fulfilled in the chosen people of England—a point which is repeatedly driven home in stake-side apophthegms grafted onto the lips of insouciant martyrs. 'Be of good comfort, Mr Ridley, and play the man,' remarks Hugh Latimer to his fellow sufferer as the fire is kindled at his feet; 'we shall this day light such a candle by God's grace in England, as I trust shall never be put out.'[15] There is even an oblique but pointed reminder to Elizabeth of her covenantal obligation, in the form of a death-bed prayer (based on Psalm 33: 12) put into the mouth of her saintly brother, Edward VI: 'O Lord, thou knowest how happy it were for me to be with thee; yet for thy chosen [ones'] sake send me life and health that I may truly serve thee. O my Lord God, bless thy people and save thine inheritance. O Lord God, save thy chosen people of England.'[16] Published early in the new reign, Foxe's martyrology was a source of hope and consolation at a time when the nation's future was far from secure. The unflinching faith of the Marian victims, narrated in dilated tales of persecution heightened by lurid woodcuts, inspired Protestant readers with a conviction of election and a willingness to endure no less in the national cause than their martyred predecessors. And by 1578, although the Catholic threat had not disappeared, the national covenant was secure enough for Edwin Sandys, the Archbishop of York, to praise Elizabeth ('a right Samuel, . . . a prince mild as Moses, just as Samuel, peaceful as Solomon, zealous as David') for her work in weeding the ecclesiastical garden of its 'popish trash', and to describe the English church as *de facto* inheritrix of all the pledges of election and divine favour: 'This is the flourishing vineyard of the Lord; the beautiful ark of covenant, wherein are reposed the treasures of God, the golden pot with manna, the rod of Aaron, and the tables of Moses. No church under heaven is more enriched with treasures and gifts of God. . . . The Lord may justly say to us, as to his people of old, "What might I do for my vine, which I have not done?"'[17]

The theme of England's special status in Jacobean times is perhaps nowhere more forcefully articulated than in the ten

sermons which Lancelot Andrewes delivered at Whitehall between 1606 and 1618 on the anniversary of the Gunpowder
Treason. The message is, in each case, essentially the same: there
can be no doubt that England is the new Israel and James a
providential agent, for never, not even in sacred history, had God
effected a more spectacular deliverance or manifested His favour
more conspicuously than in saving England on this occasion. In
Sermon II (1607), for example, Andrewes confesses that, although his text (Psalm 126) celebrates Israel's deliverance from
Babylon and the restoration of Zion, yet still 'this *Delivery* of theirs
(such as it were) falls short of that of ours as on this day,
wherewith yet I shall be faine to match it'.[18] He proceeds almost
immediately to drive home the vocational significance of England's recent redemption by proposing a hypothetical emenda-
tion of his text: 'If we might but change that one word, and instead
of reading, *When the Lord turned away the captivity of Sion*, we might
thus read, *When the Lord turned away the blowing up of Sion*, every
word else [of Psalm 126], would suit well and keep perfect
correspondency' with England's experience.[19] So remakable, indeed is this instance of prevenient deliverance that 'I may safely
say, *Quae regio in terris*, What *land* is there, whether the *fame* of it is
not gone, where it is not spoken of? and we by means of it
renowned and made famous over all the earth; even to *Turks* and
Infidels (for, thither also it is come, how GOD *hath dealt with us*).'[20]

With the Parliamentary ascendancy in the 1640s the doctrine of
national election became the political cornerstone of Puritan
covenant theology. In the very first sermon delivered before the
Long Parliament in November 1640, Cornelius Burges picked up
the theme where Andrewes had left it two decades earlier and he
adapted it to a specifically Puritan context. Taking as his subject
the history of the covenants between Israel and the Lord, he lost
no time in underlining the contemporary application of the
theme, for recent history indicated plainly that England, as the
new Israel, should bind herself to God by covenant: 'Consider . . .
how many, great, admirable, and even miraculous deliverances
God hath given us; what great things hee hath done for us. No
Nation under heaven can say more to his praise, in this kinde,
than we have cause to do. Our great deliverancés out of *Babylon*,
from the *Spanish Invasion*, from the *Gun-powder Treason*, and from
many other evils and feares, do all call upon you for a Covenant.'[21]

When the House of Commons inaugurated a series of monthly

fast days early in 1642,[22] the preachers of the Puritan brotherhood
were provided with a regular opportunity to influence policy by
propounding their interpretation of history directly to the govern-
ing body itself. On these occasions the staples of Puritan prop-
aganda were patriotism and prophetism. Wholly committed to
the belief that England was an object of divine intention, the
preachers never tired of reminding the members of Commons that
they were the representatives of a people in covenant with God,
and they repeatedly admonished Parliament of its covenantal
responsibility to perfect the work of reformation. 'Surely God hath
a good will to England,' declared one such preacher in 1641, 'he
hath done *great* and will doe greater *things* for *England*, and you
Right Honourable [Members of Commons] hath he raised up to
be instrumentall in these waies of his glorious mercies towards
us.'[23] The close correspondence between England and Israel as
elect nations made comparison inevitable; and, in fact, it became
a cardinal assumption of the Puritans that the Old Testament
contained the blueprint for the required reconstruction of the
English church and state. Israel's experience of election provided
an invaluable guide and pattern for the nascent English
theocracy—a conviction which is reflected even in the short titles
of many of the sermons delivered to the Long Parliament between
1642 and 1647. The following can serve as a representative
sample: Thomas Goodwin's *Zervbbabels Encovragement to Finish the
Temple* (1642), William Sedgwick's *Zions Deliverance and her Friends
Duty* (1642), John Strickland's *Gods Work of Mercy, in Sions Misery*
(1643), John Durye's *Israel's Call to March out of Babylon unto
Jerusalem* (1645), and Simeon Ash's *Gods Incomparable Goodness unto
Israel* (1647). In the language of Canaan itself the Puritan
prophet-preachers called upon their countrymen to obey the
divine will and to succeed where Israel had failed.

At the formal inauguration of the monthly fast programme on
23 February, 1642, members of Commons gathered in St Margaret's, Westminster, to hear sermons delivered by two of Milton's Smectymnuan friends. In the morning Edmund Calamy
exhorted them in *Gods free Mercy to England*, and later the same day
Stephen Marshall addressed them in a sermon entitled *Meroz
Cursed*. The fundamental conviction of both preachers was that
the English were a covenanted people lacking only the full
presence of God's church in their midst and that the whole nation,
symbolically represented in Westminster, was engaged in a corporate act of repentance and humiliation appropriate to the

nascent people of God. The close relationship of Milton with the Smectymnuans in 1642 lends a particular interest to these two sermons, and a brief look at Calamy's *Gods free Mercy to England* will be useful for the light it sheds both on the nature and concerns of Puritan apologetics and on Milton's place in the tradition.

In his preamble Calamy states his theme and defines his own role as a prophetic messenger conveying the word of God to His chosen people. England, he warns the Long Parliament, is in grave danger of forfeiting her election through disobedience and sins against the national covenant. There is, of course, no doubt of England's elect status: 'Now God hath brought England into the *schoole of mercy*, and hath placed it *in the highest forme*, and hath made it Captaine of the schoole.' However, since it 'cannot bee denied but that ... England hath done much against God', Calamy's intention on the present occasion is to recall the nation to her divine mission by laying 'the sins of England against God in one scale, and the mercies of God to England in the other scale, and [calling] upon you this day to bee humbled'. And he assures the Honourable Members that his right to interpret the divine will to them springs from his calling as *lingua Dei*; for, as the Lord once sent an angelic messenger from Gilgal to the people of Israel (Judges 2: 1–5), so 'God hath sent me hither this day as his Angell upon the same Embassage, I am to reminde you of Gods mercies to us: And of our ingratitude against him'.[24]

Like most Puritan preachers in Stuart England, Calamy divides his subject into 'doctrines' from which follow numerous 'reasons' and 'uses' demonstrating the contemporary relevance of the 'doctrines'. *Gods free Mercy to England* contains four 'doctrines'. The first, 'That God doth sometimes shew mercy to a Nation when it least *deserves*, and least *expects* it', is used to establish the fact that England has received an abundance of unmerited grace; it is indeed wonderful that God should do all that He has '*for such a Nation*, and *not for other Nations*: Not for *Germany*, not for *Ireland*. Although we drinke as deep of the cup of sinne as they, yet that God should give us no cup, but a cup full of mercy to drink off; to make us like Goshen when all other Protestant Nations are plagued as Egypt, O what a rare Circumstance is this!'[25]

Calamy's second doctrine is that '*Englands mercies come from the God of England*', and it elicits the following observation:

> ... we may truly say with *David, If the Lord had not beene on our side, if the Lord had not beene on our side when men rose up against us,*

they had swallowed us up quick, and the streames had gone over our soules:
There is not onely the *finger* of God, but the *hand*, even the *right
hand*; the *arme*, even the *strong arme* of Jehovah, the onely
wonder-working God in Englands mercies.[26]

But God's great mercy implies an active responsibility on the part
of those who have received it. It is not enough simply to praise
Him for such blessings: 'We must improve *Englands mercies* to the
glory of the *God of England*.' Since the Lord 'hath made England a
miracle of mercy', then 'let England bee a *miracle* of obedience: A
Christian in England must not onely *servire Deo, sed & adulari*, as
Tertullian saith: Hee must bee *rich* in good works as God hath been
rich in mercy.'[27] And this call for active duty leads, in the third
doctrine, to the corollary that the election is contingent rather
than absolute, that its object and purpose are extrinsic, not
intrinsic: 'Be it known unto you, *O house of England*, It is not for
your sakes, for you are a stiff-necked people, but for my holy
names sake.'[28]

The fourth doctrine, which follows naturally from the third,
restates the 'generall doctrine' of God's mercies with a call to
repentance and a warning about the inevitable punishment for
disobedience: 'The great God hath freed this Nation from Egypt,
and Babylon, from the Gun-powder treason, and from many
slaveries. Now if we prove unthankfull after all these mercies, wee
may justly expect *to be re-inslaved*.'[29] In spite of the many sins of
which the nation is guilty, the Lord has nevertheless chosen to
preserve and even bless her, for '*God hath dealt with England not
according to his ordinary rule, but according to his Prerogative. England* (if I
may so speake with reverence) is a *Paradox to the Bible*.'[30] However,
if the nation is to reap the fruits of this superabundance of grace,
she must not continue in sin: 'If the beginnings of hope that now
appeare, and these inclings of better dayes will not work upon us
to *humble* us *for, and from sinne*: God will take away all our hopes,
and all his mercies from us, and give them to a Nation that will
make better use of them.'[31] By way of conclusion Calamy sets out
some of England's particular sins. Of these, the gravest is her
reticence to accept the offer of grace by refusing to carry forward
the divinely ordained reformation of the church. As many of the
captive Israelites had grown fond of life in Babylon and refused to
return to Jerusalem when the Lord sent King Cyrus to deliver
them, so now in England 'there are many that like their former

condition under the innovations so well, that they had rather continue in Babylon still, than accept of the reformation offered'.[32] And thinking both of himself and, as well, of such parliamentary agents of reform as Pym and Essex, Calamy closes his peroration with a warning to the Honourable Members—some of whom were hostile to his message—neither to harm nor hinder the instruments whom God has chosen as bearers of His word or prosecutors of His will: '*Be ashamed to injure the instruments by which God conveies these mercies unto us.* When *Corah and his company rebelled against Moses and Aaron, then came the plague.* As wee must not *idolize*, so wee must not *injure* the *golden pipes*, through which these mercies flow unto us.'[33]

Since Milton was closely associated with the Smectymnuans in 1641–2, it is not surprising that his tone and attitude in the antiprelatical tracts should parallel those we have just examined in Calamy's sermon. Throughout the controversy over episcopacy, Milton's faith in the special calling that '*Brittains* God' had settled upon England remained firm and unshaken. The evidence of divine favour was everywhere apparent: 'the present age', as he remarked in *Animadversions* (July 1641), 'is to us an age of ages wherein God is manifestly come downe among us, to doe some remarkable good to our Church or state.' (*YP*, I, p. 703) However, while the Lord has 'ever had this Iland under the speciall indulgent eye of his providence', the danger is that now, when this favour is at its zenith, Englishmen might shrink from the task of perfecting the reformation and prefer to follow the prelates. If this were to happen, if the nation were to obey voices other than God's, then there was every reason to believe that the Lord would withdraw His favour: 'O if we freeze at noone after their[34] earely thaw, let us feare lest the Sunne for ever hide himselfe, and turne his orient steps from our ingratefull Horizon justly condemn'd to be eternally benighted.' (Ibid., p. 705) Although he had little faith in the ability and covenantal conviction of the average Englishman, Milton was convinced that 'a full and perfect reformation' of the church was the divinely appointed task of the Long Parliament, which he lauded in *An Apology for Smectymnuus* (April 1642) as 'some divine commission from heav'n . . . to take into hearing and commiseration the long remedilesse affliction of this kingdom'. It was observed, indeed, that God was with them and blessed their proceedings, that He 'hath bin pleas'd to make himselfe the agent, and immediat performer of their desires;

dissolving their difficulties when they are thought inexplicable, cutting out wayes for them where no passage could be seene' (*YP*, I, p. 927). And in the closing sentence of *The Reason of Church-Government* (January or February 1642), the English prophet called upon Parliament to let its 'severe and impartial doom imitate the divine vengeance' by bringing 'such a dead Sea of subversion upon [the Laudian church], that she may never in this Land rise more to afflict the holy reformed Church, and the elect people of God' (*YP*, I, p. 861).

Milton construed his calling as a prophet of reformation in terms of a divine commission and, like Calamy, interpreted his personal vocation in the light of what he conceived to be the sacred mission of his nation. Despite youth and inexperience he believed himself guided by 'the supreme inlightning assistance' (*YP*, I, p. 749) of God when he entered the polemical fray and penned replies against learned opponents like Joseph Hall. The employment of 'those few talents which God had . . . lent me' was determined by the national covenant, for the 'ease and leasure' that he had enjoyed since his Cambridge days was a period of intellectual and spiritual preparation for that time 'when the cause of God and his Church was to be pleaded' (ibid., pp. 804–5). The office of spokesman, he informed his Anglican opponents in *An Apology for Smectymnuus*, 'goes not by age, or youth, but to whomsoever God shall give apparently the will, the Spirit, and the utterance' (ibid., p. 875). And, like the Old Testament prophets on whose experience his own was patterned, the author of *The Reason of Church-Government* knew from personal knowledge that, 'when God commands to take the trumpet and blow a dolorous or a jarring blast, it lies not in mans will what he shall say, or what he shall conceal' (ibid., p. 803).

The doctrine of national election is a cardinal assumption throughout the antiprelatical tracts; its presence is everywhere felt, but its truth is too apparent to require detailed explication or defence. By the time Milton wrote *Areopagitica* (November 1644), however, the situation had begun to change, and this pamphlet contains the most sustained and passionate expression in all of his prose of the conviction that the English were the nascent people of God:

Lords and Commons of England, consider what Nation it is wherof ye are, and wherof ye are the governours: a Nation not slow and dull, but of a quick, ingenious, and piercing spirit, acute to invent, suttle and sinewy to discours, not beneath the reach of any point the highest that human capacity can soar to .... Yet that which is above all this, the favour and the love of heav'n we have great argument to think in a peculiar manner propitious and propending towards us. Why else was this Nation chos'n before any other, that out of her as out of *Sion* should be proclam'd and sounded forth the first tidings and trumpet of Reformation to all *Europ*.[35] And had it not bin the obstinat perversnes of our Prelats against the divine and admirable spirit of *Wicklef*, to suppresse him as a schismatic and *innovator*, perhaps neither the *Bohemian Husse* and *Jerom*, no nor the name of *Luther*, or of *Calvin* had bin ever known: the glory of reforming all our neighbours had bin completely ours. But now, as our obdurat Clergy have with violence demean'd the matter, we are become hitherto the latest and backwardest Schollers, of whom God offer'd to have made us the teachers. Now once again by all concurrence of signs, and by the generall instinct of holy and devout men, as they daily and solemnly expresse their thoughts, God is decreeing to begin some new and great period in his Church, ev'n to the reforming of Reformation it self: what does he then but reveal Himself to his servants, and as his manner is, first to his English-men; I say as his manner is, first to us, though we mark not the method of his counsels, and are unworthy. (*YP*, II, pp. 551–3)

The passionate intensity of this passage, the earnest combination of exhortation and admonition, is to be explained by the ideological rift between Milton and the Presbyterian divines of the Westminster Assembly.

In August 1643 Milton had dedicated *The Doctrine and Discipline of Divorce* to the 'Parliament of England, with the Assembly' and had reminded both bodies that 'Yee have now, doubtlesse by the favour and appointment of God, yee have now in your hands a great and populous Nation to Reform' (*YP*, II, p. 226). But by 1643 Milton's idea of the course of reformation had begun to undergo a significant alteration, with profound implications for his alliance with the Presbyterians. In the antiprelatical tracts his assumption had been that the final end of reformation would be quickly achieved once the bishops had been removed; he had called for a 'speedy and vehement' reformation in the belief that the Kingdom of God was at the door and that the English New Jerusalem would be established immediately upon the destruction of the Laudian Babylon. Time and experience, however, taught him otherwise. Continuing abuses at all levels of society pointed clearly to the necessity of continuing reformation, and he began to appreciate that national regeneration would be a protracted undertaking, a task requiring the best efforts of the best men. Since 'Good and evill . . . in the field of this World grow up together almost inseparably', reconstruction must take the form of a progressive search for truth rather than, as the Presbyterians maintained, that of rebuilding according to a clearly revealed pattern: 'To be still searching what we know not, by what we know, still closing up truth to truth as we find it (for all her body is *homogeneal*, and proportionall) this is the golden rule in *Theology* as well as in Arithmetick.' (*YP*, II, p. 551)

Prompted by the failure of his marriage to Mary Powell, Milton's first attempt to close up to truth centred on the question of divorce; and he published his findings in a pamphlet which, as we have seen, he dedicated to Parliament and the Westminster Assembly together. His idealism, however, blinded him still to the repressive implications of the Presbyterian cause that he had supported with such headlong enthusiasm since 1641. His Smectymnuan friends and their fellows had at heart only the reform of church government along rigid and preconceived lines, and, that achieved, they proposed to shut the gates firmly against the stream of reformation. They were, therefore, not prepared to entertain innovations on divorce, and Milton's pamphlet was received by members of the Assembly with a mixture of asperity and patronising humour. The hostile reception accorded *The Doctrine and Discipline of Divorce* convinced Milton that the Assembly was a serious impediment to further reformation. And since it was clear that truth could have no impartial hearing from the Presbyterian Assembly, he addressed his next pamphlet— *The Judgement of Martin Bucer* (July 1644)—to the Long Parliament alone.

By the time *Areopagitica* was published five months later the rift was complete, for Milton was convinced that in instigation if not in very deed the Licensing Order was the work of the Assembly attempting to suppress points of view inconsistent with its own dogma. Themselves recently victims of oppression, the Presbyterians had now resorted to repression in an effort to force the

consciences of their countrymen: 'But now the Bishops abrogated
and voided out of the Church, as if our Reformation sought no
more, but to make room for others into their seats under another
name, the Episcopall arts begin to bud again.' (*YP*, II, p. 541) If
England were to resume her 'wonted prerogative, of being the first
asserters in every vindication' of God's glory, then Parliament
must be ready to use 'their wholesome and preventive shears' to
cut off the Assembly together with its abettors the Scottish
commissioners like Robert Baillie ('Scotch What-d'ye-call').[36]
And, as Ernest Sirluck has noted, it was to convince Parliament of
the gravity of the Presbyterian threat to the national covenant
that Milton in *Areopagitica* distinguished firmly between the Assembly and the nation, and in order to 'reveal the dimensions of
the gap, he [portrayed] the character of the nation'—a nation
that history had shown to be 'the peculiar favorite of heaven' (*YP*,
II, p. 175).

Like St Paul, Milton was coming to see that 'they are not all
Israel, which are of Israel'. The national mission depended on an
elect remnant smaller than he had expected; for, with the defection of the Assembly, the task of renovation was transferred
wholly to the safekeeping of the 'wise and faithful labourers'
sitting in Parliament. Upon them alone devolved the onerous
responsibility of transforming a 'knowing' and divinely favoured
people into 'a Nation of Prophets, of Sages, and of Worthies' (*YP*,
II, p. 554). There was, however, a real apprehension on Milton's
part that Parliament, like the Assembly, might prove unequal to
its commission; and there is a note of strained and fearful optimism in his vision of that time—now close at hand he dared
hope—'wherein *Moses* the great Prophet may sit in heav'n rejoyc-
ing to see that memorable and glorious wish of his fulfill'd, when
not only our sev'nty Elders, but all the Lords people are become
Prophets' (ibid., pp. 555–6). The rhetoric is designed to serve a
definite purpose. It is a prophetic vision offered in order to
confirm the 'sev'nty Elders' of the English Sanhedrin in their
covenantal duty. Led by Parliament, the nation must imitate a
rejuvenated Samson; she must become like a mighty eagle soaring
in heaven and deaf to the timorous cries of the Westminster
Assembly:

Methinks I see in my mind a noble and puissant Nation rousing
herself like a strong man after sleep, and shaking her invincible

locks: Methinks I see her as an Eagle muing her mighty youth, and kindling her undazl'd eyes at the full midday beam; purging and scaling her long abused sight at the fountain it self of heav'nly radiance; while the whole noise of timorous and flocking birds, with those also that love the twilight, flutter about, amaz'd at what she means, and in their envious gabble would prognosticat a year of sects and schisms. (*YP*, II, pp. 557–8)

He implores Parliament to transform these similes into metaphors, to translate vision into reality. And yet, as the exhortations of Israel's prophets often fell on deaf ears because the rulers had been seduced by evil counsel, so he fears that Parliament may disregard prophetic utterance and be led astray by the impious advice of the Presbyterian Assembly.

Milton's fears were, in fact, justified by the event. The Assembly continued to sit until 1649 and remained an important influence in decision-making until well into 1647; moreover, the Presbyterian members in Commons successfully resisted the call for further reformation from the growing Independent faction in Parliament and the Army. Milton's anguish over the obstruction of reformation and subversion of the national mission by the reactionary Presbyterian majority reached its nadir in the spring of 1648 with his composition of a *Character of the Long Parliament* and his translation of Psalms 80 to 88. As a group these nine psalms deal with the disobedience of the chosen people and the Lord's righteous anger, and they stress the need for a national renewal which can be achieved only by divine intervention. These themes are well illustrated in Milton's rendering of verses five to eight of Psalm 82:

> They know not nor will understand,
> 　　In darkness they walk on,
> The earth's foundations all are moved
> 　　And out of order gone.
>
> I said that ye were gods, yea all
> 　　The sons of God most high
> But ye shall die like men, and fall
> 　　As other princes *die*.

Rise God, judge thou the earth *in might*,
This *wicked* earth redress,
For thou art he who shalt by right
The nations all possess.

The prayer for renewal and divine guidance was eventually answered in a swift-moving series of events which began with Colonel Pride's ejection of the Presbyterian members from Commons in December 1648 and ended with the decisive action of the Army and Rump in bringing Charles Stuart to trial and execution in January 1649. 'The sum is', Milton declared of this latter event in *Eikonoklastes* (October 1649), 'they thought to limit or take away the *Remora* of his negative voice, which like to that little pest at Sea, took upon it to arrest and stopp the Common-wealth stearing under full saile to a Reformation.' (*YP*, III, p. 501) The new Israel had been given a second chance. And God's English prophet was not slow to warn the new rulers of their responsibilities and tell them that, although they had received manifest tokens of divine favour, that grace would be withdrawn for failure to carry forward the work of reformation. Even when addressing himself to a European audience in *Pro Populo Anglicano Defensio* (February 1651), he was not adverse to admonishing the Rump directly: 'should you, ... after having found the divine power so favourable to yourselves and so stern towards your foes, fail to learn ... that you must fear God and love justice, then ... you shall soon find that God's hatred of you will be greater than was his anger towards your foes or his kindly grace towards you above all people now on earth.' (*YP*, IV, i, p. 536)

By the time the *Defensio Secunda* appeared in May 1654 the longed-for consummation of reformation, the establishment of the English New Jerusalem, seemed almost within grasp. Despite the misgivings he must have felt at the abrupt dissolution of the Rump and institution of the Protectorate, Milton—unlike Hutchinson and Vane who retired from active political life—continued to serve the Council of State. And with a buoyant idealism recalling the tone of *Areopagitica* ten years earlier, he took up his pen to praise his nation: 'I was born at a time in the history of my country when her citizens, with pre-eminent virtue and nobility and steadfastness surpassing all the glory of their ancestors, invoked the Lord, followed his manifest guidance, and after accomplish-

ing the most heroic and exemplary achievements since the foundation of the world, freed the state from grievous tyranny and the
church from unworthy servitude.' (*YP*, IV, i, pp. 548–9) By 1654,
however, 'the whole burden of affairs' had fallen on Oliver
Cromwell. And for Milton, who had been disappointed by the
Westminster Assembly and the Long Parliament, the Lord Protector represented the last refuge of a dream. Yet Cromwell was
the instrument of Providence, an elect remnant of one; the signs
were unmistakable, and England need have no fear while her
destiny lay in his hands: 'For while you, Cromwell, are safe, he
does not have sufficient faith even in God himself who would fear
for the safety of England, when he sees God everywhere so
favorable to you, so unmistakably at your side.' (Ibid., p. 670)

Like Cicero, Cromwell is *pater patriae*, the father of his country;
and he is of all Englishmen 'the man most fit to rule' (ibid.,
p. 672). There is, however, a note of apprehension in this last
phrase. In 1652 Milton had counselled this man, who had been
'Guided by faith and matchless Fortitude' on the battlefield, that
'peace hath her victories / No less renownd then warr' (*Sonnet 16*).
Would God's warrior, now king in all but name, be as adept in the
arts of government and peace as he had been on the field at
Marston Moor and Naseby? The task is not an easy one, and
Milton turns aside from his encomium to warn the Lord Protector
of the heavy burden he has assumed: 'These trials will buffet you
and shake you; they require a man supported by divine help,
advised and instructed by all-but-divine inspiration.' (*YP*, IV, i,
p. 674) The tone is less assured here than it was only four pages
earlier. Cromwell is the indispensable man, 'the man most fit to
rule'—but will he prove equal to 'this most exalted rank' to which
he has been 'raised by the power of God beyond all other men'?
Only the issue will decide. And what if Cromwell and the nation
should prove unfaithful to their election and their covenanted
mission? Then, 'be sure that posterity will speak out and pass
judgment':

It will seem to posterity that a mighty harvest of glory was at
hand, together with the opportunity for doing the greatest
deeds, but that to this opportunity men were wanting. Yet there
was not wanting one who could rightly counsel, encourage, and
inspire, who could honor the noble deeds and those who had
done them, and make both deeds and doers illustrious with
praises that will never die. (Ibid., pp. 685–6)

This statement is far more than an expression of 'the abiding faith of genius'.[37] It is a prophet's self-vindication and an acknowledgement of inspired duty accomplished.

When Cromwell died in September 1658, the task of rebuilding was still far from complete; but the death of the Lord Protector was, effectively, that also of the Puritan experiment. Discord and indecision in a series of ineffectual Parliaments declared only too clearly that men were indeed wanting for the 'mighty harvest of glory'. For Milton, as Arthur Barker has observed, 'the triumphant vindication of divine justice in 1649 had been the achievement of the remnant in whom God's grace had worked effectively; but such was the wilful degeneracy of the many, and the weakness even of those who should have been God's champions, that the triumph was short-lived. The disintegration of the Commonwealth when the goal was within reach followed from a corrupt repudiation of divine grace and a wilful rejection of England's glorious destiny.'[38] Milton himself bore his prophetic burden to the end. Sustained and prompted by God, he took up the trumpet to blow several sharp and jarring blasts in the pamphlets of 1659–60, warning his countrymen that if they were to desert God and prove unfaithful to election they would never 'be voutsaf't heerafter the like mercies and signal assistances from heaven in our cause' (*YP*, VII, p. 423).

On 29 May 1660 Charles II made his triumphal entry into the capital; and *the good Old Cause*, to which Milton had given two decades of selfless labour and on whose altar he had sacrificed his eyesight, went down to the pealing of churchbells and shouts of joyous Londoners. Milton took sanctuary in the house of an unknown friend in Bartholomew Close. Never again, either in prose or verse, did he speak of his nation's providential destiny. The hopes of the Lord and his blind prophet for the renovation of a covenanted English church and state were seeds cast on stony ground and had sprouted only to wither and perish.

(ii) PROPHETIC INSPIRATION

> *Then the Lord put forth his hand, and*
> *touched my mouth. And the Lord said*
> *unto me, Behold, I have put my words*
> *in thy mouth.*
> (Jeremiah 1: 9)

Like Abraham and Moses, the prophets of ancient Israel were the 'friends of God' and interpreters of the divine will. They were not in any sense, however, mere marionettes who jerked and babbled when God pulled the strings. The canonical prophets were, as E. W. Heaton observes,

> servants in God's household, and not mere tools in his hands. Their personalities were neither dissolved by fusion with the divine in any sort of 'mystic union', nor yet swept aside by the violence of any non-moral ecstatic afflatus. When they were commissioned as 'men of God', they remained *men*—and that is why they can so powerfully mediate to human persons the self-disclosure of the personal God.[39]

And William Kerrigan summarises the same position in this way: 'Christianity tends to equate freedom with obedience: to become truly free, a man chooses to obey his God and assumes the yoke of the Gospels. Christian liberty is serving the Lord. Thus Origen wrote that the prophets "voluntarily and consciously . . . collaborated with the Word that came to them" . . . . Though chosen, the free man chose to be so. Prophecy was at once the record of the Spirit and the autobiography of His free instrument.'[40] Since Kerrigan in *The Prophetic Milton* (1974) has examined in considerable detail Milton's indebtedness to the theological tradition of defining and categorising prophetic inspiration, there could be little point in rehearsing the evidence again here and I shall therefore confine the discussion to Milton's view of his own inspiration in the prose works.[41]

Milton's prophetic inspiration is the natural concomitant of his poetic inspiration. Indeed, both in the *Nativity Ode* and *The Reason of Church-Government* he discusses his poetic vocation in prophetic terms, and it is therefore not surprising to find that in the prose works he readily transfers his sense of election and inspiration from a call to serve as God's poet-priest to a call to serve as His prophet of reformation. Arthur Barker is almost certainly right in arguing that it was an 'enthusiastic belief that the completion of England's reformation would bring with it the long-sought release of his poetical powers [that] swept Milton into the ecclesiastical controversy'.[42] Yet it must be added that his experience as prophet effectively transformed his view of his poetic role, for it not only focused his sense of vocation but channelled it in new directions and deepened his belief in inspiration. Prophecy may have initially been subservient to poetry in 1642, but by 1660 poetry had become the servant of prophecy. And the distance travelled over these two decades may be measured by comparing the qualified and unformed statements of inspiration in the early poetry and prose with the declarations of divine guidance in the invocations in *Paradise Lost* and *Paradise Regained*. Milton never experienced the sudden, blinding infusion of divine grace described by so many of his Puritan contemporaries in their spiritual autobiographies and records of religious conversion. Rather, his sense of divine prompting and guidance developed gradually, becoming stronger and more intense as he passed from experience to experience. He came to political and ecclesiastical controversy already equipped with an idealist's conviction of calling and mission. During the twenty years of polemical warfare, however, that faith was tested in the arena of *Realpolitik*, where theory was transformed into fact and aspiration into actuality. The task of justifying God's ways to men requires speaking not simply *of* God but *for* God––and it is precisely this development from priest to prophet that lies at the heart of Milton's vocational education in the prose works and accounts for the fact that his view of inspiration deepens appreciably from the early to the later poetry.

  Following in the tradition of Sidney and Jonson, Milton's early theoretic statements about poetry and poetic inspiration are moderate and well-balanced, combining a modified Platonic view of inspiration with an Aristotelian conviction that poetry is a mimetic *art*. As I suggested in Chapter 2 (pp. 58–61), he regarded poetic genius as a divinely implanted talent nurtured and perfected by human study and endeavour. The position is happily summarised by Sidney in *An Apologie for Poetrie* (1595):

  A Poet no industrie can make, if his owne *Genius* bee not carried vnto it: and therefore it is an old Prouerbe, *Orator fit, Poeta nascitur*. Yet confesse I alwayes that as the firtilest ground must bee manured, so must the highest flying wit haue a *Dedalus* to guide him. That *Dedalus*, they say, both in this and in other, hath three wings to beare it selfe vp into the ayre of due commendation: that is, Arte, Imitation, and Exercise.[43]

Without denying the legitimate claims of either nature or grace this account of poetic 'making' steers a middle course between the

Scylla of mere empirical intellection and the Charybdis of irrational afflatus. It rejects, on the one hand, the extreme rationalism
of theorists like Thomas Hobbes, who flatly denied the possibility
of divine aid and scoffed at poets who wished 'to be thought to
speak by inspiration, like a Bagpipe'.[44] And it tempers, on the
other hand, the excesses of the *furor poeticus* tradition in which the
poet loses all rational control over his work and functions merely
as the amanuensis of deity:

> We are kindled in such fashion
> With heat of the Holy Ghost
> (Which is God of mightes most),
> That he our pen doth lead,
> And maketh in us such speed
> That forthwith we must need
> With pen and ink proceed . . . .[45]

Like Sidney, Milton avoided both of these extremes. Although
there are several sonorous descriptions of inspiration in the early
poetry (*Vacation Exercise* and *Elegies* 5 and 6), they are largely
conventional. Apart from the *Nativity Ode*, the claims to inspiration in the early verse are theoretical rather than practical, a
yearning for visionary experience rather than an acknowledgement of it. And from *Il Penseroso* to *Lycidas*, as I have argued in
Chapter 2, the hoped-for 'prophetic strain' remains only an
aspiration.

After Milton's return from Italy, however, the 'inward prompting' of God—experienced hitherto only occasionally—became
more frequent and 'grew daily upon me' (*YP*, I, p. 810). The
conviction of divine guidance deepened still further in the period
of the antiprelatical tracts and issued, for the first time since the
Nativity Ode, in concrete claims to inspiration, imparted through
the medium of conscience or reason: 'And if any man incline to
thinke I undertake a taske too difficult for my yeares, I trust
through the supreme inlightning assistance farre otherwise; for
my yeares, be they few or many, what imports it? so they bring
reason, let that be lookt on.' (Ibid., p. 749) The prompting is
indirect, but it is actual—a fact rather than a hope. And it may be
added that Milton's belief in divine direction was certainly
encouraged—perhaps even directly influenced—by the views
expressed by his Smectymnuan friends and many other Pres-

byterian divines in the early 1640s. Customarily these men construed their invitations to preach before the members of Commons as a divine mandate. Stephen Marshall, for example,
bluntly declared to the House in 1640 that 'the speciall errand I
have to deliver from the Lord, is to assure you . . . . That God will
be with you, while you be with him'; a year later Edmund Calamy
informed them that 'God hath sent me hither this day as his
Angell'; and in April 1642 Thomas Goodwin interpreted his
invitation as a call to serve as God's spokesman: 'You were
pleased so far to owne me, as to betrust me with this service, to be
God's mouth in publique unto you.'[46] These assertions are
grounded in a firm conviction of inspired duty and there is no
reason to doubt their sincerity.

Milton's view of inspiration in 1641–2 is expressed most clearly
in the autobiographical preface in *The Reason of Church-Government*,
where he compares his calling to that of the Old Testament
prophets. Like Jeremiah, he sees himself as 'a man of strife and
contention', a man prompted to speak against his own will. What
he feels compelled to say will be unpopular and ill-received by
many, but 'when God commands to take the trumpet and blow a
dolorous or a jarring blast, it lies not in mans will what he shall
say, or what he shall conceal'. Moreover, since poetry rather than
prose is his preferred medium, 'the genial power of nature' calls
him in another direction. But 'these tumultuous times' demand
obedience to the inward call of God and not the leisurely indulgence of one's natural inclinations. Even if he has only 'the use,
as I may account it, but of my left hand' in a prose controversy, he
must speak as God commands; and the spectre of divine reproach
is a spur to action:

> Thou hadst the diligence, the parts, the language of a man, if a
> vain subject were to be adorn'd or beautifi'd, but when the
> cause of God and his Church was to be pleaded, for which
> purpose that tongue was given thee which thou hast, God
> listen'd if he could heare thy voice among his zealous servants,
> but thou wert domb as a beast. (*YP*, I, pp. 804–5)

Although there is nothing formulaic or insincere in these assertions of divinely ordained duty, they do not represent a full and
unqualified identification of the speaker with the tradition of Old
Testament prophecy.[47] Anxious to justify his intrusion into ec-

clesiastical controversy and to declare the genuine nature of his prompting, he draws an analogy between his own experience and that of Jeremiah (cf. above, pp. 79–80) — and then quickly passes on to a long and eloquent discussion of his poetic plans and aspirations. He thinks of himself as a poet rather than a prophet.

The next stage of Milton's confirmation in his prophetic vocation comes in the divorce tracts. In *The Doctrine and Discipline of Divorce* (August 1643) he left the beaten track of controversy and set off on his own, acknowledging, however, that divine grace had sustained him on this journey into a new realm of polemical endeavour: 'I trust, through the help of that illuminating Spirit which hath favor'd me, to have done no every daies work.' (*YP*, II, p. 340) Whereas his involvement in the 'wayward subject against prelaty' had been against his will, the problem of divorce was much nearer to home and he was strongly motivated to employ his left hand in rescuing this neglected truth when called upon to do so. And his belief both in his own ability and in the immediacy of divine prompting was correspondingly deeper and stronger. This faith was severely tested, however, by the hostile reception of the pamphlet. Yet adversity served a constructive purpose, for it further confirmed his sense of calling and supernatural guidance. References to inspiration increase in number in the prose works of 1644, and the discovery that Martin Bucer had anticipated Milton's own views on divorce led to the most uncompromising declaration of divine direction that he had so far claimed:

> If therefore God in the former age found out a servant, and by whom he had converted and reform'd many a citie, by him thought good to restore the most needfull doctrine of divorce from rigorous and harmfull mistakes on the right hand, it can be no strange thing if in this age he stirre up by whatsoever means whom it pleases him, to take in hand & maintain the same assertion. Certainly if it be in mans discerning to sever providence from chance, I could allege many instances, wherein there would appear cause to esteem of me no other then a passive instrument under some power and counsel higher and better then human, working to a general good in the whole cours of this matter. For that I ow no light, or leading receav'd from any man in the discovery of this truth, . . . he who tries the

inmost heart, and saw with what severe industry and examination of my self, I set down every period, will be my witnes.
(*The Judgement of Martin Bucer*, July 1644; *YP*, II, p. 433)

Although the statement is cautiously hedged with
conditionals — 'if', 'could', 'would appear' — it claims a more
profound and direct supernatural prompting than anything in the
antiprelatical tracts. Urged by God's secretary Conscience and
directed by His gift of *recta ratio*, Milton had singlehandedly
defended an unpopular truth, and the Lord had rewarded his
faith and obedience by showing him that Bucer had served as a
divine instrument in the same cause: 'at length it hath pleas'd
God, who had already giv'n me satisfaction in my self, to afford
me means wherby I may be fully justify'd also in the eyes of men.'
(Ibid., p. 435) The significance of Bucer's treatise was that it
provided Milton with documentary evidence that he had supported God's own cause; it verified both his authority in speaking
and the divine source of the inspiration to which he laid claim.
Indeed, he was certain that the divorce issue had been a trial of his
prophetic vocation: 'For God, it seems, intended to prove me,
whether I durst alone take up a rightful cause against a world of
disesteem, & found I durst.' (Ibid., p. 434) He emerged from the
experience with the unshakable conviction that he was not only
God's servant but also His spokesman. He could claim with
Jeremiah that 'the Lord put forth his hand, and touched my
mouth. And the Lord said unto me, Behold, I have put my words
in thy mouth' (Jer. 1: 9).

After 1643 Milton's sense that he was 'God's mouth in publique' is assumed as an axiom. There is, however, a noticeable
deepening of emotional commitment to his prophetic calling in
the years following the onset of total blindness in February 1652.
The loss of his sight — a traumatic counterpoint to his recent
grand victory over Salmasius and the acclaim of all
Europe — emphasised his isolation from his fellow men and his
utter dependence on God. It was, moreover, an event that de-
manded vocational redefinition. And his reassessment of his
calling and his usefulness to God in these altered circumstances
issued both in *Sonnnet 19* ('When I consider how my light is spent')
and in the *Defensio Secunda* in magnificent reaffirmations of election and divine support:

although by no means exempt from the disasters common to humanity, I and my interests are nevertheless under the protection of God. . . . When I speak, not on behalf on one people nor yet one defendant, but rather for the entire human race against the foes of human liberty, amid the common and well-frequented assembly (so to speak) of all nations, I have been aided and enriched by the favor and assistance of God. Anything greater or more glorious than this I neither can, nor wish to, claim. (*YP*, IV, i, pp. 557–8)

His identification with the prophets of Israel is here complete. And speaking of the special grace and illumination accorded to blind men in general, he assumes his prophetic stance to deliver the following inspired *defensio pro se*:

To be sure, we blind men are not the least of God's concerns, for the less able we are to perceive anything other than himself, the more mercifully and graciously does he deign to look upon us. Woe to him who mocks us, woe to him who injures us. He deserves to be cursed with a public malediction. Divine law and divine favor have rendered us not only safe from the injuries of men, but almost sacred, nor do these shadows around us seem to have been created so much by the dullness of our eyes as by the shade of angels' wings. And divine favor not infrequently is wont to lighten these shadows again, once made, by an inner and far more enduring light. (Ibid., p. 590)

The style and tone are those of Isaiah and Jeremiah, and so, too, is the confident assurance of divine aid and protection. Indeed, the passage might well have been written by any one of the canonical prophets as a defence of his personal sanctity and prophetic calling.[48]

It is against the background of Milton's sense of prophetic vocation in the later prose that one should approach the claims to inspiration in the invocations in *Paradise Lost* and *Paradise Regained*. These invocations have often been discussed by other readers with such acuity and sensitivity that I shall content myself with making only one or two basic points.

The invocation with which *Paradise Lost* opens is addressed to two quite separate 'deities'—the poet's Muse and the Holy

Spirit. By convention, epic poetry always begins with an appeal to supernatural authority for guidance and support. Characteristically, however, Milton adapts conventions to suit his own particular situation—as he does, for example, by transforming the traditional pastoral elegy in *Lycidas*. The same is true in *Paradise Lost*, for the Muse whom he invokes to inspire his song is not an accredited 'sister of the sacred well' on Mount Helicon. She is, rather, a 'heavenly Muse' whose affinities are with other pools and other mountains:

> Sing heavenly Muse, that on the secret top
> Of Oreb, or of Sinai, didst inspire
> That shepherd, who first taught the chosen seed,
> In the beginning how the heavens and earth
> Rose out of chaos: or if Sion hill
> Delight thee more, and Siloa's brook that flowed
> Fast by the oracle of God; I thence
> Invoke thy aid to my adventurous song. . . .
>
> (I, 6–13)

She is, in fact, the inner voice that led Moses as he composed the Pentateuch and guided the prophets as they set down their inspired visions. But why is she distinguished from the Spirit, and why does the poet appeal 'chiefly' to the latter? First, it needs to be noted that their functions are separate: while the Muse is asked to 'inspire' the poet, the Spirit is asked to teach him ('Instruct me, for thou know'st', 19) and to render him a vessel fit to reveal holy things:

> what in me is dark
> Illumine, what is low raise and support;
> That to the highth of this great argument
> I may assert eternal providence,
> And justify the ways of God to men.
>
> (23–6)

Moreover, they are addressed in different terms and represented by different symbols: the Muse who is asked to 'sing' is defined largely in terms of speech and sound, whereas the didactic Spirit is described as imparting light and illumination. Nor is this all. The

tone of the 'two' invocations is quite distinct. The request to the
Muse is confident and full of daring, anticipating an 'adventurous
song' that

> with no middle flight *intends* to soar
> Above the Aonian mount, while it pursues
> Things unattempted yet in prose or rhyme.
> (14–16; italics mine)

The prayer addressed to the Holy Spirit, on the other hand, is a
humble petition, in which the speaker is well aware of his human
frailty and in which his prospective success in the undertaking is
expressed in the subjunctive:

> That to the highth of this great argument
> I *may assert* eternal providence. . . .
> (24–5; italics mine)

The distinction between the Muse who *sings* and the Spirit that
justifies is crucial to Milton's conception of inspiration in *Paradise
Lost.* I find irresistible Helen Gardner's suggestion that the
heavenly Muse represents 'the poetic embodiment of Milton's
belief in his vocation'.[49] I should prefer to state the case in this
way: the Muse is the divinely implanted poetic talent—that
'inspired guift of God rarely bestow'd, ' as he had called it in *The
Reason of Church-Government* (*YP*, I, p. 816)—which Milton has
possessed from birth and which he has nurtured and improved
over a long life of study and severe application. On the threshold
of the great poem for which his whole life has been a preparation,
he personifies his own creative energy and calls upon it to fulfil the
end for which it was given, by pursuing 'Things unattempted yet
in prose or rhyme'.[50] And he can afford to be confident, to speak of
a flight that '*intends* to soar', because he is now ready to begin and
has done all in his power to cultivate the poetic gift entrusted to
him. But neither the original talent nor that talent as improved by
human industry and study is wholly adequate for the great
enterprise upon which he is embarking; and so Milton turns in the
second section of the invocation to the Holy Spirit, humbly
beseeching that, through the operation of His Spirit, God will
provide him with the subsequent or supporting grace needed to
bring the work successfully to completion. The work of the Spirit

is to purify the vessel and enlighten the poet with knowledge that is unattainable except by direct revelation, knowledge that no amount of human industry can acquire unaided. The same theme is restated at the climax of the invocation to Light in Book III:

> So much the rather thou celestial Light
> Shine inward, and the mind through all her powers
> Irradiate, there plant eyes, all mist from thence
> Purge and disperse, that I may see and tell
> Of things invisible to mortal sight.
>
> (III, 51–5)

Whether or not the 'celestial Light' here invoked is synonymous with the Holy Spirit is a question too vexed and complex to allow brief analysis in the present discussion. However, given the place of the Spirit in Puritan theology generally[51] and, as well, the parallels between the invocation here and that to the Spirit in Book I, I am inclined to see them as identical. But perhaps rigid identification is unnecessary; for, as Ronsard notes in his *Abbregé de l'art poétique françois* (1565), 'les Muses . . . ne nous representent autre chose que les puissances de Dieu, auquel les premiers hommes avoyent donné plusieurs noms pour les divers effectz de son incomprehensible majesté.'[52] It may be enough to know that the 'celestial Light' is an aspect of God's providence, without seeking to pin the symbol onto a collector's display-board with its precise identity subscribed.

To return for a moment to Book I: what is the significance of this bipartite invocation shared between Muse and Spirit in terms of Milton's view of inspiration? If the argument about these two figures outlined above is accepted, then it seems to me that the question is easily answered. Milton's experience as God's spokesman in the prose works taught him to place himself in the tradition of Old Testament prophecy. And in that tradition, as I pointed out at the beginning of this section, inspiration is distinct from irrational afflatus and, in fact, bears no relation to it. The prophets are men, free men, who voluntarily co-operate with God and consciously accept the service 'imposed' on them. They will to relax the will, in order to declare God's will. In the same way *Paradise Lost* is the record of the collaboration between the Poet and God, that is, between a free speaker and the divine word. In the opening invocation these two figures are invoked separately: through the 'heavenly Muse' Milton declares his own readiness to begin, and through the invocation to the Spirit he calls upon God to sustain and direct the work.

In later invocations the two functions are fused, as is natural since there is no distinction between instrument and Word once the request for inspiration has been granted. Indeed, in succeeding invocations the emphasis shifts from requests for inspiration to acknowledgements of its receipt. This change is particularly evident in Book IX, where the course of the narrative constrains the poet to change his note from pastoral to tragic,

> If answerable style I can obtain
> Of my celestial patroness, who deigns
> Her nightly visitation unimplored,
> And dictates to me slumbering, or inspires
> Easy my unpremeditated verse:
> Since first this subject for heroic song
> Pleased me long choosing, and beginning late. . . .
>
>   (IX, 20–6)

This is a remarkable blending of free choice and blind dictation. 'He reminds us', Kerrigan comments on these lines, 'of those mystics who hit the target by not aiming, of those biblical prophets who wrote the words of God in books that bear their own names. Milton is both author and amanuensis. He has both everything and nothing to do with *Paradise Lost*.'[53]

And it may be said in conclusion that *Paradise Regained* takes up the theme of inspiration from the point reached in Book IX of *Paradise Lost*. The invocation with which *Paradise Regained* begins brings together the contributions of both the author who 'sings' and the Spirit who 'inspires'; and it stresses the necessary co-operation between the human instrument and the divine prompter, between the poet as free speaker and the poet as an inspired medium of God's continuing self-revelation:

> I who erewhile the happy garden sung,
> By one man's disobedience lost, now sing
> Recovered Paradise to all mankind,
> By one man's firm obedience fully tried
> Through all temptation, and the tempter foiled

In all his wiles, defeated and repulsed,
And Eden raised in the waste wilderness.
  Thou spirit who led'st this glorious eremite
Into the desert, his victorious field
Against the spiritual foe, and brought'st him thence
By proof the undoubted Son of God, inspire,
As thou art wont, my prompted song else mute,
And bear through highth or depth of nature's bounds
With prosperous wing full summed to tell of deeds
Above heroic, though in secret done,
And unrecorded left through many an age,
Worthy t' have not remained so long unsung.

          (I, 1–17)

4 Paradise Lost

When he took occasion in *The Reason of Church-Government* to 'covnant with any knowing reader' about his poetic aspirations, Milton had not yet decided definitely on the subject or form of the great work that he promised to compose 'some few yeers' hence, once the nation 'had ... infranchis'd her self from [the] impertinent yoke of prelaty' and he had been freed from ecclesiastical controversy to return to his interrupted poetic preparation. However, despite his indecision over theme and mode, there were certain aspects of the projected poem that he was able to describe with precision and conviction, even in 1642. In the first place, having chosen 'these British Ilands as my world', he would compose a work of *national* significance (perhaps on a theme drawn from English history) and would write it in the vernacular. He was still committed to the resolve, first articulated in the *Vacation Exercise* of 1628, 'to fix all the industry and art I could unite to the adorning of my native tongue; not to make verbal curiosities the end, that were a toylsom vanity, but to be an interpreter & relater of the best and sagest things among mine own Citizens throughout this Iland in the mother dialect' (*YP*, I, pp. 811–12). Secondly, the prospective poem, set firmly in the *docere cum delectatione* tradition of Christian humanist poetics, would be didactic; it would seek to inculcate virtue and morality by 'teaching over the whole book of sanctity and vertu through all the instances of example with such delight to those especially of soft and delicious temper who will not so much as look upon Truth herself, unless they see her elegantly drest' (ibid., pp. 817–18). Thirdly, since the religious poet's gift of song is 'of power beside the office of a pulpit, to imbreed in a great people the seeds of vertu, and publick civility ... [and] to celebrate in glorious and lofty Hymns the throne and equipage of Gods Almightinesse' (ibid., pp. 816–17), Milton himself would stand to his audience in the relation not only of teacher but also of inspired poet-priest mediating divine truth to his fellow men. And finally, he knew that his promised poem would be the product of human industry guided and sustained by divine grace, that its execution depended upon 'devout prayer to that eternall Spirit who can enrich with all utterance and knowledge' together with the poet's own contributions of 'industrious and select reading, steddy observation, [and] insight into all seemly and generous arts and affaires' (ibid., pp. 820–1).

Each of these expectations was eventually fulfilled in *Paradise Lost*—though not always in exactly the way in which Milton had originally intended. On the one hand, his sense of divine guidance and inspiration, deepened by his experience as a prophet of reformation in the prose works, came to rich fruition in the invocations in *Paradise Lost* (see pp. 108–12). On the other hand, however, his plan to compose a great national poem underwent substantial revision. The initial conception had been firmly based on apocalyptic expectations and a conviction of England's special status in the designs of Providence. As I suggested earlier (p. 78), the original plan was to write a poem celebrating the (imminent) establishment of the English New Jerusalem and calling upon God's Englishmen to prepare themselves both spiritually and morally for the advent of the earthly Kingdom and the reign of the saints which was to precede the Parousia. Within this context of millennial optimism poetry and prophecy were inextricably intertwined, and the promised poem was intended to glorify God for His signal mercies to the English nation and to exhort the nation to continuing reformation and obedience to her covenantal mission. But the failure of the Puritan theocracy—or rather abortive *series* of theocracies—made necessary a fundamental revision of the original conception formulated in the early 1640s.

When Milton began the composition of *Paradise Lost*, probably in 1658 but perhaps earlier in the decade,[1] the need to admonish his fellow countrymen of their high calling and to impress upon them their covenantal responsibility was a matter of immediate and pressing concern. By the time the Protectorate was established in 1653 the national mission as Milton conceived it had been abandoned by the Presbyterians on the theological right and by many of the sects on the Puritan left; the national destiny lay precariously in the hands of Oliver Cromwell and his dwindled remnant of advisers and supporters—a remnant which shrank yet further in the years between 1653 and 1658. After the Lord Protector's death in September 1658, the political situation became acute, then desperate and, finally, hopeless. Throughout this period of national disintegration, as the shadows of returning night lengthened over the wan face of his departing dream, Milton laboured tirelessly—but in vain—to rouse the consciences of his countrymen (or at least the 'sensible and ingenuous' among them) and to recall them to the continuing need for regeneration. The slender hopes of national rebirth that he still cherished in the pamphlets of 1659–60, however, were erased forever by the Restoration in May 1660; and the depth of Milton's despair may be gauged by *Paradise Lost*, a poem originally planned to honour a restored Paradise in England. Significantly, England is never mentioned in the epic; indeed, even in Michael's brief résumé of church history from the time of the Apostles to the Last Judgment (XII, 502–43) there is no reference to English affairs. On the contrary, with no mention of the Reformation at all—whether in England or on the Continent—Michael's narrative traces the progressive decline of the church from its apostolic purity, a descent arrested only by the Day of Judgment:

> truth shall retire
> Bestuck with slanderous darts, and works of faith
> Rarely be found: so shall the world go on,
> To good malignant, to bad men benign,
> Under her own weight groaning till the day
> Appear of respiration to the just,
> And vengeance to the wicked. . . .
>
> (XII, 535–41)

At first sight the collapse of the Puritan theocracy and final abnegation of the national covenant at the Restoration might seem to have left Milton as a poet-prophet without either a cause or a poetic theme—but such, of course, was not the case. He simply turned his attention in *Paradise Lost* from national to individual vocation and regeneration; as Tillyard succinctly expresses it, 'The "paradise within" is the substitute for the paradise on earth, now proved to be impossible of achievement.'[2] The transition, however, is not as abrupt as it may appear when stated so baldly. Throughout the period of the public prose Milton served as God's voice to the chosen people of England. The nation as a whole was bound by the national covenant and Milton's role, as prophet, was to exhort his countrymen to fulfil the obligations which the covenant imposed upon them. Nevertheless, while all were called, not all responded; and, even among those who did initially respond, the incidence of backsliding accelerated alarmingly after 1643. As increasing defection from the national mission made it ever clearer that 'they are not all Israel, which are of Israel', Milton was constrained to alter his prophetic stance in order to adapt it to this new disquieting situation. He did so, I believe, in two important respects. In the first place, his expectations of the general English populace diminished rapidly and his assessment of them became correspondingly harsher—in 1644 they were potentially 'a Nation of Prophets, of Sages, and of Worthies', by 1649 they had been demoted to 'an inconstant, irrational, and Image-doting rabble', and in 1660 the 'perverse inhabitants' of England were dismissed with asperity as 'a misguided and abus'd multitude'.[3] There is a change, too, in the tone of Milton's prophetic voice as the prose progresses, for the buoyant optimism of the antiprelatical tracts, reminiscent of Deutero-Isaiah, modulates gradually but inexorably through the divorce and regicide tracts toward the stern Amos-like pessimism of the pamphlets of 1659–60. In the second place, as the task of fulfilling the national vocation devolved upon an (ever decreasing) elect remnant representing the 'true' England, Milton's emphasis shifts perceptibly from national election in its broadest sense to a concern for individual calling and renovation. From *Areopagitica* on, the prose works stress the importance of private religious experience, and there is a growing prominence accorded such topics as conscience, the inner light, and the role of *recta ratio*. Indeed, by the time one reaches the tracts of 1659–60, the actual political theories there propounded—although these are the pamphlets' ostensible *raisons d'être*—are less important than the spiritual doctrines that underpin them; for, in the final analysis, these last pamphlets must be approached as essays on the right use of Christian liberty and oblique statements of the regenerative process on which that individual liberty depends.

The internalisation of Eden, then, and the search for the 'fit audience, though few'[4] was under way well before the composition of *Paradise Lost* was begun. But Milton's longest and most important prose discussion of the 'paradise within' is found not in the eristic pamphlets but rather in his anatomy of the mechanics of spiritual rebirth in *De Doctrina Christiana*. This treatise is of special interest to readers of *Paradise Lost* both because its composition overlaps that of the epic[5] and also because its exposition of doctrine is frequently an indispensable guide to understanding the poem's theological emphases. There is a sense in which *De Doctrina Christiana* may properly be regarded as a 'prose gloss' on *Paradise Lost*—but there are dangers involved in any literal or insensitive application of this precept.[6] To use the treatise as an ideological template for the epic is to ignore the qualitative difference between prose statements and poetic statements; and the result is invariably crippling to the latter. Milton's concern in *Paradise Lost* is not with the forensic exposition of doctrine but rather with its mimetic representation within a narrative framework; and in a similar way, the critic must endeavour to imitate his author by applying the doctrinal assertions of *De Doctrina Christiana* to the epic with sensitivity, insight, and imagination—*laxis effertur habenis*. It is a case of the letter killing but the spirit giving life.

While many aspects of Milton's theology in *De Doctrina Christiana* might be (or have already been) profitably explored for the light they can throw on *Paradise Lost*, there is perhaps none so fruitful as his view of personal vocation, renovation, and regeneration. Not only are these doctrines important cornerstones in Milton's soteriology, but they appear to have been matters of central concern to him over a considerable period of time. As he struggled to articulate his theological system, he found himself returning again and again to these themes. Arthur Barker, indeed, has pointed out that 'The extant revisions and additions made in the manuscript of *De Doctrina* all focus attention on his preoccupation with redemption and the process of regeneration and the Christian liberty resulting from the process; the most obvious clusters of revisions occur in the chapters on Christ's mediatorial office, on man's "natural renovation" and "calling", on his "supernatural renovation" and "regeneration" and "being planted in Christ", on the Covenant of Grace, including Law and Gospel, on Christian liberty.'[7] Barker's contention is that Milton's last poems 'use ... all the doctrines to which the manuscript revisions call attention' and 'elaborate and represent his notions about the process of regeneration by filling in, mimetically, what *De Doctrina* leaves confused, its operation even under pre-Christian dispensations'.[8] These observations are, I believe, both profound and exciting.

Milton asserts categorically in his chapter on divine decrees in

De Doctrina Christiana that 'by virtue of his wisdom God decreed
the creation of angels and men as beings gifted with reason and
thus with free will' (*YP*, VI, p. 164). The doctrine of free will
is the keystone of his soteriology in the prose treatise (cf.
Introduction)—and it is also the theological centre of *Paradise
Lost*. Not only is it a doctrine invoked in numerous asides and
allusions throughout the poem, but it is also a subject elaborated
in set-speeches delivered by most of the principal speakers: God in
III, 98–128 and V, 233–45; Satan in IV, 66–72; Raphael in V,
520–43 and VIII, 635–43; Adam in IX, 343–56; and Michael in
XII, 82–96. There are two significant implications of Milton's
doctrine of free will which merit brief mention here, although I
shall defer examining their poetic ramifications for the moment.
First, divine decrees are *absolute* with respect to God Himself
(whose perfection is immutable) but *contingent* with respect to
creatures (whose perfection is mutable): 'On the one hand is the
universal process of God's ways; on the other the process of
individual experience which fulfils itself in the degree to which it
corresponds with God's ways. . . .'[9] In other words, God's decrees,
which are an aspect of His internal efficiency (*DDC*, I, iii; *YP*, VI,
p. 153), are necessarily as eternal and invariable as God Himself
who has promulgated them; however, the fulfilment of these
immutable decrees depends upon mutable, potentially inconstant
agents endowed with free will. Second, free will presupposes the
possibility of choice; it implies, that is, the existence of (mutually
exclusive) alternatives between which an individual may freely
choose. In the postlapsarian predicament the choice is between
known good and known evil;[10] in the prelapsarian situation it is
between known good and potential evil, for, as unfallen Adam
explains to Eve after her dream,

> Evil into the mind of god [i.e. angel] or man
> May come and go, so unapproved, and leave
> No spot or blame behind.
>
> (V, 117–19)

In either case the choice ultimately resolves itself into an option to
obey God's declared will and an option to disobey the divine will
by acceding to the promptings of one's selfish will. Free will, then,
involves choosing between God and the self; and what free will
provides is the opportunity to grow either toward God or away

from Him. Self-knowledge requires the abnegation of self-will, for the predicate of self-knowledge is God, not the self; that is to say, self-knowledge means knowledge of the self *in* God and in relation to God—*sum quia in Deo sum*. Paradoxically, then, to attain self-knowledge the free agent must freely will to relax the will, so that his own individual will may become continuous with God's will.[11] The poetic elaboration of this paradox—expressed in antithetical images of reason and passion, abstinence and appetite, light and darkness—leads (as we shall see) to the heart of Adam's vocation and education both as pre- and postlapsarian man.

But a vocation to self-knowledge is not restricted to the human protagonists alone. In the moral universe of *Paradise Lost* all 'creatures' are endowed with free will; all are called to respond positively to the promptings of the divine will revealed to them through the faculty of *recta ratio* and to serve freely as instruments of that will. 'What God consistently gives his responsive creatures', Barker writes, 'is an opportunity to respond to his providential processes—and to all creatures in his own good time.'[12] At the same time, however, every situation by which a free agent is confronted offers the possibility of wrong choice. The most obvious instance, perhaps occurs in the case of Abdiel, who follows Satan initially but whose right reason leads him to check his revolt from God as soon as he recognises his potential disobedience for what it is:

> the seraph Abdiel faithful found,
> Among the faithless, faithful only he;
> Among innumerable false, unmoved,
> Unshaken, unseduced, unterrified
> His loyalty he kept, his love, his zeal;
> Nor number, nor example with him wrought
> To swerve from truth, or change his constant mind
> Though single.
>
> (V, 896–903)

Abdiel's zealous obedience provides the most striking instance of spiritual heroism in the poem because it is the most dramatic example of loyalty and unswerving rectitude. Nevertheless, as Stanley Fish points out, 'Abdiel has always been heroic since he has always been free to disavow his allegiance to God, and to date he has declined to do so, at every moment of his life. The reader just happens to be there when Abdiel is being heroic in a conspicuously dramatic context.'[13] In a similar way, but in less histrionic circumstances, each character in the epic is invited in every act (physical or mental) that he performs to reconfirm his elect status as a son of God; and every situation provides him with an opportunity for disobedience and the wilful repudiation of his calling. Conversely, a positive response to one's calling frequently results in gains in self-knowledge. Both Abdiel and Michael, for example, are taught important lessons about the limits of angelic power by their respective failures in armed combat against the rebellious Satan; Raphael, too, is educated in the inadequacy of his own understanding and the limits of angelic percipience as he struggles to fulfil his commission of enlightenment by accommodating divine truths to human sense and responding (as best he can) to Adam's requests for instruction.[14]

Free will and the opportunity for responsive growth are also extended to Christ. Although Milton reserves his full treatment of this theme for the characterisation of the incarnate Son in *Paradise Regained*, he anticipates this later presentation by depicting Christ in *Paradise Lost* as a free agent who willingly responds to his messianic vocation. In pronouncing prospective doom on Man for his foreseen transgression, the Father declares that Adam

> with his whole posterity must die,
> Die he or justice must; unless for him
> Some other able, and as willing, pay
> The rigid satisfaction, death for death.
>
> (III, 209–12)

This judgment is greeted by 'silence in heaven' until the Son freely offers himself in atonement for man's sin:

> Account me man; I for his sake will leave
> Thy bosom, and this glory next to thee
> Freely put off, and for him lastly die
> Well pleased. . . .
>
> (238–41)

What is significant about Christ's offer is not only that it is an act of spontaneous free will but also that it is made without foreknow-

ledge of the result. His response is based on faith and his trust in
God's goodness:

> on me let Death wreak all his rage;
> Under his gloomy power I shall not long
> Lie vanquished; thou hast given me to possess
> Life in my self for ever, by thee I live,
> Though now to Death I yield, and am his due
> All that of me can die, yet that debt paid,
> Thou wilt not leave me in the loathsome grave
> His prey, nor suffer my unspotted soul
> For ever with corruption there to dwell;
> But I shall rise victorious, and subdue
> My vanquisher, spoiled of his vaunted spoil;
> Death his death's wound shall then receive, and stoop
> Inglorious, of his mortal sting disarmed.
> I through the ample air in triumph high
> Shall lead hell captive maugre hell, and show
> The powers of darkness bound. Thou at the sight
> Pleased, out of heaven shalt look down and smile,
> While by thee raised I ruin all my foes,
> Death last, and with his carcass glut the grave:
> Then with the multitude of my redeemed
> Shall enter heaven long absent, and return,
> Father, to see thy face, wherein no cloud
> Of anger shall remain, but peace assured,
> And reconcilement. . . .
>
> (241–64)

Milton's reader, his understanding directed by scriptural allusion
(e.g. 1 Cor 15: 54–5), immediately recognises this speech as an
accurate résumé of Christ's mission of salvation and its promised
consummation at the end of time. But the reader's perspective
here is not Christ's—for the reader, who knows the Bible, understands the narrative partly as history (fulfilled revelation) and
partly as prophecy (revelation yet to be fulfilled), whereas for
Christ the whole action is prospective. This point is important,
for, if the reader fails to distinguish between what he *knows* and
what Christ *predicts* about his mission, he runs the risk of serious
misinterpretation, either by ascribing to the Son a prescience
which (for Milton) he does not possess or, more grievously, by

interpreting the Atonement offer as a pre-arranged scenario between the Father and the Son.

In fact, however, the scene is intended to function as a trial of the Son's vocational obedience. The request for a mediator, an invitation extended to the entire heavenly host, is designed as a test of the Son's willingness to respond to his calling and to fulfil freely the decree of conditional mercy on behalf of fallen men.[15] Indeed, with due allowance for the nature of its divine participants, the scene is a poetic representation of what Milton elsewhere calls a *good temptation*: 'Good temptations are those which God uses to tempt even righteous men, in order to prove them. He does this not for his own sake—as if he did not know what sort of men they would turn out to be—but either to exercise or demonstrate their faith or patience.' (*DCC*, I, viii; *YP*, VI, p. 338) God, of course, who is omniscient, knows that the Son will accept the role decreed for him ('man shall find grace', III, 131); but He no more forces the Son's obedience here than He does the disobedience of Adam and Eve in Book IX. Like Adam, Christ is a free agent, and he responds to his calling without constraint or necessity. Moreover, his response to the Father's offer of mercy for man is prompted by his knowledge of God and not by his *fore*knowledge of events: God has promised him eternal life and he knows, therefore, that He will 'not leave me in the loathsome grave' as Death's prey, but rather 'I shall rise victorious, and subdue/ My vanquisher'. The Son's willing submission to His Father's will and unquestioning faith in His promises, however, strengthens his vocational awareness and does enable him to forecast, without absolutely foreknowing, the *general pattern* of events—he 'foresees' the Resurrection, for example, but not the Crucifixion—and the essentials of his messianic mission.

Having offered himself in atonement, the Son 'attends the will/ of his great Father', and 'Admiration seized/ All heaven, what this might mean' (270–2). The Father does not hold them long in suspense. He discloses a further detail about His Son's career (*viz.* incarnation by virgin birth), outlines the method of salvation by revealing the doctrines of solifidianism and imputed merit, and rewards Christ's obedience by exalting him over all other creatures—

Because thou hast
. . . .
been found

By merit more than birthright Son of God,
Found worthiest to be so by being good,
Far more than great or high; because in thee
Love hath abounded more than glory abounds,
Therefore thy humiliation shall exalt
With thee thy manhood also to this throne,
Here shalt thou sit incarnate,
. . . .

all power
I give thee, reign for ever, and assume
Thy merits; under thee as head supreme
Thrones, princedoms, powers, dominions I reduce:
All knees to thee shall bow, of them that bide
In heaven, or earth, or under earth in hell.

(305–22)

The Father concludes his speech with further revelations concerning the Last Judgment, Millennium, and exaltation of the just. And finally, the council in heaven closes as the host take up their harps to hymn the Father's mercy and to praise the Son's responsive submission to His Father's providential purpose:

No sooner did thy dear and only Son
Perceive thee purposed not to doom frail man,
So strictly, but much more to pity inclined,
He to appease thy wrath, and end the strife
Of mercy and justice in thy face discerned,
Regardless of the bliss wherein he sat
Second to thee, offered himself to die
For man's offence.

(403–10)

After his incarnation the Messiah will face more trials of vocational obedience and will learn further facts about his calling—but that story is reserved for *Paradise Regained* and for a later chapter.

The central vocational interest in *Paradise Lost* is, of course, centred on Adam's responses—both prelapsarian and postlapsarian—to God's prompting and providential processes; and what applies to Adam directly is intended, by inference and analogy, to be seen as applicable to the poem's reader as well.[16] Although it is impossible in a single chapter to give these topics the detailed attention they merit, I shall attempt at least to elaborate some of the more important patterns.

ADAM AND EVE: PRELAPSARIAN EDUCATION AND *THEOPOIĒSIS*

As Barbara Lewalski has demonstrated in a brilliant essay, Milton's Eden is distinguished from the paradisic gardens both of classical mythology and of traditional exegesis by virtue of the fact that Edenic life in *Paradise Lost* is characterised not by static and stable perfection but rather by 'radical growth and process.'[17] From their first moments of life Adam and Eve grow in self-knowledge and in knowledge of their world and their Creator. The poem's imagery makes it clear that they are not only gardeners placed in Eden by the 'sovereign Planter' (IV, 691) but that they are themselves part of the garden and are responsible for perfecting their own natures, for cultivating the 'paradise within' of which the external garden is the physical correlative: 'Adam and Eve, like the Garden, have natures capable of a prodigious growth of good things, but which require constant pruning to remove excessive or unsightly growth, constant direction of overreaching tendencies, constant propping of possible weaknesses, and also, one supposes, further cultivation through art.'[18] And Professor Lewalski concludes her argument by pointing out that Milton's treatment of the prelapsarian state effects a redefinition of the Life of Innocence that is 'virtually unique':

> Milton's vision of the prelapsarian life admits no dichotomy between the states of Innocence and Experience: they are not, as in Blake, 'two contradictory states of the human soul'. Rather, the Edenic portion of *Paradise Lost* displays the process whereby Adam and Eve grow in knowledge and acquire experience within the State of Innocence, and thereby become steadily more complex, more conscious of manifold challenges and difficulties, more aware of large responsibilities, and by this very process, more complete and more perfect.... Such an imagination of the State of Innocence sets the Fall in the proper tragic perspective in the poem, as the event which blasted man's opportunity to develop—without suffering, violence, despair and death, though not in the least without tension and trial—the rich resources and large potentialities of the human spirit.[19]

Gifted with free will and endowed with right reason, our first parents are set in Eden and vested with the responsibility of working out the full potential of their protogenic humanity. Their vocation, then, is pre-eminently a calling to self-definition; and, as each new experience occasions a response and leads them a step further on the path of self-discovery, they grow in vocational awareness and are instructed in the limits of human knowledge and power. Their education proceeds, however, by trial and error, leaving room not only for mistake and misjudgment[20] but also for wilful disobedience and self-interest. As Arthur Barker observes, 'Every prelapsarian incident in the poem involves for Adam and Eve (as for all its other creatures) a "calling", and every prelapsarian incident illustrates the possibility of refusal.'[21] Their benevolent Creator has provided them with all things necessary to proper development. He has granted them *recta ratio* to distinguish good from evil and has sown within them 'the seeds of sufficient determining' (*YP*, II, p. 679); and in every new situation they experience He is their guide, unobstrusively calling them to respond to the unseen prompting of His divine will. But they are free to refuse. Indeed, Satan is not the only—or even the major—threat to their happiness, for unfallen man is potentially his own worst enemy—as is clear both from Eve's narcissistic response to her reflection in the pool (IV, 453–69) and Adam's admission of profane passion (VIII, 530–59). And the point is reinforced at a critical moment before the Fall when Adam 'fervently' reminds his headstrong spouse, as she sets off alone with blithe insouciance to exercise her fugitive and cloistered virtue, that

> best are all things as the will
> Of God ordained them, his creating hand
> Nothing imperfect or deficient left
> Of all that he created, much less man,
> Or aught that might his happy state secure,
> Secure from outward force; within himself
> The danger lies, yet lies within his power:
> Against his will he can receive no harm.
>
> (IX, 343–50)

From the violence of physical attack they are protected by the arm of Omnipotence. The real danger is internal and lies in their use of free will; for, as God had earlier remarked, 'I formed them free, and free they must remain,/ Till they enthrall themselves' (III, 124–5). Thus, the essence of their prelapsarian education hinges on right response to the 'good temptations' (cf. p. 124) presented in every new situation that they encounter.

In Milton's Eden education is synonymous with responsive growth. The *terminus a quo* of the educative process is the mere self or (to borrow a phrase from *King Lear*) 'unaccommodated man'; the *terminus ad quem* is accommodated man, that is, the individual self fulfilled and realised in God. Paradoxically, then, self-knowledge is the result of self-abnegating self-determination, and true liberty is only achieved by denying personal freedom and binding one's self to God. This paradox is developed in *Paradise Lost* through the doctrine of 'mutable perfection'—a theme which Raphael elaborates for Adam's benefit in an important speech in Book V:

> O Adam, one almighty is, from whom
> All things proceed, and up to him return,
> If not depraved from good, created all
> Such to perfection, one first matter all,
> Indued with various forms, various degrees
> Of substance, and in things that live, of life;
> But more refined, more spirituous, and pure,
> As nearer to him placed or nearer tending
> Each in their several active spheres assigned,
> Till body up to spirit work, in bounds
> Proportioned to each kind. So from the root
> Springs lighter the green stalk, from thence the leaves
> More airy, last the bright consummate flower
> Spirits odorous breathes: flowers and their fruit
> Man's nourishment, by gradual scale sublimed
> To vital spirits aspire, to animal,
> To intellectual, give both life and sense,
> Fancy and understanding, whence the soul
> Reason receives, and reason is her being,
> Discursive, or intuitive; discourse
> Is oftest yours, the latter most is ours,
> Differing but in degree, of kind the same.
> Wonder not then, what God for you saw good
> If I refuse not, but convert, as you,
> To proper substance, time may come when men

With angels may participate, and find
No inconvenient diet, nor too light fare:
And from these corporal nutriments perhaps
Your bodies may at last turn all to spirit,
Improved by tract of time, and winged ascend
Ethereal, as we, or may at choice
Here or in heavenly paradises dwell;
If ye be found obedient, and retain
Unalterably firm his love entire
Whose progeny you are.

(469–503)

This speech is more than an embellished restatement of the common Neoplatonic conception of man's assigned station on the *scala naturae* or chain of being. What Raphael is saying, in fact, is that neither man's place nor that of other creatures in the hierarchy of being is fixed and unalterable. Using the traditional plant image as well as his own angelic digestive process as analogies, he explains the potential for growth that is inherent in the entire *natura naturata*. In the prelapsarian situation, all of created nature—and, for Milton, creation is *de Deo* not *ex nihilo* (*DDC*, I, vii; *YP*, VI, p. 308)—is perfect because it is *ex substantia Dei*, yet mutable because its perfection is relative rather than absolute. Within this context of mutable perfection individual beings are assigned to 'their several active spheres' where they strive, 'in bounds/ Proportioned to each kind', to transform corporeal into spiritual substance.

But man's position in the creaturely hierarchy and his place in the process of potential growth is unique. It is also more complex than that of other creatures, for man's nature is more complex. According to Sir Thomas Browne, 'Man [is] that great and true *Amphibium*, whose nature is disposed to live, not onely like other creatures in divers elements, but in [the] divided and distinguished worlds' of matter and spirit.[22] The dualism of human nature complicates man's vocational duty, for (unlike the creatures below him in the *scala naturae*) he is conscious of his responsibility and is, therefore, directly accountable for his actions and decisions. Inferior beings respond to God's providential processes by instinct, but men (and angels) do so by choice. Like the other creatures, mankind is created 'perfect'—that is, perfect relative to his assigned station in the hierarchy of being; however, since he possesses reason and free will, his 'mutability'—that is, his potential for growth either toward or away from God—lies strictly within his own power and his free use of these divine faculties:

> God made thee perfect, not immutable;
> And good he made thee, but to persevere
> He left it in thy power, ordained thy will
> By nature free, not over-ruled by fate
> Inextricable, or strict necessity;
> Our voluntary service he requires,
> Not our necessitated. . . .
>
>   (V, 524–30)

Like the angels above him (notice Raphael's shift from 'thee' to 'our'), Adam is called to serve his Creator voluntarily through responsive choices which both confirm and advance his spiritual status.

At their creation Adam and Eve have two injunctions placed upon them: a negative command instructing them not to taste the fruit of the interdicted tree, and a positive command enjoining them to 'Be fruitful, multiply, and fill the earth,/ Subdue it, and throughout dominion hold' (VII, 531–2). Thus, prelapsarian obedience involves both abstinence and active involvement, both a 'thou shalt not' and a 'thou shalt'. The negative command, arbitrary and unimportant *per se*, is a 'good temptation' which is designed to test our first parents' unquestioning faith and obedience. The positive command—to subdue the earth and hold dominion over it—is more complex, because more is involved in fulfilling it. Adam and Eve, as has been pointed out, are not only Eden's gardeners but are also themselves part of the garden they are instructed to cultivate, and their responsibility for pruning 'wanton growth' (IX, 211) extends inward as well as outward. They are called to govern and direct the growth of human nature as well as of external nature; and, as Adam is led to see, the striving for upward growth in the natural world provides a pattern and *exemplum* for man's ideal development:

> O favourable spirit, propitious guest,
> Well hast thou taught the way that might direct
> Our knowledge, and the scale of nature set

> From centre to circumference, whereon
> In contemplation of created things
> By steps we may ascend to God.
>
> (V, 507–12)

Alastair Fowler (*PM*, p. 705 n) finds a parallel for Milton's prelapsarian teleology in the Pauline doctrine of change from corruptible to incorruptible in 1 Corinthians 15. This analogue, however, obscures perhaps more than it reveals. In the first place, whereas St Paul's reference is to a postlapsarian change of state from mortality to immortality, the change envisaged for unfallen Adam and Eve is one of degree rather than of kind—a change from relative to absolute perfection. Second, while the postlapsarian transformation takes place 'in a moment, in the twinkling of an eye, at the last trump' (1 Cor. 15: 52), the prelapsarian ascent to God is seen to be a slow and gradual process. God Himself describes what is involved when He decrees the creation of man and his establishment on earth:

> [I] will create
> Another world, out of one man a race
> Of men innumerable, there to dwell,
> Not here, till by degrees of merit raised
> They open to themselves at length the way
> Up hither, under long obedience tried,
> And earth be changed to heaven, and heaven to earth,
> One kingdom, joy and union without end.
>
> (VII, 154–61)

God's use of the word 'merit' both underscores the distinction between pre- and postlapsarian man and, as well, throws into stark relief the real tragedy implied in the Fall—namely, the irremediable loss of man's potential for self-development. In the unfallen world Adam and Eve have not only an opportunity but also a vocational obligation to grow toward God; they are able to earn heaven by their own merit, to ascend by stages to absolute perfection by obedient response to their Creator's will. After the Fall, however, man may co-operate in the work of salvation but he cannot contribute to it; capable of earning nothing for himself, the sinner is raised to heaven only because Christ's merit is, by legal fiction, imputed to him (see above, p. 17). Man's good works are efficacious before the Fall but not after it; human merit is purely a prelapsarian phenomenon.

An important *leitmotiv* running through Adam and Eve's prelapsarian education is that man must govern his development and keep it 'within bounds'. Poetically, this theme is elaborated largely through images of appetite. In the early books the word *appetite* is reserved for gustatory desire: IV, 330; V, 85 and 305; VII, 49. However, Raphael develops the metaphorical implications of the image in an instructive speech in Book VII:

> Yet what thou canst attain, which best may serve
> To glorify the maker, and infer
> Thee also happier, shall not be withheld
> Thy hearing, such commission from above
> I have received, to answer thy desire
> Of knowledge within bounds; beyond abstain
> To ask, nor let thine own inventions hope
> Things not revealed, which the invisible king,
> Only omniscient, hath suppressed in night,
> To none communicable in earth or heaven:
> Enough is left besides to search and know.
> But knowledge is as food, and needs no less
> Her temperance over appetite, to know
> In measure what the mind may well contain,
> Oppresses else with surfeit, and soon turns
> Wisdom to folly, as nourishment to wind.
>
> (115–30)

Like all other created beings, man has been assigned his own sphere of activity—a sphere bounded and proportioned to his specific nature, needs and potential. Human happiness and spiritual growth depend on living within prescribed limits. To attempt to surpass those limits in knowledge, to attempt to become more than human (as Satan had tried to become more than archangelic), is both presumptuous and sinful. Knowledge, Raphael argues, ceases to be wisdom when it becomes an end in itself rather than a means toward understanding, within permissible limits, the nature of man and God. And in a later speech he warns Adam of the penalty for intellectual overreaching when he admonishes him to 'govern well thy appetite, lest Sin/ Surprise thee, and her black attendant Death' (VII, 546–7).

In Book VIII the theme of ungoverned appetite is developed in a way that demonstrates clearly Milton's architectonic skill. Although the book has not, for the most part, been kindly treated by the critics, it is one of the most interesting sections of the poem from a structural point of view. At the end of Book VII, having finished his account of the Creation, Raphael invites further inquiries from Adam: 'if else thou seek'st/ Aught, not surpassing human measure, say' (VII, 639–40); and his offer leads in the opening lines of Book VIII to Adam's queries about the nature and construction of the universe. By observation and through the use of reason Adam has worked out for himself the essentials of the geocentric theory of Ptolemaic cosmology—but 'something yet of doubt remains' (VIII, 13), and he raises some of the Copernican objections to the Ptolemaic theory and asks his angelic tutor to solve the difficulty for him. (Eve, who has been listening until now, sees the technical direction that the discussion is taking and retires to her nursery to tend her flowers, leaving the men to their talk.) Raphael is sympathetic to Adam's curiosity and does not condemn his desire for astronomical knowledge: 'To ask or search I blame thee not, for heaven/ Is as the book of God before thee set' (66–7); and he supplements Adam's observations with additional scientific facts and speculative suggestions. But he does not resolve the issue of geocentric and heliocentric astronomy for Adam, because there are limitations placed on man's knowledge and Adam is not entitled to absolute understanding of God's mysterious ways. While astronomical speculation is permitted as an academic exercise, Raphael makes it clear that absolute knowledge on the topic is both unnecessary and forbidden, and he counsels Adam not to solicit his mind with the mysteries of divine Providence: 'heaven is for thee too high/ To know what passes there; be lowly wise:/ Think only what concerns thee and thy being' (172–4). And the Archangel's warning draws from Adam a positive recognition of the vanity and potential danger of speculating about things remote from human life:

> to know
> That which before us lies in daily life,
> Is the prime wisdom, what is more, is fume,
> Or emptiness, or fond impertinence,

> And renders us in things that most concern
> Unpractised, unprepared, and still to seek.
>
> (192–7)

Having seen that 'wisdom' involves recognising one's proper limitations and acquiring only so much knowledge as is appropriate to the human condition, Adam abandons the 'high pitch' of astronomical speculation and proposes to 'descend/ A lower flight, and speak of things at hand/ Useful' (198–200). He narrates to Raphael, who was away on an errand when man was created, what he remembers of his creation and his first few hours of life; he speaks of his intuitive sense that he had been formed by 'some great maker', tells of his installation in Eden, his meeting with his Creator, his naming of the animals, and the fashioning of Eve from his rib. But the creation of Eve brought a problem in its wake:

> here passion first I felt,
> Commotion strange, in all enjoyments else
> Superior and unmoved, here only weak
> Against the charm of beauty's powerful glance.
>
> (530–3)

And, after the dangerous speculation that the Creator may have blundered in not arming him sufficiently against this threat, he continues:

> For well I understand in the prime end
> Of nature her the inferior, in the mind
> And inward faculties, which most excel,
> In outward also her resembling less
> His image who made both, and less expressing
> The character of that dominion given
> O'er other creatures; yet when I approach
> Her loveliness, so absolute she seems
> And in her self complete, so well to know
> Her own, that what she wills to do or say,
> Seems wisest, virtuousest, discreetest, best;
> All higher knowledge in her presence falls
> Degraded, wisdom in discourse with her
> Loses discountenanced, and like folly shows;

> Authority and reason on her wait,
> As one intended first, not after made
> Occasionally; and to consummate all,
> Greatness of mind and nobleness their seat
> Build in her loveliest, and create an awe
> About her, as a guard angelic placed.
>
> (540–59)

Adam is here on the verge of idolatry, and it is not surprising that having heard this confession Raphael should reply 'with contracted brow'. Not only has Adam questioned the Creator's judgment but he has given carnal passion precedence over sacred love. Playing Socrates to Adam's Agathon, Raphael undertakes to set his pupil's affections in right tune by summarising for him the Platonic doctrine of love in the *Symposium*:

> What higher in her society thou find'st
> Attractive, human, rational, love still;
> In loving thou dost well, in passion not,
> Wherein true love consists not; love refines
> The thoughts, and heart enlarges, hath his seat
> In reason, and is judicious, is the scale
> By which to heavenly love thou mayst ascend,
> N t sur in carnal pleasure, for which cause
> Among the beasts no mate for thee was found.
>
> (586–94)

True love is ennobling, not enslaving; it leads from flesh to spirit, from profane to sacred. Although these ideas are the common property of Renaissance Neoplatonism, Milton is using them here to develop with respect to passion the point he had made earlier in relation to knowledge. Passion is to love as knowledge is to wisdom; and, as 'knowledge is as food, and needs no less/ Her temperance over appetite', so too passion is an appetite that must be governed by reason and will: 'take heed lest passion sway/ Thy judgment to do aught, which else free will/ Would not admit' (635–7).

While the two subjects—astronomy and passion—which dominate Book VIII seem at first sight to have little in common, their relationship is of considerable importance. In the first place, knowledge (exemplified by astronomy) and passion are established as appetites which must be controlled and kept within proper bounds. Both unbridled speculation and ungoverned passion are sinful and threaten man's decreed growth toward God. Secondly, the two topics focus on different aspects of man's dual nature. As Castiglione had asserted over a century before Milton began *Paradise Lost*, 'Man of nature indowed with reason, placed (as it were) in the middle betweene these two extremities, may through his choice inclining to sense, or reaching to understanding, come nigh to the coveting sometime of the one, sometime of the other part.'²³ Sharing his physical senses with the creatures below him and his reason with the angels above him, man—that 'great and true *Amphibium*'—may sink toward the beasts in passion or rise toward the angels in understanding; but excess in either direction is unlawful. And so it is that Adam learns in the astronomy discussion that it is sinful to attempt to become more than man by pursuing forbidden knowledge; and in the discussion of passion he learns that it is equally improper to become less than a man by pursuing blindly his brutish instincts without the restraining hand of reason. Adam, in short, must neither a Faustus nor an Antony be. And thirdly, the discussions in Book VIII prepare the way, poetically,²⁴ for the falls of Adam and Eve. In the amalgam of reason and passion that makes up the two different sexes, Adam represents reason modified by passion and Eve passion exalted by reason. However, the overreacher theme—first discussed in Book VII with Eve present—anticipates Eve's fall, which results from an unbridled appetite for knowledge; Adam, on the other hand, falls by surrendering his will to his passion and his admission of unregulated passion to Raphael is thus proleptic of his transgression through uxoriousness. Ironically, then, the traditional roles of the human protagonists are reversed in the Fall: Eve, the inferior being, characterised more by passion than reason, sins by trying to become more than human by seeking forbidden knowledge; Adam, the rational principle, sins in becoming less than human by rejecting reason for passion. Their transgressions—Eve's attempt at divinity and Adam's submission to sense—thus become violations of the systematic government of universal degree; and, as Shakespeare notes in *Troilus and Cressida*, the intricate hierarchical structure of 'degree, priority, and place' is upset with fatal consequences when lower beings usurp the rightful functions and stations of their superiors, or *vice versa*: 'Take but degree away, untune that string,/ And hark what discord follows.' (I, iii, 109–10)

The controlled images of appetite that we have been tracing in Books VII and VIII rise to their climax in Book IX. Satan's temptation of Eve is expressed in terms of appetite.[25] When Eve, surprised to hear 'Language of man pronounced/ By tongue of brute' (IX, 553-4), enquiries of serpent-Satan how he came to acquire the power of speech, he replies that the fruit of a certain tree is responsible. He was drawn by the sweet odour, 'Grateful to appetite' (580); and

> To satisfy the sharp desire I had
> Of tasting those fair apples, I resolved
> Not to defer; hunger and thirst at once,
> Powerful persuaders, quickened at the scent
> Of that alluring fruit, urged me so keen.
>
> (584—8)

And the gratification of physical appetite led immediately to that of intellectual appetite:

> Thenceforth to speculations high or deep
> I turned my thoughts, and with capacious mind
> Considered all things visible in heaven,
> Or earth, or middle, all things fair and good. . . .
>
> (602-5)

The conjunction of food and knowledge as appetites recalls to the reader, though not to 'unwary' Eve, Raphael's earlier warning that 'knowledge is as food, and needs no less/ Her temperance over appetite' (VII, 126-7). Led on by curiosity and the tempter's flattering sophistries, Eve finds herself at the foot of the forbidden tree at an awkward time of day:

> Fixed on the fruit she gazed, which to behold
> Might tempt alone, and in her ears the sound
> Yet rung of his persuasive words, impregned
> With reason, to her seeming, and with truth;
> Mean while the hour of noon drew on, and waked
> An eager appetite, raised by the smell
> So savoury of that fruit, which with desire,
> Inclinable now grown to touch or taste,
> Solicited her longing eye. . . .
>
> (735-43)

She rehearses Satan's arguments, as though to confirm them in her own mind, and then 'her rash hand in evil hour/ Forth reaching to the fruit, she plucked, she ate' (780–1). Oblivious to all else, her whole attention is centred on the satisfaction of physical and intellectual appetite:

> Back to the thicket slunk
> The guilty serpent, and well might, for Eve
> Intent now wholly on her taste, naught else
> Regarded, such delight till then, as seemed,
> In fruit she never tasted, whether true
> Or fancied so, through expectation high
> Of knowledge, nor was godhead from her thought.
>
> (784–90)

Her selfish desire is without bounds—'Greedily she engorged without restraint' (791)—and at the very outset of her postlapsarian career she compounds her transgression by adding to disobedience the deadly sin of gluttony.

Sated at length, her selfish thought turns to Adam, and the jealous fear that he may wed 'another Eve' and 'live with her enjoying' (828–9) prompts the further selfish determination that he must fall too. Adam, however, needs no convincing—for idolatrous passion wins an instantaneous victory over reason: 'How can I live without thee . . . ?' (908) In the fall of Adam, as in that of Eve, unbridled appetite looms large in the imagery. Eve offers her husband the fruit with 'liberal hand' (997), and

> Adam took no thought,
> Eating his fill, nor Eve to iterate
> Her former trespass feared, the more to soothe
> Him with her loved society, that now
> As with new wine intoxicated both
> They swim in mirth, and fancy that they feel
> Divinity within them breeding wings
> Wherewith to scorn the earth. . . .
>
> (1004–11)

Their gluttony issues, however, not in flights of speculation, but in the satisfaction of a more mundane appetite—an appetite particularly well suited to one who has lost all through passion:

> he on Eve
> Began to cast lascivious eyes, she him
> As wantonly repaid; in lust they burn.
>
> (1013–15)

And they are no more temperate in sexual indulgence than in their edacious licence with the interdicted apples: 'they their fill of love and love's disport/ Took largely' (1042–3). But the fruits of lust are measured not in delight, as was formerly the case with their love-making, but only in 'grosser sleep/ Bred of unkindly fumes' (1049–50) and in troubled dreams.

Waking from sleep, the guilty pair attempt to hide their shame with 'broad smooth leaves' (1095), but they can no more hide themselves from God or from themselves with fig-leaves than Satan can escape the burning hell he carries within him by vain attempts at flight. They wake to find their eyes opened and minds darkened; and lust and shame give way to mutual recrimination in a passage where the images of raw appetite and intemperance culminate in anguished awareness of a guilt which they are powerless to remedy or purge:

> They sat them down to weep, nor only tears
> Rained at their eyes, but high winds worse within
> Began to rise, high passions, anger, hate,
> Mistrust, suspicion, discord, and shook sore
> Their inward state of mind, calm region once
> And full of peace, now tossed and turbulent:
> For understanding ruled not, and the will
> Heard not her lore, both in subjection now
> To sensual appetite, who from beneath
> Usurping over sovereign reason claimed
> Superior sway.
>
> (1121–31)[26]

As Balachandra Rajan comments, 'They cannot revoke the defiance of order which they have set in motion, they cannot rewrite and they can barely recollect the law of nature which their transgression has defaced. Within the microcosm chaos is come again and degree is suffocated in lawless, murderous misrule.'[27] They have irreparably rent the veil of innocence protecting them from ill and have leapt forth, shorn of strength and native righteousness, into a self-ordained life of degradation and depravity and death. And Milton closes this book that has told of man's first disobedience and the sins that blasted human bliss and potential, with one savage and tragic pun: 'Thus they in mutual accusation spent/The fruitless hours. . . .' (1187–8).

ADAM AND EVE: POSTLAPSARIAN EDUCATION AND REGENERATION

After the completion of 'the mortal sin/ Original' (IX, 1003–4) the vocational emphasis in *Paradise Lost* shifts abruptly from self-regulating generation to divinely directed *re*generation. In Books IV–IX Adam and Eve are themselves charged with the responsibility—and glorious opportunity—of completing the work of generation begun at their creation by working out their own destiny and earning heaven by their own merit. In Books X–XII, however, the initiative for self-development is lost completely and the task of restoration and growth is achieved *ab extra*, for the renovation and regeneration of fallen man is the work of God alone. Once his faculties of free will and right reason (lost at the Fall) have been partially restored by prevenient grace—the first step in his supernatural renovation—then postlapsarian man is able to co-operate in his regeneration, but he cannot himself contribute in a positive way to it. If he continues to respond to the vocation by which God invites him to accept regeneration, his reason and will are strengthened and he grows progressively towards God as the divine image is gradually restored in him—but this work of restoration depends entirely on divine initiative and on imputed righteousness, neither man's own energy nor merit having any place in the process. This is, essentially, Milton's view of renovation and regeneration in *De Doctrina Christiana*[28]—and these doctrines are elaborated poetically in the last three books of *Paradise Lost*, where the pattern of Adam and Eve's postlapsarian education traces the ascent from death and despair to life and spiritual rebirth.

Book X of *Paradise Lost* is concerned with the immediate effects of the Fall. The action in this book is dramatic and fast-moving with rapid changes of locale—from heaven to earth to hell, then back to heaven, and finally to earth again. At the cosmic level these scenic transitions draw attention to the universal implications of the Fall and, as well, to the ironic reversal whereby evil, even as it seems to triumph, is made to recoil upon itself. But the cosmic sweep of the action, important as it is, must not be permitted to obscure the importance of what happens in the hearts and minds of the newly fallen human protagonists. Almost half of Book X is devoted to Adam and Eve's response to their situation, and the two sections which take place in Eden—the judgment scene (90–228) and the first stages of regeneration (720–1104)—mark the beginnings of their postlapsarian education.

As Book X opens, God decrees the 'mortal sentence' on man for his transgression and transfers the task of judgment itself to His 'Vicegerent Son'. Christ responds immediately to this vocation—

> Father Eternal, thine is too decree,
> Mine both in heaven and earth to do thy will
> Supreme, that thou in me thy Son beloved
> Mayst ever rest well pleased—
>
> (68–71)

and descends to earth to pass judgment on Adam and Eve. But his mission is two-fold, for he comes as 'mild judge and intercessor both/ To sentence man' (96–7). In dramatic terms this duality of function is of great importance, and the effect of the scene depends on the reader's approaching it from Adam and Eve's perspective. They appreciate the Son's role as judge because the inevitability of judgment for their transgression has been revealed to them (VIII, 323–36); but they do *not* yet know of the Son's role as mediator and of the possibility of restoration that he will earn for them. The significance of this point will be clear if we look briefly at the episode. When the Son arrives in Eden and calls to Adam and Eve, the guilty pair, knowing (as it seems to them) exactly what is in store, promptly hide themselves and at last emerge from the sheltering thicket with something more than reluctance:

> Love was not in their looks, either to God
> Or to each other, but apparent guilt,
> And shame, and perturbation, and despair,
> Anger, and obstinacy, and hate, and guile.
>
> (111–14)

It is not only guilt and shame that shows in their faces; in their total depravity they have acquired the truculent and deceitful qualities of Satan—obstinacy, hate, guile—and they share too his despair. They have also inherited the Arch Fiend's technique of equivocation, although they are not yet practised enough to use it adeptly: Adam attempts to prevaricate with his Judge but is quickly forced to confess his transgression—though not *his* guilt: 'She gave me of the tree, and I did eat' (143). Eve, in turn, blames the serpent: 'The serpent me beguiled and I did eat' (162). Although the Son formally passes sentence of physical death on them, it is clear from their responses that even before the indictment is pronounced they are spiritually dead—a state which Milton defines as characterised by 'the loss of that divine grace and innate righteousness by which, in the beginning, man lived with God' (*DDC*, I, xii; *YP*, VI, p. 394). Sunk in self-willed depravity, they are incapable of any but selfish thoughts and actions; the divine image in them is wholly defaced, and they are powerless to restore it either in part or in whole. Absolute degeneracy is the merited fruit of their sin; and they deserve the sentences served on them: for Eve, pain in childbirth and subjection to her husband; for Adam, physical labour and death for himself and his posterity.

But Christ has come not only to condemn but also to promise restoration. He anticipates his mediatorial office on two occasions in the judgment scene, but the significance of his words and deeds at this stage is lost on Adam and Eve whose regeneration has not yet begun. First, he judges the serpent *before* passing sentence on the human pair, and the judgment of the serpent contains, 'Though in mysterious terms, judged as then best' (X, 173), a messianic prophecy:[29]

> Between thee and the woman I will put
> Enmity, and between thine and her seed;
> Her seed shall bruise thy head, thou bruise his heel.
>
> (179–81)

At this point Adam has no idea what this might mean. Later, he remembers these words and, although his exegesis suffers from literalism, he experiences the beginnings of illumination (X, 1028–40). It is not, however, until much later when Michael tells him of the Nativity that Adam understands that Christ is the prophesied 'seed of woman' and that the Incarnation signals the time when the serpent 'Needs must . . . his capital bruise/ Expect with mortal pain' (XII, 383–4)—though even here he is still disposed to see the contest between Christ and Satan in physical terms, and Michael finds it necessary to explicate the prophecy's spiritual meaning. To return to Book X: the second prolepsis is the Son's act of clothing the sinners:

> then pitying how they stood
> Before him naked to the air, that now
> Must suffer change, disdained not to begin
> Thenceforth the form of servant to assume,
> As when he washed his servants' feet so now
> As father of his family he clad
> Their nakedness with skins of beasts, or slain,
> Or as the snake with youthful coat repaid;
> And thought not much to clothe his enemies:
> Nor he their outward only with the skins
> Of beasts, but inward nakedness, much more
> Opprobrious, with his robe of righteousness,
> Arraying covered from his Father's sight.
>
> (211–23)

The significance of this event is lost on Adam and Eve. They know that the Son has clothed them in a physical sense, but they do not yet understand the spiritual meaning of his act because the Covenant of Grace has not been revealed to them. Only when Michael explains the doctrines of justification by faith and of imputed righteousness (XII, 402–35) will Adam come to appreciate fully how Christ, as Mediator, clothes man's inner nakedness and covers his spiritual blemishes with his robe of righteousness to make the sinner acceptable in his Father's sight.

The judgment scene, then, serves a double purpose. On the one hand, it fulfils the demands of divine justice; on the other hand, it anticipates—albeit in veiled terms—the process of divine mercy by which good will be brought out of evil. Moreover, the scene is intended as a dramatisation of fallen man's vocation to salvation:

> the voice of God they heard
> Now walking in the garden, by soft winds
> Brought to their ears, while day declined, they heard,
> And from his presence hid themselves among

> The thickest trees, both man and wife, till God
> Approaching, thus to Adam called aloud. . . .
>
> (97–102)

Sunk still in carnal self-interest and lacking any faith in God's goodness and mercy, the human pair do not respond willingly to this calling. At this stage, before their regeneration has begun, their depravity and darkened reason (symbolised by the declining day) blind them to the Son's charitable purpose, and in the voice borne to them by 'soft winds' they hear only accents of doom. For Adam and Eve here, as later for Simon Peter on the occasion when Jesus becomes a servant to wash his Disciples' feet—Milton's allusion in lines 214–15 is not without its point—the spiritual significance of Christ's symbolic acts of calling and purifying sinners (whether by washing their feet or clothing their naked bodies) is not understood: 'What I do thou knowest not now; but thou shalt hereafter.' (John 13: 7) Grace is offered before man knows that he requires it.

The first stages of Adam and Eve's regeneration are dramatised at the end of Book X. The section opens with Adam's long soliloquy (720–844)—a speech that Kester Svendsen denominates the 'tragic recognition scene' in which Adam confesses his guilt and accepts it as justly his.[30] In this dramatic monologue Adam Agonistes, surrounded by the mounting chaos in the natural order as Nature grows red in tooth and claw, turns inward in anguished self-examination: 'He has nowhere to turn and no one to turn to except his conscience. His sense of guilt is his only companion, and he wrestles with it as with an adversary.'[31] Reason (partially restored by supernatural renovation) and passion struggle for supremacy within his breast, and reason is confirmed and strengthened as it answers the objections raised by selfish passion. But reason's victory at this early stage is largely pyrrhic, for Adam's recognition of guilt—

> On me, me only, as the source and spring
> Of all corruption, all the blame lights due—
>
> (832–3)

is a conviction earned only at the price of hopelessness, terror, and despair:

> O conscience! into what abyss of fears

And horrors hast thou driven me; out of which
I find no way, from deep to deeper plunged!

(842–4)

Outstretched on the inhospitable earth, Adam invokes death and curses his creation, and the entrance of Eve only prompts him to a frenzied denunciation of his spouse and of woman and matrimony in general. But Eve's penitence and willing—if wishful—desire to take all the punishment for their sin upon herself disarms his anger and evokes his pity. Passionate irrationality yields to rational assessment of their situation, and Adam's forgiveness of Eve leads him to see that God may likewise forgive him. They are now truly embarked on the road to recovery. Adam's faith in God's mercy is an important step forward, for it enables him to place the judgment scene in perspective and to believe in the certainty of salvation even before it is revealed:

Undoubtedly he will relent and turn
From his displeasure; in whose look serene,
When angry most he seemed and most severe,
What else but favour, grace, and mercy shone?

(1093–6)

In *De Doctrina Christiana* Milton declares that the effects of regeneration are repentance and faith, and he distinguishes five degrees of repentance: 'recognition of sin, contrition, confession, abandonment of evil and conversion to good' (*DDC*, I, xix; *YP*, VI, p. 468). By the end of Book X of *Paradise Lost* (as has often been noticed) the beginnings of faith have manifested themselves in Adam and Eve and, as well, the human pair have risen up the first three rungs of the ladder of repentance:

they forthwith to the place
Repairing where he judged them prostrate fell
Before him reverent, and both confessed
Humbly their faults, and pardon begged, with tears
Watering the ground, and with their sighs the air
Frequenting, sent from hearts contrite, in sign
Of sorrow unfeigned, and humiliation meek.

(1098–1104)

But it must be remembered that regeneration (the product of faith and repentance) is contingent upon renovation, and renovation is the work of God alone. By supernatural renovation God restores some measure of fallen man's free will and reason, and it is only because of this divine activity that regeneration is possible:

> Thus they in lowliest plight repentant stood
> Praying, for from the mercy-seat above
> Prevenient grace descending *had removed*
> The stony from their hearts, and made new flesh
> Regenerate grow instead. . . .
>   (XI, 1−5; italics mine)

By natural renovation (vocation) God calls upon men to accept His offered grace. Refusal is always possible; however, if a man responds to grace, his partially restored faculties are strengthened and he grows gradually towards God as the divine image is restored in him. The renovation of Adam and Eve begins in the judgment scene with their calling to Christ and the gift of imputed righteousness; it proceeds as they start to respond to the divine initiative and to show the early signs of faith and repentance at the end of Book X; and it is brought to completion as Adam continues to co-operate with grace in his responsive obedience to Michael's revelations in Books XI and XII.

Knowing how 'variable and vain' is man's heart if 'Self-left', God sends Michael to earth on an errand of justice and mercy: he is to expel the sinful pair from Eden, but he is also instructed to bring them to a full spiritual understanding of their promised redemption. However, while the command of expulsion is absolute, the decree of mercy (since it depends on man's willing response) is conditional:

> If patiently thy bidding they obey,
> Dismiss them not disconsolate; reveal
> To Adam what shall come in future days,
> As I shall thee enlighten, intermix
> My Covenant in the woman's seed renewed;
> So send them forth, though sorrowing, yet in peace.
>   (XI, 112−17)

Theologically, Michael's mission is necessary, for the remaining stages of Adam's repentance (abandonment of evil and conversion to good) cannot be accomplished without revelation. In the fallen world, where good is only known by evil (that is, by conscious separation from evil), Adam must be educated both in the forms of evil with all their baits and seeming pleasures and also in the forms of goodness and its rewards. Only after he has learned the worst that Satan, Sin and Death have to offer and after he is aware of the full significance of Christ's atoning sacrifice is Adam in a position to choose rationally between good and evil. A full understanding is the necessary prerequisite of informed choice, and it is with the object of providing Adam with this understanding that Michael reveals to him the course of human history.

Although Michael's pedagogical mission is necessary from a theological point of view, its artistic importance (and success) has frequently been questioned and most of the three centuries of readers lying between us and Milton have been disparaging in their comments on Books XI and XII. The tradition extends from Addison, who lamented that 'the Author has been so attentive to his Divinity, that he has neglected his Poetry', to C. S. Lewis, who argues that 'Such an untransmuted lump of futurity, coming in a position so momentous for the structural effect of the whole work, is inartistic'.[32] Recent criticism has done much, however, to achieve a more balanced perspective, and Milton's art and architectonic skill in the last books have been ably defended by F. T. Prince, Joseph H. Summers, Lawrence Sasek, and H. R. MacCallum.[33] These readers have shown that the process of Adam's enlightenment is highly dramatic and have demonstrated how Milton's careful arrangement of historical material creates 'a dialectical pattern of ascent which leads Adam from type to truth, from flesh to spirit':

> Michael's aim is to bring Adam to a full and spiritual understanding of the Son's prophecy concerning the war between the seed of the woman and the serpent. He leads Adam toward his goal by a series of graded steps, each one but the last inconclusive, and each consequently capable of misinterpretation. Yet as he proceeds he does sow within Adam 'the seeds of a sufficient determining', so that by the close of the story every part takes its place in a total design.[34]

The final books are characterised, dramatically and poetically, by the dynamic interaction between the typological progression of

the scriptural narrative and Adam's growing vocational awareness and conviction as he responds to the unfolding history of the
world. Each new situation presents an opportunity for mistake
and misjudgment. Adam is often hasty and occasionally pre-
sumptive in his responses, and Michael finds it necessary to
correct and guide him to the proper stance. However, as he
accepts each new experience, Adam's responses gradually sharpen and he becomes more aware of his human responsibilities and
more capable of executing those responsibilities. His developing
perception of the prophesied bridge spanning the gulf between
human depravity and divine goodness leads from his initial
despair over the consequences of his sin and his mounting horror
at his descendants' capacity for evil, to a full and *personal* understanding of redeeming grace and a willing reconciliation with
God's providential purpose.

The stages by which Adam's education progresses have been
well documented by the critics mentioned above, and I have here
neither space nor reason to rehearse their findings. There is,
however, one point which to my knowledge has not so far been
noticed but which, it strikes me, is of considerable importance.

At the beginning of Book XI the penitent Adam and Eve are
compared, in one of the very few classical allusions in the last
books, to Deucalion and Pyrrha:

> nor important less
> Seemed their petition, than when the ancient pair
> In fables old, less ancient yet than these,
> Deucalion and chaste Pyrrha to restore
> The race of mankind drowned, before the shrine
> Of Themis stood devout.
>
> (9–14)

The prayers of Deucalion and Pyrrha and their earnest hope of
restoring their desolate world with divine aid provides an appropriate parallel to the penitent invocations of Adam and Eve whose
attention is likewise focused on the future of mankind in a world
destroyed by crimes against deity; and, like their pagan counter-
parts, they hope that the world may be restored through them.
Nevertheless, despite its importance as an index to the immediate
situation, the Deucalion allusion serves another—and more
significant—purpose in the structure of the closing books of
Paradise Lost.

For the seventeenth-century reader the reference to Deucalion would immediately call to mind the figure of Noah, of whom Deucalion was the mythic analogue. The identification was conventional in the period:

> Who doth not see drown'd in Deucalions name,
> (When earth his men, and sea had lost his shore)
> Old Noah . . . ?[35]

Milton stresses the correspondence, and it is clear that he intends the early reference to Deucalion and 'The race of mankind drowned' as a prolepsis of his later account of Noah and the Flood. Deucalion's 'devout' prayer to Themis on Mount Parnassus prefigures Noah's 'uplifted hands, and eyes devout' (XI, 863) on Mount Ararat, and the oracle from the goddess in the classical myth parallels the signs vouchsafed to Noah in the form of a dove and a rainbow arching in the cloudy sky (XI, 857–62). Moreover, as Ovid declares of Deucalion that *non illo melior quisquam nec amantior aequi/ vir fuit* (*Metamorphoses*, I, 322–3), so Michael denominates Noah the 'one just man alive' (XI, 818) and Adam rejoices on hearing of

> one man found so perfect and so just,
> That God vouchsafes to raise another world
> From him, and all his anger to forget.[36]
> (XI, 876–8)

But Noah, of course, is traditionally a type of Christ: the covenant with Noah anticipates (albeit imperfectly) the Covenant of Grace, and the flood which destroys all save Noah and his family looks forward to that time when 'this world's dissolution shall be ripe' (XII, 459), when the sinful earth shall be wasted by fire and the righteous received into eternal bliss. And it is not surprising to find that Milton's account of the Flood is, as H. R. MacCallum demonstrates, 'resonant with typological implications'.[37]

The figures of Deucalion, Noah and Christ, then, form an allusive triptych[38] involving three hills (Parnassus, Ararat, and Calvary), three distinct yet related covenants between God and man, and three new beginnings for mankind where, in each instance, the central figures stand poised between 'the world destroyed and world restored'—a redemptive point from which man proceeds 'as from a second stock' (XII, 3, 7).[39] Not only are

Deucalion, Noah and Christ symbolically linked through situation and imagery, but also—and this is the most significant point—they appear at moments of great structural importance: Deucalion at the beginning of Book XI, Noah at the end of Book XI, but his influence spills over into the opening lines of Book XII, and Christ at the end of Book XII. Through these strategically placed narratives Milton establishes a subtle and elaborate framework for the entire historical account recorded in the last two books of *Paradise Lost*. The three stories are not isolated and discontinuous, but cumulative and organically related; their significance, like Adam's spiritual growth, is realised only as process. The ascent implied in the movement from the pagan fiction of Deucalion, to the historical narrative of the patriarch Noah, to the fulfilment of these prefigurative types in the life and work of Christ, provides a graded symbolic frame that parallels the progression from 'shadowy types to truth, from flesh to spirit' (XII, 303) which constitutes the pattern of Adam's spiritual and educational experience in the closing books of the epic.

5 *Samson Agonistes*

The most remarkable aspect of *Samson Agonistes* is its internalisation of the action.[1] Samson's movement back to God, his recovery of his lost pre-eminence and power, is recorded, not in terms of the hero's actions, but rather in terms of his progressively more acute spiritual awareness. It is in the spiritual movement of the drama that the Aristotelian 'middle', which Dr Johnson found wanting in the play, is to be found. Indeed, most of Milton's modern readers would readily endorse Arthur Barker's facetiously accurate reversal of Dr Johnson's charge: 'Samson's experience is so far from having no middle that it is in effect all middle.'[2]

Almost without exception, recent commentators have read *Samson Agonistes* as a study in regeneration, and many have argued that the pattern of Miltonic soteriology set out in *De Doctrina Christiana* provides an important gloss on the poetic handling of Samson's spiritual development. These readers have pointed out that the hero is renovatingly called in the opening soliloquy, that he freely chooses to respond to this vocation, and that the process of his spiritual rebirth is patterned on the Miltonic doctrines of renovation and regeneration. The position is admirably summarised by Anthony Low:

> When Samson is led in from the prison, he is in what amounts to a state of spiritual death, into which he has fallen as a result of his betrayal of God's trust. He laments his blindness and captivity, he feels a bewildered sense of spiritual malaise and guilt, but before he can make any progress toward recovery he must first learn to understand and to confront his sin. This he does, undergoing the process known as conversion (that is, a turning of the soul from evil to good) and regeneration (spiritual rebirth or renewal). In Milton's view, regeneration is impossible without the assistance of God's grace, since man in a fallen state cannot satisfy God's justice or merit his help. At the same time, however, the individual must freely choose to cooperate

with grace and with the opportunities for spiritual renovation that providence offers him. . . . Much of the process [of regeneration] can only be assumed, because it takes place inwardly and is reflected only indirectly by Samson's outward behavior and conversation; but that it occurs is clear. . . . Finally, Samson follows the 'progressive steps' of repentance: 'conviction of sin, contrition, confession, departure from evil, conversion to good'. It would be wrong, I believe, to associate these steps too closely or schematically with the structure of the play, even though one is tempted to do so by the fact that there are five steps of repentance and the play consists of five episodes or acts. One may say roughly, however, that Samson is convicted of sin, becomes contrite, and confesses his guilt in the first part of the play—including his soliloquy and the interviews with the Chorus and Manoa. Although these three steps each might be said to begin at some indefinite point in the first part of the play, all of them plainly culminate in the interview with Manoa. In his interview with Dalila, Samson can be said to depart from evil—and also, perhaps, in his interview with Harapha, when he dismisses much of what he has formerly been. His final conversion to good takes place between the two visits of the Public Officer.[3]

Such theological interpretations have shed considerable light on the mimetic pattern of Samson's renovating movement from death-in-life to life-through-death—a spiritual journey from darkness to light and from loss to restoration that is mirrored in the play's time scheme, which takes us from early morning to the catastrophic finale in Dagon's temple at high noon. But vocation and the possibility of spiritual growth are not limited to Samson alone. Both Manoa and the Chorus are called through Samson's experience and invited to respond to the renovating grace extended to them as well; and that they do respond—each according to the degree of grace given to him (cf. pp.14–15)—is clear from the 'new acquist/ Of true experience' gleaned from their personal involvement in the great events which they have witnessed—an acquisition of private spiritual experience that sends them from the stage 'With peace and consolation . . ./ And calm of mind all passion spent' (1755–8). In a similar way, Dalila and Harapha are called to co-operate with universal grace, and Samson's development must be seen as being, potentially, an analogue of the regenerative experience offered to but declined by them. Their wilful behaviour sends them off self-condemned and self-blinded; and ironically, as Anthony Low points out, 'their visit to Samson proves to be an "evil temptation" for them, which encourages them to sink further into error, at the same time that they serve as "good temptations" to strengthen him'.[4]

Samson's vocational experience, however, is both deeper and more complex than that of any of the other characters. He is not only called, like those around him, to respond to God's redemptive purpose by a *vocatio generalis*, but he is also called by a *vocation specialis* which sharply distinguishes his spiritual *agon* from theirs: 'God, whenever he chooses, invites certain selected individuals . . . more clearly and more insistently than is normal.' (*YP*, VI, p. 455) Samson is not an ordinary man; he is a Judge, an Israelite *shôphet* elect above the rest of mankind: 'when the Lord raised them up judges, then the Lord was with the judge' (Judges 2: 18). Throughout *Samson Agonistes* stress is laid on the hero's unique status as a divinely commissioned instrument. In his opening soliloquy Samson declares that his 'breeding' had been 'ordered and prescribed/ As of a person separate to God,/ Designed for great exploits' (30–2), and the theme of special election is reinforced in the speeches of Manoa and the Chorus and is often cogently restated by Samson himself: 'I was no private but a person raised/ With strength sufficient and command from heaven/ To free my country.' (1211–13) But, as these formulations indicate, Samson's *vocatio specialis* involves a special responsibility—for those whom the Lord has 'solemnly elected' (678) to serve Him are called as agents of His will and not for their own sake. Samson, however, when first we meet him in the prison-house at Gaza, has proven unfaithful to the divine trust. Motivated by self-interest and guilty of presumption, he has wilfully abrogated his mission and cut himself off from the source of his strength. And before he can be reinstated as God's 'faithful champion' and fulfil his predicted role as Israel's deliverer, he must be educated in the limits of power and he must learn, like the Christ of Milton's epics, to deny the promptings of self-will so that he may truly serve as the instrument of deity, not pre-empting but co-operating with grace and freely performing God's acts in God's own time.

In the poetic fabric of *Samson Agonistes* the related themes of regeneration and election, of general and special vocation, are

developed together and skilfully interwoven. As the drama begins, the hero is presented to us as a 'fallen' man in a double sense:
he is both an heir of Adam's transgression and a peccant agent
(apparently) dismissed from divine service. Both of these states
are transcended as the play progresses and as Samson grows
through his ever more positive response to the graded series of
temptations offered to him by Manoa, Dalila, Harapha, and the
Philistian Officer. The various confrontations cause him to manifest faith and repentance; and, as the process of his regeneration
advances, the divine image defaced in Eden is gradually restored
in him. Correlative with—and, indeed, contingent upon—this
spiritual metamorphosis is the educational growth which transforms him from a self-motivated agent operating on what he
presumes to be God's will to a chastened instrument responding
only to the intimate impulse of the 'rousing motions' by which
God calls him to active service.

SAMSON AND THE CHORUS: LINES 1–325

In the first act of the drama the significance of the hero's fallen
state is explored by contrasting past and present, and the theme of
vocation is introduced in terms of an unresolved tension between
prophecy and fact, between Samson's promised calling as God's
champion and Israel's deliverer and his actual position as a
Philistian bondslave whom God, it seems, has rejected. Led from
the confines of his prison, Samson laments that, while the cessa-
tion of labour afforded by Dagon's feast may grant some ease to
his body, it allows none to his mind, which is the more assailed by
those 'restless thoughts' that rush upon him like a swarm of angry
hornets

>   and present
> Times past, what once I was, and what am now.
> O wherefore was my birth from heaven foretold
> Twice by an angel, who at last in sight
> Of both my parents all in flames ascended
> From off the altar, where an offering burned,
> As in a fiery column charioting
> His godlike presence, and from some great act
> Or benefit revealed to Abraham's race?

Why was my breeding ordered and prescribed
As of a person separate to God,
Designed for great exploits; if I must die
Betrayed, captived, and both my eyes put out,
Made of my enemies the scorn and gaze;
To grind in brazen fetters under task
With this heaven-gifted strength? O glorious strength
Put to the labour of a beast, debased
Lower than bond-slave! Promise was that I
Should Israel from Philistian yoke deliver;
Ask for this great deliverer now, and find him
Eyeless in Gaza at the mill with slaves,
Himself in bonds under Philistian yoke. . . .

(21–42)

Samson is more than a fallen Hercules or Prometheus, more than a tragic image of despoiled strength or thwarted heroism. Despite the noble self-pity that he manifests in the face of adversity, he is spiritually dead—a state characterised by 'the loss of that divine grace and innate righteousness by which, in the beginning, man lived with God' (*YP*, VI, p. 394). In this state Samson, like the newly fallen Adam and Eve in Book IX of *Paradise Lost*, is incapable of any but selfish thoughts and actions, and his lack of faith is attested in his querulous vocational doubts.

But Samson's renovation has already begun when the curtain rises:

A little onward lend thy guiding hand
To these dark steps, a little further on;
For yonder bank hath choice of sun or shade,
There I am wont to sit, when any chance
Relieves me from my task of servile toil,
Daily in the common prison else enjoined me,
Where I a prisoner chained, scarce freely draw
The air imprisoned also, close and damp,
Unwholesome draught: but here I feel amends,
The breath of heaven fresh blowing, pure and sweet,
With day-spring born; here leave me to respire.

(1–11)

The 'guiding hand' by which he is led forth is the hand of God as

well as that of the (purposely) unnamed figure who pilots him up
the dark steps and across to the embankment, and the sweet
breath of heaven 'With day-spring born' is emblematic of the
secret operation of inspiring grace and, as well, of the possibility
for rebirth. Responsive choice is possible from the outset: the
steps, now dark, up which he stumbles out of the prison prefigure
the latent stages of his enlightenment and regeneration; and, as
the embankment gives him 'choice of sun or shade', so he is free to
respond or not to the gentle leading of the unseen hand that guides
him from an imprisonment that is as much spiritual as it is
physical.

His initial response to renovating grace issues, as we have seen,
in peevish vocational murmurings against the ways of Providence. With the aid of restored right reason, however, he takes his
first step on the road to recovery almost simultaneously, by
admitting—albeit reluctantly—the possibility of personal responsibility for his present deplorable condition:

> Yet stay, let me not rashly call in doubt
> Divine prediction; what if all foretold
> Had been fulfilled but through mine own default,
> Whom have I to complain of but myself?
>
> (43-6)

Samson's sense of guilt and recognition of sin, however hedged
with conditionals and question marks, provides the starting-point
for his gradual return to God—for conviction of sin is the first of
those 'progressive steps' of repentance outlined by Milton in *De
Doctrina Christiana* (cf. above, p. 145). Remorse, however, is not
repentance, and Samson's introductory footing on the path of
redemptive theology is precarious and faltering.

> O impotence of mind, in body strong!
> But what is strength without a double share
> Of wisdom, vast, unwieldy, burdensome,
> Proudly secure, yet liable to fall
> By weakest subtleties, not made to rule,
> But to subserve where wisdom bears command.
>
> (52-7)

As Adam in *Paradise Lost* had questioned the Creator's wisdom in not arming him against the threat of passion, so Samson's words here contain a tacit rebuke that he was not granted wisdom equal to his strength.

At this early stage the vague awareness of spiritual death is capable of producing in the protagonist effects which are diametrically opposed. If Samson's sense of guilt is the first step in his potential recovery, then, conversely, his sense of alienation from divine favour, nurtured by doubts concerning his ordained vocation as Israel's deliverer, leads him to the very brink of the chasm of despair. It is as 'one past hope, abandoned,/ And by himself given over' (120–1) that the Chorus first describes him, and through the first two acts of the drama he is tempted again and again to yield to despair. The mortal sin of *tristitia*, when man succumbs to it, puts him at the furthest remove from God; it is the sin for which no forgiveness is possible and, as Milton notes, it 'falls upon the reprobate alone' (*DDC*, II, iii; *YP*, VI, p. 659). If Samson despairs, he nullifies that first step in repentance which he has taken by recognising his guilt and responsibility for what has happened, and, what is worse, he effectively extinguishes any chance of regeneration or reacceptance into his promised calling.

'The principal purpose of this mainly expository first Act', according to A. S. P. Woodhouse, 'is . . . to underline Samson's remorse (not yet repentance) and his religious despair: to give us the starting point of the movement back to God—and on to the catastrophe.'⁵ While this is true, it should be added that there is nothing fated or ineluctable about this progression. Samson is not driven on by relentless *parcae* to a predestined end; his 'fate' lies in his own use of reason and free will as he is called to respond to renovating grace. It is significant, too, that Milton develops the theme of Samson's regeneration (that is, his response to the *vocatio generalis*) in terms of his growing understanding of his special vocation. His initial realisation is that he has, through sin, failed in his role as deliverer; and this recognition leads, as he discusses his two marriages with the Chorus, to further insight into the causes of his fall from favour and takes him a step further in repentance:

> The first I saw at Timna, and she pleased
> Me, not my parents, that I sought to wed,
> The daughter of an infidel: they knew not
> That what I motioned was of God; I knew

> From intimate impulse, and therefore urged
> The marriage on; that by occasion hence
> I might begin Israel's deliverance,
> The work to which I was divinely called;
> She proving false, the next I took to wife
> (O that I never had! fond wish too late.)
> Was in the vale of Sorec, Dalila,
> That specious monster, my accomplished snare,
> I thought it lawful from my former act,
> And the same end; still watching to oppress
> Israel's oppressors: of what now I suffer
> She was not the prime cause, but I myself
> Who vanquished with a peal of words (O weakness!)
> Gave up my fort of silence to a woman.
>
> (219–36)

The marriage to the woman of Timnath, although it necessitated
his transgressing ceremonial and Nazaritic law, was prompted by
God, and Samson therefore urged it on in order that he might
'begin Israel's deliverance,/ The work to which [he] was divinely
called'. The marriage to Dalila, however, through which he
sought to continue his harassment of the Philistines and further
the work of his promised vocation, was not 'motioned' by God: it
was an action undertaken by Samson alone ('I *thought it lawful*
from my former act,/ And the same end'). This is rationalisation
rather than reasoning, and Samson has erred, as Arnold Stein
points out, by interpreting intuition by analogy.[6] In taking the
woman of Timnath to wife, he had contravened the law out of
respect to the will of the Lawgiver—for God's servants are
required to obey divine commands, even when doing so means
disobeying divine laws. In marrying Dalila, however, he was
guilty of presumption: although his intentions were good, he
presumed, without that certainty provided by 'intimate impulse',
to carry forward what *he* felt to be God's plan for the liberation of
Israel.

Samson has assumed that, as an elect instrument, he must be
always *actively* engaged in God's service. What he has overlooked
is that the scheme for Israel's deliverance is God's and must be
carried out in God's time. Samson is the instrument, not the
instigator; he has not scrutinised the divine plan and he does not
know how it is to be fulfilled. Legitimately, all he can do is await

God's commands and obey them. But his mania for action leads him to presume and, in presuming, to fall from grace. Moreover, presumption is connected with a number of other sins which accentuate its gravity: loss of humility and the deadly sin of pride. The credit for Samson's glorious victories over the Uncircumcised belongs, properly, to God; however, as his career advanced, Samson had begun to take personal pride in, and personal credit for, these feats. Forgetting the real source of his strength, he had swaggered 'like a petty god/ . . . admired of all and dreaded/ On hostile ground, none daring my affront' (529–31). As his pride and self-esteem grew, his humility before God inevitably eroded and, eventually, disappeared.

Before he can be reinstated as an instrument of the divine will, Samson must be educated. First, he must learn the lesson of *humility*: instead of arrogant self-sufficiency, he must manifest absolute submission before God. Second, he must learn the lesson of *patience*: as an instrument of deity his role will not always be an active one, and he must patiently await God's commands. Third, he must learn the lesson of *faith:* in spite of his sins and in spite of his present deplorable situation, he must trust in divine mercy and have faith in the promise of his special calling. Humility, patience and faith are the spiritual antidotes to the three sins—pride, presumption, doubt—of which he is guilty as the play begins; and these three virtues, freely embraced, will bring about his regeneration and return to divine favour. It is through suffering and through a series of 'good temptations'—both aspects of the mysterious working of Providence—that Samson passes to purification and the fulfilment of his divinely ordained vocation to deliver Israel.

SAMSON AND MANOA: LINES 326–709

In the second movement of the drama, Samson is confronted by Manoa who, like the Chorus (115–74), laments his son's change of fortune. And, as Samson had done earlier, Manoa questions the 'divine justice' which raised his son to such an eminence and then, after he had made but one mistake, abandoned him:

> Why are his gifts desirable, to tempt
> Our earnest prayers, then given with solemn hand

> As graces, draw a scorpion's tail behind?
> For this did the angel twice descend? for this
> Ordained thy nurture holy, as of a plant;
> Select, and sacred, glorious for a while,
> The miracle of men: then in an hour
> Ensnared, assaulted, overcome, led bound,
> Thy foes' derision, captive, poor, and blind
> Into a dungeon thrust, to work with slaves?
> Alas methinks whom God hath chosen once
> To worthiest deeds, if he through frailty err,
> He should not so o'erwhelm, and as a thrall
> Subject him to so foul indignities,
> Be it but for honour's sake of former deeds.
>
> (358–72)

Beneath this questioning of divine justice lie the implicit questions, 'How can Samson now be of service to God? What is his role now in the work of Israel's deliverance—or is he no longer of use?' And, although Samson reproves his father for his presumptuous indictment of divine prediction, it is obvious that he is troubled by his words. Manoa has, indeed, touched a sore spot, for (we recall) these are precisely the questions that Samson had asked himself in his opening soliloquy when he was lamenting the disparity between prophecy and fact in his career as a divine agent. Here, having acknowledged that 'I this honour, I this pomp have brought/ To Dagon', he goes on to reveal the full extent to which he has been affected by the subject of his father's queries:

> This only hope relieves me, that the strife
> With me hath end; all the contest is now
> 'Twixt God and Dagon, Dagon hath presumed,
> Me overthrown, to enter lists with God,
> His deity comparing and preferring
> Before the God of Abraham. He, be sure,
> Will not connive, or linger, thus provoked,
> But will arise and his great name assert.
>
> (460–7)

Once again he voices his sense of Heaven's desertion—and with a difference that does not bode well for his spiritual growth. Earlier, he had lifted himself above pride and self-confidence enough to realise that his marriage to Dalila had been an act of presumption; but here, when Manoa calls God's justice into doubt, Samson is plunged into near despair. And this state of mind prompts him to another presumptuous act: he assumes that God has finished with him. His only 'hope' is hopelessness. There is, he decides, no possibility that he can now fulfil his promised mission: 'all the contest is now/ 'Twixt God and Dagon.' It always has been. And this is the crux of the matter. Samson accuses Dagon of presumption, but presumption is his fault as well, for he implies that before his fall the battle had been between Dagon and himself. 'Swollen with pride', he had acted as a free agent prosecuting justice in God's name, but without His consent or authority. Now, confronted by his father's doubts (which reflect his own), he is on the point of reversing his spiritual growth and nullifying the progress he has made.

It is at this point that we have the explicit wording of the first temptation. Manoa, who (ironically) has been trying to ransom his son, advises:

> Be penitent and for thy fault contrite,
> But act not in thy own affliction, son,
> Repent the sin, but if the punishment
> Thou canst avoid, self-preservation bids;
> Or the execution leave to high disposal,
> And let another hand, not thine, exact
> The penal forfeit from thyself; perhaps
> God will relent, and quit thee all his debt.
> . . . . .
> Reject not then what offered means, who knows
> But God hath set before us, to return thee
> Home to thy country and his sacred house,
> Where thou may'st bring thy off'rings, to avert
> His further ire, with prayers and vows renewed.
>   (502–20)

Manoa counsels liberty, ease, peace in retirement from active service, and the expiation of error in 'prayers and vows renewed'. On the human level, this advice to one who has suffered much seems reasonable enough; however, since chastisement is often 'the instrumental cause of repentance' (*DDC*, I, xix; *YP*, VI, p. 469), Samson should not attempt to avoid punishment. The

main point of Manoa's temptation hinges once again on the sin of
presumption: Manoa presumes that Samson's mission is over and
that God has no further need of him—and he asks his son to *act* on
this assumption.

Samson admits that his father is probably right, that his days as
God's sword against the Philistines are almost certainly over:

> Now blind, disheartened, shamed, dishonoured, quelled,
> To what can I be useful, wherein serve
> My nation, and the work from heaven imposed,
> But to sit idle on the household hearth,
> A burdenous drone; to visitants a gaze,
> Or pitied object, these redundant locks
> Robustious to no purpose clustering down,
> Vain monument of strength; till length of years
> And sedentary numbness craze my limbs
> To a contemptible old age obscure.
> Here rather let me drudge and earn my bread,
> Till vermin or the draff of servile food
> Consume me, and oft-invocated death
> Hasten the welcome end of all my pains.

> (563–76)

Given Samson's lack of physical, moral and spiritual strength,
and his scepticism (aggravated to some degree by self-pity) about
his usefulness to God, one would expect that he would succumb
inevitably to Manoa's temptation. Yet he rejects it, and his reason
for doing so is not difficult to find—pride. The memory of
his former greatness will not permit him to become a 'gaze'
for curious visitors or a 'pitied object'; after the glories of his
past life, he refuses to be ransomed into senility and 'a contempt-
ible old age obscure'. Moreover, his belief in the necessity of
action—even action for action's sake—finds the prospect of
'sedentary numbness' and sitting 'idle on the household hearth,/
A burdenous drone' repulsive. Thus, he rejects Manoa's temptation, but he does not *overcome* it. He does the right thing for the
wrong reason.

Manoa's temptation only succeeds in bringing Samson's present situation squarely before him; and his father's well-
intentioned but purely empirical assessment of the situation
serves only to plunge Samson further into the Slough of Despond:

> So much I feel my genial spirits droop,
> My hopes all flat, nature within me seems
> In all her functions weary of herself;
> My race of glory run, and race of shame,
> And I shall shortly be with them that rest.
>
> (594–8)

Not wishing to 'omit a father's timely care', Manoa bustles off to 'prosecute the means of [his son's] deliverance/ By ransom or how else' (602–3) — leaving Samson in the hands of another Father who is also, though by a higher means, concerned with delivering him from prison and the grave.

SAMSON AND DALILA: LINES 710–1060

In the third movement of the drama Samson is confronted by Dalila, who 'like a stately ship' sweeps in,

> With all her bravery on, and tackle trim,
> Sails filled, and streamers waving,
> Courted by all the winds that hold them sway.
>
> (717–19)

The imagery suggests that the confrontation will take on the character of a naval engagement, a battle between a dangerous merchantman whose armament is cleverly hidden from view and a broken warship wandering rudderless on a sea of doubt. The encounter, however, is to be contested with rhetoric, not with cannon. Dalila's temptation is that of *concupiscentia oculorum* (temptation by fraud or persuasion) and, Michael Krouse observes, 'it is she, more than either Manoa or Harapha, who tries to persuade Samson.'[7]

The mere arrival of Dalila, his 'accomplished snare', is enough to lift Samson from the near despair into which Manoa's visit had thrown him: 'My wife,' he cries, 'my traitress, let her not come near me' (725). Despite seeming penitence, Dalila is still a fraudulent temptress who has, it would appear, taken to heart Lady Macbeth's advice to 'looke like th' innocent flower,/ But be the Serpent under 't' (*Macbeth*, I, v, 74–5). Although his response is initially prompted by wounded pride and the rankling memory of how he had been 'effeminately vanquished', the return of Samson's fighting spirit renders him psychologically capable of meeting her challenge. His point by point refutation of her arguments forces him to employ his partially restored *recta ratio*, and the result is that this faculty is confirmed and strengthened as he confutes her specious reasoning. He does not, then, simply reject her temptation, as he had Manoa's; he overcomes it—and achieves a measure of self-knowledge in the process.

With feigned penitence and 'still dreading thy displeasure, Samson', Dalila has come—moved, she avers, by 'conjugal affection'—to ask pardon for her 'rash but more unfortunate misdeed' (747). Samson, smarting from the effects of this 'rash' deed, sees through her immediately; he accuses her of 'feigned remorse', the object of which is to regain his trust and then to lead him to transgress once more. Having failed in her first attempt, Dalila tries a different approach: she admits her error in publishing the secret of his strength, but maintains that weakness and the fear of losing him (either to another woman or on the field of battle) had prompted the decision and that she had not foreseen the consequences of her action. Samson is not deceived, either by the tears or the polished rhetoric: 'All wickedness is weakness: that plea therefore/ With God or man will gain thee no remission.' (834–5) Thwarted again, Dalila adjusts the ground of her argument a third time: public duty and religion 'took full possession of me and prevailed' (869). Samson remains undeceived.[8]

In one final attempt, Dalila suggests that she intercede on his behalf with the Philistian lords,

> that I may fetch thee
> From forth this loathsome prison-house, to abide
> With me, where my redoubled love and care
> With nursing diligence, to me glad office,
> May ever tend about thee to old age
> With all things grateful cheered, and so supplied,
> That what by me thou hast lost thou least shalt miss.
>
> (921–7)

The temptation here is to sloth and physical ease and, except that Dalila adds the note of carnal indulgence, it is precisely the temptation that Manoa had earlier offered his son. This time, however, Samson is ready and has no difficulty in overcoming the temptation:

> Thy fair enchanted cup, and warbling charms
> No more on me have power, their force is nulled,
> So much of adder's wisdom I have learnt
> To fence my ear against thy sorceries.
>
> (934-7)

When she realises that Samson will not again be duped, Dalila begins to show her true colours and stalks off in a fit of *hubris,* 'a manifest serpent by her sting/ Discovered in the end, till now concealed' (997-8). And the nautical imagery with which the episode began is rounded off by the Chorus in a rhetorical question: 'What pilot so expert but needs must wreck/ Embarked with such a steers-man at the helm?' (1044-5)

The encounter with Dalila does not teach Samson humility, patience, or faith, but it does succeed in raising him out of the apathy, hopelessness, and despair into which Manoa's visit had thrown him. The important point is that he has refuted her specious arguments and has, with the aid of right reason, overcome—not merely rejected—her attempts to draw him again 'into the snare/ Where once I have been caught' (931-2). At this stage, however, his reaction to temptation is too self-motivated (his pride is piqued) for positive spiritual growth; but he will learn the necessity of selfless service in the encounters with Harapha and the Public Officer, to which the trial by Dalila is the necessary prelude.

SAMSON, HARAPHA, AND THE PUBLIC OFFICER: LINES 1061 - 1440

In the fourth movement, Samson is confronted by two instruments of force: Harapha, the giant of Gath, and the Philistian Officer. The taunts of Harapha and commands of the officer are, in terms of his regeneration, the most significant of Samson's trials.

Harapha, the first to arrive, says that he has heard much of the Hebrew's martial feats and now is come 'to see of whom such noise/ Hath walked about' (1088-9). He laments that they had not met earlier, on the battlefield, so that he might have vindi-

cated Philistian glory—but now, alas, 'that honour,/ Certain to
have been won by mortal duel from thee,/ I lose, prevented by thy
eyes put out' (1101–3). Samson's reflex reaction to this cowardly
taunt is to challenge the Philistian giant to a trial by single
combat. Harapha, who has come only to scoff, is shaken by the
spirited challenge, and he attempts to take refuge in the charge
that Samson's strength is the product of 'spells/ And black
enchantments', of 'some magician's art' that 'Armed thee or
charmed thee strong' (1132–4). Almost without realising what he
is saying, Samson replies:

> I know no spells, use no forbidden arts;
> My trust is in the living God who gave me
> At my nativity this strength, diffused
> No less through all my sinews, joints and bones,
> Than thine, while I preserved these locks unshorn,
> The pledge of my unviolated vow.
>
> (1139–44)

Harapha's taunts have drawn from Samson, almost unawares, an
expression of hope—the first in the poem. During Manoa's visit
he had given over all hope of his divine mission: 'all the contest is
now/ 'Twixt God and Dagon'; but here, forgetting his earlier
sense of heaven's desertion, he unconsciously assumes once more
his role as God's instrument. And, shortly, his reflex assertion
yields to sincere conviction, a positive and conscious declaration
of faith:

> All these indignities, for such they are
> From thine, these evils I deserve and more,
> Acknowledge them from God inflicted on me
> Justly, yet despair not of his final pardon
> Whose ear is ever open; and his eye
> Gracious to readmit the suppliant;
> In confidence whereof I once again
> Defy thee to the trial of mortal fight,
> By combat to decide whose god is God,
> Thine or whom I with Israel's sons adore.
>
> (1168–77)

The dispute with Dalila had succeeded in lifting Samson from near despair, and his despair—as the Manoa episode illustrated—was born of self-centred remorse. Once his attention is focused on the spiritual rather than on the temporal or physical aspects of his situation, the door is open to returning humility and faith. Harapha's gibes have called forth a latent belief in God's mercy, a hope of 'final pardon'. Samson has always believed in divine justice, and from the beginning has accepted personal responsibility for his condition; however, because his thoughts had centred too much on himself (on what he *is* as compared with what he *was*), he had begun to doubt and, finally, to despair that God tempers justice with mercy. But here, now guided by right reason and piqued more by Harapha's derisive suggestion that Heaven has deserted him than by the slight to his own pride, Samson asserts that there is no cause to doubt divine mercy or despair of pardon, for God's 'ear is ever open; and his eye/ Gracious to readmit the suppliant'. The important word here is *suppliant*. Samson has become a humble petitioner imploring God's mercy, and his returning faith leads him to hope for—indeed, to expect with certainty—His final pardon.

If the verbal encounter with the giant of Gath causes Samson to reassert his faith and humility before God, it does not teach him the necessity of patience. Without God's sanction, he challenges Harapha to a 'trial of mortal fight,/ By combat to decide whose god is God'. Truly, the active inactivity of standing and waiting for divine commands does not come easily or naturally to Samson. As was the case in his determination to marry Dalila, his motive here is, in itself, good. Yet his defiant and (largely) selfless challenge puts him on the verge of committing another presumptuous act, of sacrificing the spiritual headway he has made through one negligent, though well-meaning, act. It is, ironically, a sudden burst of pride that prevents his carrying this presumptuous threat into execution: he disdains to fight a 'vain boaster' who uses every excuse to avoid combat—he (Harapha) cannot fight a blind man, cannot demean himself to duel with a slave, and so on. And Samson contemptuously dismisses the Philistine *braggadocio* in high scorn:

> Go baffled coward, lest I run upon thee,
> Though in these chains, bulk without spirit vast,
> And with one buffet lay thy structure low,
> Or swing thee in the air, then dash thee down

To the hazard of thy brains and shattered sides.

(1237–41)

Many critics have not regarded the summons of the Public Officer as a separate and significant trial, and yet, in many ways, it is the most significant of Samson's temptations, for he must learn that as an instrument of the divine will he is permitted to act only when God commands. It is the function of the temptation presented by the Philistian Officer to teach him the necessity of patience, of standing and waiting. After the Chorus has ironically observed that Samson's lack of sight 'May chance to number [him] with those/ Whom patience finally must crown' (1295–6), the Officer enters and orders that Samson follow him to the temple, where a festival is being held in Dagon's honour. Although Samson advances his fidelity to Hebrew law as his reason for refusing to comply, it is apparent that his refusal is also motivated by wounded pride:

> Have they not sword-players, and every sort
> Of gymnic artists, wrestlers, riders, runners,
> Jugglers and dancers, antics, mummers, mimics,
> But they must pick me out with shackles tired,
> And over-laboured at their public mill,
> To make them sport with blind activity?
>
> (1323–8)

Again he is on the point of doing the right thing for the wrong reason. However, when the Officer reminds him that he should obey for his own safety's sake, Samson remembers that his own safety is not important, that his strength is God's gift and must not, especially now that he has hope of pardon, be profaned in 'feats and play before their gods' (1340).

Ultimately, then, Samson refuses to accompany the Officer because he realises that, in doing so, he would be breaking God's law and prostituting his 'consecrated gift/ Of strength' (1354–5) to the amusement of idol-worshippers. His choice is to obey God's law or the Philistines' command—and, since he has free will, the choice is his alone:

> the Philistian lords command.
> Commands are no constraints. If I obey them,

> I do it freely; venturing to displease
> God for the fear of man, and man prefer,
> Set God behind: which in his jealousy
> Shall never, unrepented, find forgiveness.
>
> (1371–6)

It is a confirmation of Samson's faith and humility that, in the end, he gives credence to the supreme value: he determines to obey God's law, whatever the consequences to himself. But he goes further, for he declares that God

> may dispense with me or thee
> Present in temples at idolatrous rites
> For some important cause.
>
> (1377–9)

He will not obey the Philistines' command—but if, he says, *God* were to command his presence at the pagan temple, he would obey without hesitation and without question. For the moment, however, he has received no such direction and so is forced to decline to accompany the Officer. He has finally learned that they also serve who only stand and wait.

Entirely baffled by Samson's determination to disobey the Officer, the Chorus can only observe in uncomprehending astonishment, 'How thou wilt here come off surmounts my reach.' (1380) No one in the play understands fully the reasons for Samson's decision and, at this point, he is completely isolated from everyone—except God. Until God indicates otherwise, Samson is resolved to pass his days in patient waiting; he has become at last a true hero, one who exemplifies that 'better fortitude/ Of patience and heroic martyrdom' of which Milton had sung in *Paradise Lost*. His regeneration is now complete. Having learned and accepted the lessons of humility, faith and patience, Samson has been renovated and sanctified 'both soul and body ... to God's service and to good works' (*DDC*, I, xviii; *YP*, VI, p. 461). And it is precisely at this point, at the culmination of his regenerative experience, that Samson is made aware by 'intimate impulse' of the *vocatio specialis* recalling him to divine service: 'I begin to feel/ Some rousing motions in me which dispose/ To something extraordinary my thoughts.' (1381–3) Directed by the Spirit of God, he is now prepared to accompany the Philistian Officer:

> I with this messenger will go along,
> Nothing to do, be sure, that may dishonour
> Our Law, or stain my vow of Nazarite.
> If there be aught of presage in my mind,
> This day will be remarkable in my life
> By some great act, or of my days the last.
>
> (1384–9)

He does not know the particulars of the duties to which God, through the Officer, is summoning him, but he is fully aware of the vocational significance of the 'rousing motions': he has been readmitted to divine service, and his prophesied mission is to find expression in some glorious action—perhaps his last. In going to the pagan temple, Samson transgresses the Law out of respect to the will of the Lawgiver—an action paralleled in his marriage at God's command to the Timnite woman.[9] His career has come full circle, and it is once again as God's active champion that Samson, humbled and trusting in the yet unrevealed will of his divine Master, freely follows the Officer to Dagon's festival and to the fulfilment of the promise of his nativity.

MANOA AND THE CHORUS: LINES 1441–1758

If 'true experience' and an understanding of God's ways to men are achieved by Samson in the first four movements of the play, then it is the function of the fifth and final movement to educate Manoa and the Chorus—in the degree appropriate to them[10]—in these same virtues.

At the beginning of this last movement, Manoa arrives to share with the Chorus his hope that he can ransom his son from the Philistines. Manoa, who operates on a lower level of awareness than either Samson or the Chorus, judges everything in purely human terms. And, as Don Cameron Allen notes, the characterisation of Manoa is perhaps Milton's broadest irony, for, wanting a true conception of God's mysterious ways, Manoa unwittingly substitutes himself for God.[11] Like God, Manoa is concerned with his son's redemption; however, whereas Manoa (characteristically) thinks of redemption only in physical and monetary terms,

> For his redemption all my patrimony,
> If need be, I am ready to forgo
> And quit,

(1482–4)

God's concern is purely spiritual. Manoa, writes R. B. Wilken-feld, 'would just change Samson's physical location—from a prison house to a domestic house—without transforming the inner man'.[12] Ironically, while Manoa has been treating with the Philistian lords about his son's physical redemption, Samson has, with God's aid, undergone a spiritual transformation that has released him from bondage to sin and death; and, moreover, as Manoa and the Chorus speak of the former's attempts to ransom his son, Samson is simultaneously performing that one final act which will at once secure his physical release from Philistian bondage and mark the resolution, in action, of his spiritual metamorphosis and prophesied vocation to deliver Israel from Philistian control.

Awareness on a lower level, however, is not confined to Manoa alone. The Chorus has not recognised the significant spiritual pattern of Samson's responses to his visitors in the earlier movements of the drama. Nor, it will be remembered, have they understood Samson's decision initially to disobey the Officer's command or his ultimate resolution, prompted by the 'rousing motions' of God's call, to accompany the Officer to Dagon's festival. 'The Chorus', writes Joseph Summers,

> is often wrong in typically unheroic ways, and . . . only as a result of the action does it acquire 'true experience' and understanding. Those Danites, friends and contemporaries of Samson, represent the 'conventional wisdom' of the drama; but the premise of the poem is that conventional wisdom is inadequate for tragic experience.[13]

Neither the Chorus nor Manoa can share directly in Samson's special calling, which implies a degree of grace greater than that offered to them; but they are expected to see in Samson's career an analogue, pitched at a higher level than is required of them, of their own vocation to rebirth—and an *exemplum* of the spiritual heroism that frees the responsive servant from the prison of sin and death.

At lines 1596–1659, the Messenger describes in detail the circumstances of Samson's death. He relates that, in spite of the scorn and derision which rang out at his appearance, Samson was 'patient and undaunted' and that he stood before destroying the temple

> with head a while inclined,
> And eyes fast fixed . . . as one who prayed,
> Or some great matter in his mind revolved.
>
> (1636–8)

Even here Samson has free will. The act of pulling down the temple is an act of responsive choice, a free action in which the will of the instrument co-operates with, and is submerged in, the will of God. Moreover, although neither Samson nor the other characters are aware of it, the Hebrew champion's deed is resonant with prefigurative values: his posture in the temple—arms outstretched to the massy pillars—adumbrates a later event, and his physical deliverance of his nation from bondage likewise anticipates, on a smaller scale, the Messiah's mission of universal salvation.

Finally, for the Chorus and for Manoa the spiritual pattern of Samson's victory begins to take form. With the degree of grace and revelation available to them, the members of the Danite Chorus recognise that 'living or dying' Samson has 'fulfilled/ The work for which [he was] foretold/ To Israel' (1661–3), and they appreciate that he has not died ignobly or unheroically but as God's servant and guided by His 'uncontrollable intent'. They are, too, vaguely aware of the magnitude of the events they have witnessed and, albeit with unconscious irony, they are led to articulate their sense of momentous occurrence in an image which later generations in another dispensation were to reserve exclusively (or nearly so) for the Resurrection:

> But he though blind of sight,
> Despised and thought extinguished quite,
> With inward eyes illuminated
> His fiery virtue roused
> From under ashes into sudden flame,
> . . . .
> So virtue given for lost,

> Depressed, and overthrown, as seemed,
> Like that self-begotten bird
> In the Arabian woods embossed,
> That no second knows nor third,
> And lay erewhile a holocaust,
> From out her ashy womb now teemed,
> Revives, reflourishes, then vigorous most
> When most unactive deemed,
> And though her body die, her fame survives,
> A secular bird ages of lives.
>
> (1687–1706)

The frame of reference is temporal ('secular' means 'lasting for ages') rather than eternal, and the fame envisaged is but terrestrial—yet, for all that, the Chorus's phoenix is an eager fledgling, straining upward for a transcendent reality. Manoa, predictably, approaches the matter of Samson's death from a more empirical angle; but even he, with his limited vision, finds consolation and a measure of spiritual insight: 'Samson hath quit himself/ Like Samson', he declares, and has conferred upon Israel

> Honour . . . and freedom, let but them
> Find courage to lay hold on this occasion,
> To himself and father's house eternal fame;
> And which is best and happiest yet, all this
> With God not parted from him, as was feared,
> But favouring and assisting to the end.
>
> (1715–20)

To these bystanders, it is apparent that Samson's recovery of lost virtue has restored him to his rightful place as God's 'faithful champion'. His victory, they realise, is as much spiritual as physical—his victory over himself as significant as that over the flower of Philistia. With new understanding and a new sense of religious purpose gleaned from Samson's exemplary experience, the Hebrew Chorus takes its leave at the end of the play:

> All is best, though we oft doubt,
> What the unsearchable dispose
> Of highest wisdom brings about,
> And ever best found in the close.

> Oft he seems to hide his face,
> But unexpectedly returns
> And to his faithful champion hath in place
> Bore witness gloriously; whence Gaza mourns
> And all that band them to resist
> His uncontrollable intent,
> His servants he with new acquist
> Of true experience from this great event
> With peace and consolation hath dismissed,
> And calm of mind all passion spent.
>
> (1745–58)

And, lest we miss the point of this *nunc dimittis*, the reader—with his knowledge of written revelation and typology—is also expected to lay down *Samson Agonistes* with new insight into the mysterious workings of Providence: 'For mine eyes have seen thy salvation, Which thou hast prepared before the face of all people; A light to lighten the Gentiles, and the glory of thy people Israel.' (Luke 2: 30–2)

6 *Paradise Regained*

BOOK I: THE VOCATIONAL FRAMEWORK

Paradise Regained begins with an identity crisis.[1] When the young Jesus arrives at the Jordan to receive baptism, he does not seem in any way different from those other 'sons of God' thronging the banks and awaiting the purifying touch of John the Baptist. His obscurity and anonymity are, however, shortlived. The 'great proclaimer' recognises him to be the Messiah—and, immediately thereafter, there comes the divine annunciation establishing his heavenly lineage:

> on him baptized
> Heaven opened, and in likeness of a dove
> The Spirit descended, while the Father's voice
> From heaven pronounced him his beloved Son.
>
> (29–32)

From this point onward, the Son's identity is a problem only for Satan.

The annunciation at Bethabara does not lead (as one might expect) either to an explanation of the event from the mouth of God or to Christ's own understanding of the revelation, but rather to Satan's reaction and the calling of a council of devils. As in *Paradise Lost*, Satan is the first speaker in the poem. Although the events at the Jordan have been factually set down by the narrator, the first interpretation of these events belongs to Satan—and, for Satan, the crux of the annunciation is the identification of his adversary. Is this 'man' whom John has baptised the same as he who defeated the rebel angels and cast them, flaming, headlong from the height of heaven? And what did the Father mean in proclaiming him 'my beloved Son'?—for the phrase (as Satan later observes) is ambiguous:

> The Son of God . . . bears no single sense;
> The Son of God I also am, or was,
> And if I was, I am; relation stands;
> All men are Sons of God. . . .
>
> (IV, 517–20)

The pattern of Satan's temptations and the inevitability of his defeat are predetermined by the fact that he never progresses beyond the identity problem and so is never able to meet Jesus, who has no doubt about the sense in which he is *the* 'Son of God', on any common spiritual or intellectual ground.

Aristically, Milton had to face the problem of making the satanic position credible. If the dramatic conflict between Christ and Satan were to succeed aesthetically, then the confrontation in the desert would have to be made plausible for readers already aware of the outcome. Christ would win, of course, and Satan would lose; but, if any degree of dramatic intensity were to be maintained, then the satanic position must not seem hopeless and utterly doomed from the outset. Milton solved this difficulty in part by stressing the Son's humanity, his fallibility, and by presenting him as an 'exalted man' rather than an incarnate deity. But he added another and more subtle dimension to the characterisation of his protagonists merely by permitting Satan to speak first. Before Christ actually appears in the poem or the nature of his mission is described by God, Satan is allowed to express his understanding and doubts concerning his antagonist. Thus, the reader who (like Satan) has no clear conception of how the Son will be presented is first introduced to the satanic viewpoint. For an instant, the reader is forced to share Satan's dilemma over the Son's identity and is invited, when he has no divine viewpoint to correct his understanding, to succumb to the self-deluding rhetoric of the Devil. Since the reader has been given no counter-argument with which to refute Satan's conception of Christ, it is impossible as the poem begins to reject Satan's reasoning out-of-hand; and the reader's initial understanding of Christ is thus postulated on demonic casuistry. Only gradually, as the Son fulfils his potential through responsive growth in rejecting temptation and as the reader's developing insight parallels Christ's own deepening awareness of his role, is the initial and satanic view of Christ rejected. Having been himself, in some degree, the victim of Satan's rhetoric, the reader is in a position to accept the

Devil as a formidable adversary and to suspend his disbelief willingly, for Satan seems stronger than he really is.

Satan tells those gathered in 'gloomy consistory' to hear him that only swift action is required in the face of this new threat:

> Ye see our danger on the utmost edge
> Of hazard, which admits no long debate,
> But must with something sudden be opposed,
> Not force, but well-couched fraud, well-woven snares,
> Ere in the head of nations he appear
> Their king, their leader, and supreme on earth.
>
> (94–9)

These lines stress, of course, the urgency of opposing the Son and, as well, the satanic conception of Christ as a rival, a threat to the materialistic dominion of the devils. But they also stress Satan's belief in the necessity and ultimate efficacy of action—even if it be no more than action for action's sake. Patience is, for Satan, an unknown and incomprehensible state of being, and he is in no way prepared for his encounter with the originator of Christian heroism, where obedience is often passive.

The poem's major vocational motif[2] is introduced in the Father's monologue:

> this man born and now upgrown,
> To show him worthy of his birth divine
> And high prediction, henceforth I expose
> To Satan;
> . . . .
>
> I mean
> To exercise him in the wilderness,
> There he shall first lay down the rudiments
> Of his great warfare, ere I send him forth
> To conquer Sin and Death the two grand foes,
> By humiliation and strong sufferance.
>
> (140–3, 155–60)

The trial in the desert has been engineered by God as the means of leading Christ to an understanding of his mission and asserting his Sonship. In the 'great duel' with Satan he will learn how he is to 'save his people from their sins' (Matthew 1:21), and the

spiritual conflict with the Devil will cause him to 'lay down the
rudiments/ Of his great warfare' — that is, to define in practice
(though not necessarily in action, for the moment) the tenets of
that Christian heroism which shall 'earn salvation for the sons of
men' (167). For the Son the experience in the wilderness is a
voyage of self-discovery; and the subject of the poem is, indeed,
none other than Christ's deepening self-awareness, his growing
understanding of his announced role as Saviour and his attainment through trial of that self-knowledge and that vocational
insight which are the prerequisites of his sacred mission. The
victory over Sin and Death and the ultimate defeat of Satan,
although implied in the spiritual conflict and victory described in
Paradise Regained, lie beyond the direct and immediate concerns of
the poem. Before he is sent forth to conquer 'the two grand foes,/
By humiliation and strong sufferance', the Son must be educated
in the requirements of his vocation as Messiah.

When Christ is introduced after his Father's monologue, he is
presented as 'much revolving in his breast' those vocational
problems whose resolution constitutes the substance of the poem:

> How best the mighty work he might begin
> Of saviour to mankind, and which way first
> Publish his godlike office now mature.
>
> (186–8)

Guided by the Holy Spirit, he leaves Bethabara where John had
baptised him and enters the desert alone to reflect upon the
meaning of the annunciation at Jordan and to come to a fuller
understanding of his role. As our initial view of Milton's Samson
had shown us a man caught in the disparity between fact and
prophecy in his career as Israel's deliverer, so here the events at
Bethabara have made Christ acutely aware of the discrepancy
between, on the one hand, the prophecies concerning his mission
and his inner assurances of potential, and, on the other hand, the
recognition that to date he has accomplished nothing, that his
premonitions of future achievement are 'Ill sorting with my
present state' (200). Although he knows himself to be the Messiah
and has, with the aid of Old Testament prophecy, arrived at a
general understanding of his mission, he does not know how he is
expected to begin the active work of redemption. The time to act,
to inaugurate his public ministry, has come; yet he cannot

discover either from scripture or from within himself any sure way to fulfil the authority he has derived from heaven. Nevertheless, he knows himself to be under divine protection and guidance; and so, unlike Satan—whom we have seen to be committed to a doctrine of action—Christ is prepared to await the decrees of heaven with patience:

> by some strong motion I am led
> Into this wilderness, to what intent
> I learn not yet, perhaps I need not know;
> For what concerns my knowledge God reveals.
>
> (290–3)

We are reminded almost inevitably of Samson led off to Dagon's temple by the inner summons of God's 'rousing motions'. The distinction, however, is that Christ already possesses as *Paradise Regained* begins the patience, faith and humility that the hero of *Samson Agonistes* earns through trial as the play progresses—and so, while Samson's *vocatio specialis* asserts itself in a sudden awareness of divine prompting just before the catastrophe, Christ is aware of his special calling throughout. Like Samson, however, Christ must assist divine disposal by his own responsive choices. In the postlapsarian world virtue is only truly virtue when it has survived trial and temptation—and the Son's virtue in *Paradise Regained* does not long remain fugitive and cloistered.

Satan arrives masquerading as 'an aged man in rural weeds' (314). After outlining the miseries and hardships which the desert-dweller endures, Satan invites the Son to demonstrate his divinity by turning stones into bread, and the insidiousness of this seemingly simple request is obscured by what Arnold Stein has happily termed the 'bait of charity':[3]

> if thou be the Son of God, command
> That out of these hard stones be made thee bread;
> So shalt thou save thyself and us relieve
> With food, whereof we wretched seldom taste.
>
> (342–5)

But Christ is not deceived either by Satan's disguise or by the temptation which he perceives to be a trial of his faith; and with commendable wit he turns the words back upon the tempter with the observation that 'lying is thy sustenance, thy food' (429). The essence of the temptation is this: Satan invites the Son to presume by performing a miracle, to act on the knowledge that he is the Messiah but to do so without divine approval. He asks him, that is, to take the Law into his own hands and so to become, like Satan himself, not only disobedient but also the rebellious rival of God. But Christ, knowing that obedience does not always involve activity and that he must follow God's will—whatever that may be and whenever it may be revealed—rather than the promptings of his own or another's will, has learned (in Northrop Frye's words) 'to will to relax the will, to perform real acts in God's time and not pseudo-acts in his own'.[4]

Repulsed and 'now undisguised', Satan argues himself to be the agent of Omnipotence, a kind of junior partner of God. In his divinely motivated role as official tempter, he maintains, he often freely offers his help and support to men:

> lend them oft my aid,
> Oft my advice by presages and signs,
> And answers, oracles, portents and dreams,
> Whereby they may direct their future life.
>
> (393–6)

Satan's oracular claims elicit from the Son a positive statement of messianic vocation: 'God hath now sent his living oracle/ Into the world, to teach his final will.' (460–1) Up to this point his responses have been negative: he has told Satan he will *not* do. Here, both for Satan and himself, he outlines his messianic function in positive terms and at the same time asserts the alternative which he will oppose to the satanic exhortation to presumptuous action: he is not a free agent but is rather God's 'living oracle' sent to teach God's will and not to indulge his own whims. In declaring that he is God's 'living oracle', the Son unequivocally proclaims that he is the Messiah and thus solves the identity problem which has plagued Satan since the annunciation at Bethabara. Satan, however, is unwilling to accept the identification. Only an outright miracle—such as the turning of stones into bread—would suffice to eradicate or cast uncertainty upon his assiduously fostered delusion concerning the Son's identity.

Satan terminates and at the same time extends the scope of his attack on Christ's faith with the designing suggestion that the Son should imitate his Father:

> Thy father, who is holy, wise and pure,
> Suffers the hypocrite or atheous priest
> To tread his sacred courts, and minister
> About his altar, handling holy things,
> Praying or vowing, and vouchsafed his voice
> To Balaam reprobate, a prophet yet
> Inspired; disdain not such access to me.
>
> (486–92)

The request seems innocent enough—but two important principles are involved. First, if the Son grants willing audience and even tolerance to Satan, then his obedience will be to the will of the Devil rather than to that of God. Second, obedience to God and imitation of God, though yoked together by satanic implication, are not identical motives to action. In asking the Son to imitate his Father's tolerance and mercy, Satan is inviting him to usurp and employ, as his own, attributes and functions pertaining to the Father alone. Undeceived by the tempter's efforts to draw him into an act of presumption by insistence upon what Satan erroneously supposes to be the inalienable rights of divine Sonship, Christ counters the assault on his faith by an 'act' of passive obedience:

> Thy coming hither, though I know thy scope,
> I bid not or forbid; do as thou find'st
> Permission from above; thou canst not more.
>
> (494–6)

And, uncertain how next to proceed against so formidable an opponent, a bewildered and (for the moment) defeated Satan, 'bowing low/ His grey dissimulation, disappeared/ Into thin air diffused' (497–9).

BOOK II: 'LAWFUL DESIRES OF NATURE'

Book II opens with the reaction of the Apostles to Christ's disappearance after the annunciation at Bethabara. Their doubt is not occasioned by uncertainty over Christ's identity—they know him to be the promised Saviour; rather, it springs from their imperfect understanding of the messianic mission. As with the Son himself (cf. I, 196–293), the Apostles' incomplete awareness of the divine plan precludes their understanding fully how the Messiah is to inaugurate and accomplish the task of universal redemption. Unlike Christ, however, whom the Father had hailed as 'This perfect man, by merit called my Son' (I, 166), the Disciples are average and therefore very fallible mortals. And, whereas Christ had faced the vocational uncertainty of how best to prosecute the 'authority . . . derived from heaven' (I, 289) by trusting in God for direction and resigning himself willingly to the active inactivity of standing and awaiting his Father's commands, the impatient Disciples respond to Christ's disappearance, firstly, by ever-increasing doubts and, secondly, by unnecessary and fruitless activity. With diligence and zeal they searched for their 'lost' Messiah—'but returned in vain' (24). Then, having failed to find Christ and still unable to account for his disappearance, they gather 'in a cottage low' and pray that God will return the Messiah to them. But suddenly, in mid-sentence, the tone and direction of the speech changes, by abrupt peripeteia, from doubt to certainty and from a prayer for divine intervention to a recognition of the need on man's part for faith and patience:

> But let us wait; thus far [God] hath performed,
> Sent his anointed, and to us revealed him
> . . . .
>   he will not fail
> Nor will withdraw him now, nor will recall,
> Mock us with his blest sight, then snatch him hence,
> Soon we shall see our hope, our joy return.
>   (49–50, 54–7)

Allowing for the fact that the Apostles operate in a lower stratum of awareness than Christ and that they therefore entertain doubts and fears foreign to his perfect humanity, their choric *planctus* nonetheless parallels, with some thematic variation and change of emphasis, the Son's long vocational meditation in Book I. And their patient submission to the divine will, their resolve to lay 'all our fears/ . . . on his providence' (53–4), is the same in substance and intent as Christ's earlier self-abnegating statement of absolute trust (I, 290–3). Like the Son, the Apostles have learned to will to relax the will, a spiritual state which is the apex of self-knowledge and the apotheosis of human potential.

Mary's soliloquy follows, *mutatis mutandis*, the same pattern as the Apostles' monologue. Mary is initially troubled by her son's unexplained disappearance, and she senses, too, the tension between prophecy and accomplished fact in his career. The 'troubled thoughts' raised in her heart are, however, soon quelled by the same patient faith that had resolved the Apostles' doubts: 'But I to wait with patience am inured.' (102) And so it is 'with thoughts/ Meekly composed' that Mary patiently 'awaited the fulfilling' (107–8) of the prophecies concerning her son.

After Mary's monologue, the scene shifts to the 'middle region of thick air' where Satan addresses 'all his potentates in council' (117–18). His speech, like those of the Apostles and Mary, opens on a note of uncertainty and doubt. Typically, however, and in contrast to the other speakers in Book II, Satan's doubt resolves itself into a determination to act—and he terminates the council with a renewed commitment to assertive self-expression: 'I shall let pass/ No advantage, and his strength as oft assay' (233–4).

Meanwhile, the Son has spent forty days of fasting, 'with holiest meditations fed':

> All his great work to come before him set;
> How to begin, how to accomplish best
> His end of being on earth, and mission high.
> (112–14)

Significantly, these vocational ruminations repeat the pattern to which I have drawn attention in the earlier speeches of the other characters in Book II. The Son begins with a rhetorical questioning of Providence:

> Where will this end? Four times ten days I have passed
> Wandering this woody maze, and human food
> Nor tasted, nor had appetite;
> . . . .
> But now I feel I hunger, which declares,
> Nature hath need of what she asks. . . .
> (245–7, 252–3)

But any vestige of self-centredness or doubt is quickly replaced by selfless obedience: 'yet God/ Can satisfy that need some other way,/ Though hunger still remain.' (253–5)

The thematic pattern stressed in the opening half of Book II, then, is that of doubt and impatience yielding to faith and patience. Each of the characters—the Apostles, Mary, Satan, and Christ—begins with an expression of doubt, but each, except Satan, succeeds in denying the importunate claims of his individual will and placing his trust in the divine will which, he knows, will be revealed to him in God's own time. The pattern is paradigmatic of the thematic development within the epic as a whole. *Paradise Regained* is concerned with the annihilation of the self and the stages by which the Son—whose experience is exemplary—grows toward the final attainment of this ideal of theological 'negative capability'. The protagonist of the poem is more than a symbol of salvation; he is an exemplar, a model for human imitation. The reader is being informed that he must participate in the Son's *agon* in a real, rather than in a merely ritualistic, way; and it is the function of the monologues of the Apostles and Mary to remind the reader of his co-operative responsibility for his own salvation, by reinforcing the central thematic pattern (seen in Christ's responses to Satan) of progressively devalued self-assertion. Satan, of course, is intended as a negative example: his wilfulness, contrasted with the Son's selfless passivity, makes him God's rival; and his frustration and ultimate fate are warnings of the inevitable lot awaiting those who commit themselves to the delusion of self-sufficiency.

Over half-way through Book II, the tempter reappears to renew his assaults. Reminding the Son of his hunger and urging his 'right' to 'all created things' (324), Satan causes an exquisite banquet to appear out of thin air. The banquet is designed to satisfy what Satan argues to be all 'Lawful desires of nature' (230)[5] and therefore comprehends all sensory and sensual gratifications. The satisfaction of a bodily appetite in moderation is not in itself a sin, but it may become so if an ethical or moral issue is involved. In 'temperately' declining to partake of the banquet, the Son bases his refusal not so much on the gift itself as on the source of the gift and on the satanic implications that, if Christ eats, he thereby declares his 'right' to all created things (II, 378–84). Moreover, since Satan—in his customary materialistic manner—has offered to assuage only physical hunger, the Son, who is 'fed with better thoughts that feed/ Me hung'ring more to do my Father's will' (258–9), trenchantly demands of Satan, 'And with my hunger what hast thou to do?' (389)

The tempter's next appeal is based directly on the identity and vocational issues. How does Christ propose to come to power in Israel without powerful allies and riches adequate to retain an armed force? Satan, therefore, counsels the amassing of riches and is, of course, prepared to show the Son—if he will sacrifice his patience and obedience—precisely how such wealth is to be gained. The Son readily disparages the offer of wealth without virtue, valour and wisdom: 'Wealth without these three is impotent.' (433) True kingship depends not on riches but on virtue and wisdom, and it is available to everyone, for it is nothing other than man's sovereignty over himself—a sovereignty which becomes yet more kingly when it serves as the means of leading others to self-knowledge and the knowledge of God:

> to guide nations in the way of truth
> By saving doctrine, and from error lead
> To know, and, knowing worship God aright,
> Is yet more kingly. . . ,
>
> (473–6)

This statement is the second positive vocational assertion in the poem. At the end of Book I, Christ had declared himself God's prophet. Here, at the close of Book II, he extends his vocational awareness by declaring himself his Father's priest, whose function is to teach—by both precept and example—the doctrine of salvation and to lead men from darkness into light.

BOOK III: GLORY, FALSE ZEAL, AND PARTHIA

While there is no break in the action between Books II and III, Satan's offers—which proceed through a scale of worldly values—become less material in the third book. The temptations of the second book concentrate on the lowest and most concrete objects of worldly attainment: bodily luxury (in all its forms) and material wealth. In the third book the emphasis shifts to appeals which are more abstract and, correspondingly, more subtle.

Supporting his case with the youthful accomplishments of such military heroes as Alexander, Scipio Africanus and Julius Caesar,

Satan opens Book III by arguing that it is time for the Son, who has displayed greater virtue and personal integrity than any of these pagan conquerors, to seek glory in action: 'Thy years are ripe, and over-ripe' (31). Essentially, the temptation is to presumptuous action and involves the usurpation of praises due only to the Father. Refusing to play God, the Son scorns the brutish fame of conquerors and the praise of the ignorant multitude. Against the illusory and transitory glory of earth he juxtaposes the 'true glory and renown' that is spiritual and eternal, the fame of heroes who have achieved true renown without seeking it:

> This is true glory and renown, when God,
> Looking on the earth, with approbation marks
> The just man, and divulges him through heaven
> To all his angels, who with true applause
> Recount his praises; thus he did to Job. . . .
>
> (60–4)

Glory is God's gift to the deserving and is earned by patience and obedience to the divine will rather than by self-assertive and self-motivated action. Christ *is* the Son and instrument of God, but his *right* to that title and mission depends upon his obedience to his omnipotent Father's will.

The satanic frustration, which increases as Christ rejects each successive temptation, is the result of genuine confusion on the tempter's part. It is, for example, inconceivable to Satan that the Son should scorn so lightly and categorically his offer of glory. As an abstract object of ambition, glory—which Satan has sacrificed all in an effort to gain—is the highest attainment of which the satanic mind can conceive. Glory is the reward of power and is exacted by God, who is Power itself, from all creation. Satan's God is a tyrant consumed by vanity, who wields his absolute power with arbitrary indifference; and the Son, Satan reasons, should be the reflection of his Father:

> Think not so slight of glory; therein least
> Resembling thy great Father: he seeks glory,
> And for his glory all things made, all things
> Orders and governs. . . .
>
> (109–12)

The unchecked absolutism, which Satan's distorted view of God and His glory assumes axiomatically, is an object of envy; indeed, it had been envy (coupled with pride) that had motivated his abortive rebellion against the Creator. At the same time, however, God's absolute power is—as Satan had learned to his sorrow—incompatible with any rival authority. And Satan hopes that with demonic guidance the Son may be tricked into repeating the satanic experience. If he can excite envy of the Father's power and glory in the Son, then Christ, too, will become God's rival. But Christ, seeking God's glory and not his own, easily rejects the offer of glory.

In all of his temptations Satan fails—but he never really understands why he fails. It is his inability to anticipate and, after the event, to comprehend his failures that accounts for his growing frustration and confusion. And the explanation of his ill success, although he himself does not realise it, is apparent in his 'confession' in Book III:

> all hope is lost
> Of my reception into grace; what worse?
> For where no hope is left, is left no fear;
> If there be worse, the expectation more
> Of worse torments me than the feeling can.
> I would be at the worst; worst is my port,
> My harbour and my ultimate repose,
> The end I would attain, my final good.
>
> (204–11)

There is, it seems at first, a certain nobility in this unexpected confession, and the extent of self-knowledge revealed surprises the reader who has anticipated no such despairing admission of guilt from Satan. It was, no doubt, a surprise to the Son as well. And it was intended to be so—for Satan, following his confession with a plea for intercession, expected to catch the Son off-guard and so trick him into exercising his mediatorial office prematurely and thus presumptuously, and into extending mercy (which is God's function) to one for whom both repentance and forgiveness are alike impossible.

Although designed as a ruse, Satan's confession reveals much about his distorted reasoning and explains in large measure his ill success with Christ. The importance of his words becomes apparent when they are set beside an instructive passage of satanic soliloquy in *Paradise Lost*:

> So farewell hope, and with hope farewell fear,
> Farewell remorse: all good to me is lost;
> Evil be thou my good; by thee at least
> Divided empire with heaven's king I hold
> By thee, and more than half perhaps will reign.
>   (IV, 108–12)

Satan, it is clear, is not entirely dissatisfied with his lot: ruling in Hell and on Earth as well is better than serving in Heaven. The precondition of satanic dominion, however, is the espousing of evil and the rejection of good. And Satan's view of himself is Manichean rather than Augustinian; in adopting evil as his good, Satan establishes himself—at least in his own mind—as a second positive cosmic force existing in opposition to Providence. Evil is not merely a void created by the absence of good; it is a positive thing, and the satanic 'empire' is the alternative to Heaven. Thus, when the tempter in *Paradise Regained* says,

> I would be at the worst; worst is my port,
> My harbour and my ultimate repose,
> The end I would attain, my final good,

he is obliquely arguing his claim to infernal dominion and his desire to consolidate his holdings. But his devotion to evil and his substitution of evil for good have hopelessly distorted his view of his antagonist. He thinks of the Son as his rival, a potential usurper, and attempts to treat with him as he would with a would-be Satan. Since he has inverted the relative values of good and evil, Satan is unable to appreciate either the Son's nature or mission, and his temptations are doomed from the outset because they are aimed at an *alter ego* rather than at an opposite.

The subject of Book III of *Paradise Regained* is kingship, a subject anticipated in Christ's statement about true sovereignty (kingship over the self) at the end of Book II. Kingship is the third and final aspect of Christ's office, the other two being his roles as prophet (Book I) and as priest (Book II).[6] Satan knows from scripture that Christ is to rule Israel, and he interprets the prophecy literally to mean that the Son is 'ordained/ To sit upon thy father David's throne' (152–3). And so, when the Son rejects the abstract theory of kingship and the necessity of immediate action to obtain his throne which Satan proposes, the tempter's literal-mindedness suggests that real and concrete examples of 'regal arts,/ And regal mysteries' may have more appeal than mere theory. Taking Christ up into a mountain, therefore, he displays to his view all the powerful cities and kingdoms of the earth, settling finally on Parthia, the foremost symbol of military strength and efficiency. But 'Israel's true king' has already explained to his uncomprehending antagonist that his reign is to be spiritual rather than temporal. Here he is content to observe that all arms are vanity, an 'argument/ Of human weakness rather than of strength' (401–2); his own weapons are spiritual, and his time to wield them and to establish his kingdom in men's souls has not yet come.

BOOK IV: ROME, ATHENS, AND THE TEMPLE

The offer of Parthia is quickly followed by that of Rome, the symbol of opulence, luxury and decadence. The wealth and power of Rome, argues Satan, are the keys to domination of the world. Satan's literal interpretation of the prophecies concerning the Son's messianic vocation have caused him once again to offer Christ the wrong kind of throne. Nevertheless, the repeated and uncompromising literalism of the tempter's understanding of the prophesied kingdom succeeds in drawing from the Son a further positive vocational assertion:

> Know therefore when my season comes to sit
> On David's throne, it shall be like a tree
> Spreading and overshadowing all the earth,
> Or as a stone that shall to pieces dash
> All monarchies besides throughout the world,
> And of my kingdom there shall be no end.
>
> (146–51)

Satanic obtuseness had earlier forced Christ to articulate his functions as prophet and priest; here the Son defines, both for Satan and himself, the nature and aim of his ordained kingship, a spiritual vocation which depends neither on time nor space and which is concerned with inner rather than external or worldly sovereignty.

It is at this point that Satan both impudently and, in terms of his own success, inopportunely makes clear to Christ the reason for the trial of the kingdoms:

> All these which in a moment thou behold'st,
> The kingdoms of the world to thee I give
> . . . .
>   if thou wilt fall down,
> And worship me as thy superior lord.
>   (162–3, 166–7)

The boldness of the assertion is occasioned by the desperateness of the tempter's case. Christ responds to the reiterated offer of the worldly kingdoms simply by pointing to the necessity of patient obedience to the will of Him who is alone the one superior Lord. Obedience to the Law and patient endurance have throughout been the Son's spiritual weapons against the formidable batteries of satanic casuistry; and Christ's assertion (IV, 181) that the tempter shall rue this bold and blasphemous request for worship is a reminder that the Son's passivity will give way, shortly, to the prophesied activity of bruising the serpent's head.

With meiosis heightened by the irony of satanic obtusity, the tempter observes that Christ 'seem'st otherwise inclined/ Than to a worldly crown' (212–13). Satan's belated recognition that Christ's kingdom is not a temporal one leads directly to the offer of Athens, 'the eye of Greece, mother of arts/ And eloquence' (240–1). To this point, Satan's temptations have relied on the public glory to be gained from wealth and power; but there remains, as he comes to see, a type of eminence which by its very nature appeals only to a few—the glory of knowledge and intellectual achievement, a form of glory best represented by ancient Athens. Nevertheless, Satan's perverted understanding leads him to treat the supreme accomplishments of Athenian culture—its literature, oratory, and philosophy—as mere stepping-stones to worldly power:

>   Be famous then
> By wisdom; as thy empire must extend,

So let extend thy mind o'or all the world,
In knowledge, all things in it comprehend,
All knowledge is not couched in Moses' law,
The Pentateuch or what the prophets wrote,
The Gentiles also know, and write, and teach
To admiration, led by nature's light;
And with the Gentiles much thou must converse,
Ruling them by persuasion as thou mean'st. . . .
                                        (221–30)

This temptation is the most sophisticated that Satan has been able to formulate, for it appeals precisely to that vocational desire that Christ had spoken of in his first meditation: 'By winning words to conquer willing hearts,/ And make persuasion do the work of fear.' (I, 222–3) But the Son, undeceived, rejects the offer of pagan learning, 'sagely' observing that

> he who receives
> Light from above, from the fountain of light,
> No other doctrine needs, though granted true.
>   (288–90)

In other words, those men who, like Christ and the Old Testament prophets, are God's special servants, are divinely taught; their knowledge is the gift of inspiration, and, for them, that sort of learning which is obtained by 'nature's light' is superfluous, often misleading, and invariably incomplete. The epistemological premise of *Paradise Regained* is that conventional or natural wisdom—like the conventional sorts of power and glory offered earlier by Satan—is entirely inadequate for the Son's understanding and prosecution of his vocation.

Still unable to understand the nature of the Son's prophesied kingdom—'Real or allegoric I discern not' (390)—Satan returns Christ to the wilderness where, abandoning persuasion for the tactics of fear, he afflicts the Son with 'ugly dreams' and the violence of a fierce storm. In the morning, Satan, 'Desperate of better course', removes Christ to the pinnacle of the temple at Jerusalem, where the threatened violence of the nocturnal storm is actualised:

> There stand, if thou wilt stand; to stand upright

> Will ask thee skill; I to thy Father's house
> Have brought thee, and highest placed, highest is best,
> Now show thy progeny; if not to stand,
> Cast thyself down; safely if Son of God. . . .
>
> (551–5)

The Arch Fiend is constrained at last to resort to physical violence in an effort to force Christ either to assert his divine Sonship (by casting himself safely down) or to reveal himself as an impostor (by plunging ignominiously to his death). But the limited scope of Satan's understanding proves inadequate once more to anticipate the Son's response—

> To whom thus Jesus: Also it is written,
> Tempt not the Lord thy God, he said, and stood—
>
> (560–1)

and it is Satan himself who, 'smitten with amazement' (562), falls headlong from the temple's spire.

The *act* of standing on the pinnacle both reaffirms and at the same time resolves the central structural and thematic pattern of the poem, that of a temptation to presumptuous self-assertion opposed by self-abnegating passivity and trusting obedience. In placing Christ on the pinnacle, Satan means to force the Son into performing a self-assertive act; but, surprisingly, Christ responds by manifesting once again that selfless patience and obedience to the Father that has characterised his replies to the tempter throughout the poem. Here, however, the Son's passivity is more significant: the decision to stand on the pinnacle, to confirm obedience by avoiding presumptuous action, is a decision beyond purely human accomplishment—for it is impossible to stand upon the spire without aid. The fact that Christ does stand, thereby performing the humanly impossible, marks the point at which the Son, having annihilated his individual and selfish will, is subsumed into the Father's will, of which he is henceforward the instrument.

In vocational terms, Christ's journey of self-discovery and self-understanding ends, paradoxically, with the total denial of the self. It is only as a result of his supreme act of obedient passivity on the pinnacle that he is able to enter finally upon his mission. He is carried down from the temple by angels, who end their hymn of praise with these words:

> Hail Son of the Most High, heir of both worlds,
> Queller of Satan, on thy glorious work
> Now enter, and begin to save mankind.
>
> (633–5)

Action, formerly the essence of temptation, is now, as the Son embarks on his messianic mission, enjoined as a vocational necessity. And, as the curtain falls on the last act, the 'undoubted Son of God' slips unobtrusively away to begin the task of transforming prophecy into fact.

Appendix
Milton Agonistes: The Date
of *Samson Agonistes*

There has, in recent years, been no more contentious issue among
Miltonists than the date of *Samson Agonistes*. Until thirty years ago
it was almost universally accepted that the play was Milton's last
poetic composition—an assumption based on Jonathan Richardson's assertion, in his influential *Life of Milton* (1734), that 'His
Time was Now [i.e. after 1660] Employ'd in Writing and Publishing, particularly *Paradise Lost*. and after That, *Paradise Regain'd*
and *Samson Agonistes*'.[1] This 'traditional' dating—which places
the compositon of the drama in 1667–70—came under heavy fire
for the first time in 1949, in a special Milton number of *Philological
Quarterly* containing essays by W. R. Parker and Allan H. Gilbert.
Parker argued that *Samson Agonistes* was begun in 1646–7 and
completed in 1653; Gilbert, on the other hand, assigned its
composition to the early 1640s: 'My own impression . . . is that the
tragedy is essentially an early work, following soon after the
making of the notes in the Cambridge Manuscript.'[2] Since 1949
the dispute has raged hotly and, sometimes, acrimoniously. Gilbert's suggestion has attracted no real support; but Parker's
hypothesis—forcefully reasserted by Parker himself and taken up
by a number of other scholars as well—has had considerable
influence.[3] At the same time, however, the traditional date has
been ably defended,[4] and it is fair to say that, at the present time,
scholarly opinion strongly favours a 1667–70 dating.

There remains one further dating proposal, which places the
composition of *Samson Agonistes* in 1660–1—that is, immediately
after the Restoration. Although this conjecture is an old one,
having been first suggested in 1796, it has been largely ignored
and has been advanced in a serious way by only one modern critic,
A. S. P. Woodhouse: 'I do not believe that the poem was the
product or reflection of a normal mood, but rather of a state of
depression not very difficult to imagine in the poet whose world
had collapsed around him and who was blind, disillusioned, ill,
and essentially alone. Such must have been the prevailing mood of

1660–1, when the poem, I suggest, was most probably written.'[5] Unfortunately, Woodhouse does not develop this proposal in detail—though his argument is far from being the 'ill-supported plea' that John Carey (*PM*, p. 332) claims it to be. For a number of years I have believed that a 1660–1 dating has much to recommend it; and the more I have worked with *Samson Agonistes* and the more familiar I have become with the experience and attitudes of Milton himself, the more convinced I have become of the essential rightness of Woodhouse's thesis. To my knowledge, his original motion has never been seconded—nor, although it has often been dismissed, has it been refuted. The argument, then, at least merits reconsideration.

There are some few preliminary observations to be briefly made, however, before coming to the major argument. First, nothing whatever is known for certain about the composition of *Samson Agonistes*. The contemporary biographers give us no help: Edward Phillips (1694) freely admits that 'It cannot certainly be concluded when he wrote his excellent Tragedy entitled *Samson Agonistes*';[6] the anonymous biographer says only that the drama was finished after the Restoration and gives no hint as to when it was begun; John Phillips and Toland (1698) mention it but say nothing about its composition; and neither Aubrey (1681) nor Wood (1691) even mentions the work. W. R. Parker is quite correct in asserting that 'not a scrap of evidence has ever been published to show that it was written late in Milton's life' (*MB*, II, pp. 903–4); but it is equally true—despite Parker's claims to the contrary—that there is no solid evidence to show that it was written in middle life. Certainty on the matter is beyond possibility; and any attempt—including my own—to establish when the poem was written is necessarily grounded on inference and speculation. Second, I am not convinced that Milton's imagery and poetic style provide any real help in determining the date of *Samson Agonistes*. On the one hand, the complicated statistical studies of Miltonic prosody have been inconclusive—indeed, contradictory.[7] And, on the other hand, since Milton frequently re-uses phrases and images employed in earlier pieces, I am profoundly distrustful of arguments relying on parallel images in different works as a basis for dating.[8] Third, since *Samson Agonistes* not only employs rhyme but draws attention to its use, I believe that the play must pre-date 1667, when Milton added to late issues of the first edition of *Paradise Lost*[9] a note on 'The Verse' in which he inveighs against 'the troublesome and modern bondage of rhyming' (*PM*, p. 457).

The major reason for wishing to assign *Samson Agonistes* to 1660–1 depends upon biographical considerations. Biographical readings of the play are, of course, not new. The tradition seems to begin with Bishop Thomas Newton who suggested in his *Life of Milton* (1749) that Milton was attracted to the Samson story by the similarity between his own post-Restoration situation and that of the blind Hebrew champion surrounded by the Philistines. Although others supported Newton's view, it was left for David Masson to develop fully the possibilities of the biographical approach:

But in the entire idea of the drama what else have we than a representation of the Puritan and Republican Milton in his secret antagonism to all the powers and all the fashions of the Restoration? Who are the Philistines but the partisans of the Restoration, all and sundry, its authors and abettors before the fact, and its multitudinous applauders and sycophants through the nation afterwards? Who are the Philistine lords and ladies, and captains, and priests, assembled in their seats within the covered part of the temple of Dagon on the day of festival? Who but Charles himself, and the Duke of York, and the whole pell-mell of the Clarendons, Buckinghams, Buckhursts, Killigrews, Castlemaines, Moll Davises, Nell Gwynns, Sheldons, Morleys, and some hundreds of others.... There were moments, I believe, in Milton's musings by himself, when it was a fell pleasure to him to imagine some exertion of his strength, like that legendary one of Samson's, by which, clutching the two central pillars of the Philistine temple, he might tug and strain till he brought down the whole fabric in crash upon the heads of the heathenish congregation, perishing himself in the act, but leaving England bettered by the carnage. That was metaphorical musing only, a dream of the embers, all fantastical. But was there not a very real sense in which he had been performing feats of strength under the gaze of the Philistine congregation, to their moral amazement, though not to their physical destruction? Degraded at the Restoration, dismissed into obscurity, and thought of for some years, when thought of at all, only as a shackled wretch or monster, incapacitated for farther mischief or farther activity of any kind, had he not re-emerged most gloriously? By his *Paradise Lost* already, and now by his *Paradise Regained* and this very *Samson Agonistes*, he had entitled himself to the place of preeminency in the literature of that Philistine age, the Philistines themselves being the judges. (*LM*, VI, pp. 676–7)

In our own century the biographical approach has been retained by James Holly Hanford, E. M. W. Tillyard, and A. S. P. Woodhouse. Hanford, for example, writes: 'In Samson's career as a champion of God's people [Milton] could see his own earlier heroic efforts in behalf of the good old cause. In the weakness which had betrayed him into the hands of a treacherous woman, he could read the causes of his own marriage disaster. The circumstances which surrounded his hero in blindness and captivity naturally associated themselves with the poet's immediate situation in the Restoration. The spiritual despair and the subsequent sense of God's favor represent an interpretation of the Biblical personality in the light of his own deepest personal emotion.'[10]

In recent years the biographical approach to *Samson Agonistes* has largely been ignored. Either it is thought to be one of those self-evident truths too obvious for comment or, more often, it is seen to be a 'dangerous' approach to the poem—a critical avenue known to exist but not much travelled by the better classes. These attitudes are unfortunate, for they rob the poem of a legitimate level of meaning. 'Samson', warns Anthony Low, 'is not Milton, however, regardless of how much he may reflect Milton's experience. To push autobiographical theories further, as their responsible exponents recognize, is to depart from the play itself.'[11] But surely there is a very real sense in which Samson *is* Milton—precisely because he does reflect so much of Milton's experience. Masson comes, I believe, much closer to the truth of the matter: 'The marvel, then, is that this purely artistic drama, this strictly objective poetic creation, should have been all the while so profoundly and intensely subjective. Nothing put forth by Milton in verse in his whole life is so vehement an exhibition of his personality, such a proclamation of his own thoughts about himself and about the world around him, as his *Samson Agonistes*. But, indeed, there is no marvel in the matter. The Hebrew Samson among the Philistines and the English Milton among the Londoners of the reign of Charles the Second were, to all poetic intents, one and the same person.' (*LM*, VI, p. 670)

I suggested in an earlier chapter (above, p. 81) that Milton
often used poetry as a vehicle for self-analysis and self-discovery.
In the *Vacation Exercise*, the *Nativity Ode* and *Lycidas*, as well as in
Sonnets 7, 19 and *23*, he turned to verse at critical moments in his
life, and in each case the imposition of aesthetic pattern on private
experience enabled him either to resolve a personal crisis or
transcend a personal difficulty by transposing its solution from
the realm of nature to that of grace. *Samson Agonistes* is another
case in point. Milton's own greatest *agon* occurred in the months
following the Restoration of Charles Stuart in May 1660. For
twenty years he had served as the prose prophet of the Puritan
New Jerusalem. With a full and unswerving conviction of national
destiny and of his own prophetic *vocatio specialis*, he had laboured
during these decades, sacrificing both his eyesight and his desire
to write a great national poem, because he was certain that the
Puritan cause was God's cause and that he, John Milton, had
been especially elected to serve as the voice of God's reforming
purpose to His chosen Englishmen. These 'certainties' could not
remain unquestioned, however, after May 1660; and the collapse
of the Puritan dream would necessarily have involved Milton in
vocational reassessment and redefinition—the record of this
experience being chronicled in *Samson Agonistes*.

Virtually nothing is known of Milton's activities in the spring
and summer of 1660. On the advice of friends concerned with his
safety he moved, according to Edward Phillips, 'into a place of
retirement and abscondence' in an unknown 'Friend's House in
Bartholomew-Close, where he liv'd till the Act of Oblivion came
forth'.[12] This enforced isolation gave him the opportunity, and the
need for vocational reconsideration gave him, I believe, the
motive to begin the composition of *Samson Agonistes*. And there is
much in the play's tone and theme that will support this
hypothesis. Samson's isolation, bitterness and despair, for example, almost certainly reflect Milton's own situation and feelings at
the Restoration; and blindness, which useful employment had
made bearable in the prose works of the 1650s, would have
become an intolerable burden to an active champion forced into
retirement and inactivity. But perhaps the most impressive parallels are the thematic ones. *Samson Agonistes* is full of
questions—many of which, as I have suggested in Chapter 5,
centre on the vocational issues of the hero's inner calling to

regeneration and his special calling as Israel's prophesied deliverer:

> Why was my breeding ordered and prescribed
> As of a person separate to God,
> Designed for great exploits; if I must die
> Betrayed, captived, and both my eyes put out,
> Made of my enemies the scorn and gaze. . .?
>
> (30–4)

This is precisely the sort of question which Milton, the blind prophet of national regeneration, must have asked himself in the years 1660–1. Like the degraded Hebrew champion, he must have been deeply troubled by the disparity between fact and promise in his career, between his actual position as the silenced and self-imprisoned spokesman of a lost cause and his expected career—a career underwritten by divine assurances and pledges, as recorded throughout the prose works—as God's chosen prophet and elect instrument in the work of establishing a regenerate nation. Like the fallen Nazarite, he must have wondered how he could now be useful to God, if at all; and he must have canvassed the possibility that his zeal had led him, like Samson, to presumptuous action—that he had, perhaps, been seduced into seeing the Puritan dream as the divine plan for England through his own fervency and the warmth of his own religious convictions. Perhaps Milton himself needed to be reminded that they also serve who only stand and wait.

It seems to me, then, that Samson's experience, as Milton *chose to present it* in his play, provides a correlative to Milton's own vocational concerns immediately after the Restoration. The year 1660 brought with it the need for Milton to rework the terms of his personal covenant with the Lord and *Samson Agonistes* was, I believe, the vehicle by which he was enabled to achieve emotional calm after the wreck of his hopes and vocational redefinition after the collapse of his prophetic calling. At the level of 'general vocation', he was led to see that, while Samson was no longer (as he had been in *Areopagitica*) a possible symbol for England as a corporate whole, his experience of rebirth could be used to represent mimetically the regeneration of those individual Englishmen responsive to the divine invitation to establish the 'paradise within'. In terms of 'special vocation', the fallen Samson's return to divine service provided an analogue to Milton's own discovery—a discovery made, I imagine, in the very process of composing the play—that God had not abandoned him and that he was still expected to employ his divinely implanted talents in God's service. If the Restoration was, for Milton, a political death, it was at the same time a poetic rebirth; and to the 'rousing motions' of his reanimated *vocatio specialis* we owe not only *Samson Agonistes* but *Paradise Regained* and the completion of *Paradise Lost*.

In his argument for an early dating of *Samson Agonistes*, W. R. Parker makes two points which ought, I think, to be challenged. First, he asserts that 'Milton's tragedy, like his anti-prelatical tracts, is almost devoid of theology' (*MB*, II, p. 907), and he goes on to define 'theology' as comprehending the Fall, original sin, Satan, Hell, and the concept of immortality. And, he concludes, unless *Samson Agonistes* were written early—that is, before *De Doctrina Christiana* and *Paradise Lost*—'its severe avoidance of theology . . . [is] difficult to explain' (ibid.). Precisely the reverse seems to me to be true. There is much more to Milton's theology than Parker admits: as I have pointed out both in the Introduction and in Chapter 5, the doctrines of vocation, renovation and regeneration are essential aspects of Milton's soteriology and, as well, are important themes in his *Samson Agonistes*. I would argue, then, that the drama is highly theological; and, given the nature of its theological concerns, I do not see how it is possible that the tragedy could have been composed before the doctrines on which it depends had been worked out in *De Doctrina Christiana*. In the second place, Parker, having noted that none of the alleged personal or political allusions in *Samson Agonistes* can be shown to belong to a period later than 1662, concludes as follows: 'If [these alleged allusions] seem to argue composition in 1661–2, then *Samson Agonistes* and *Paradise Lost* were composed simultaneously —which is highly unlikely in view of Milton's known habits of composition.' (*MB*, II, p. 907) Two points may be made in reply. First, we know very little indeed about Milton's habits of composition, and yet what little we do know will not support Parker's contention: the *Nativity Ode* and *Elegy 6*, for example, seem to have been composed simultaneously, and so, too, do *De Doctrina Christiana* and *Paradise Lost*, at least in the period 1658–60. Second, what is more surprising than that the two poems should have been written together is the fact that *Paradise Lost* flows on with no hint, apart from a few lines early in Book VII (lines 24–8), of the great spiritual *agon* through which its author had passed in the process of its composition. Surely it is strange that an event so momentous (both in personal and in national terms) as the Restoration should have left so little mark on the poem itself—unless, that is, there were an intervening work in which the problems raised by this event were met and resolved. The only possibility for such an intervening work is *Samson Agonistes*.

My view of the matter, then, is that *Samson Agonistes* was begun shortly after May 1660 and that it was completed, probably, in the spring of 1661. It may have been composed simultaneously with *Paradise Lost*; however, in view of the time factor and in view of Milton's need to resolve the vocational issues raised by the Restoration, I am inclined to believe that its composition interrupted and, at the same time, made it possible for Milton to continue with the writing of *Paradise Lost*. It would, of course, have been suicidal to have published a poem containing such obvious and such censorious allusions to the restored regime with the taint of traitor and regicide still on him, and Milton wisely deferred the publication of *Samson Agonistes* for a decade, by which time his former republican activities had been somewhat atoned for by good behaviour and by which time his reputation had been restored (even among Royalists) by his achievement in *Paradise Lost*. I shall conclude by allowing Professor Woodhouse, whose argument the foregoing pages have been designed to endorse and buttress with some further evidence, to summarise his own case:

> If *Samson Agonistes* were the literary solace of Milton's months of hiding, there would be reason enough for its tone of bitterness and despair, for the apparent immediacy of its political allusions to Restoration England, and incidentally for the absence of Edward Phillips when it was composed. On this view Milton would be seen as writing *Samson Agonistes* before completing *Paradise Lost* or dreaming of *Paradise Regained*, and perhaps as achieving by means of the tragedy a partial tranquillizing of his spirit necessary before he could do either.... This is the hypothesis which I would advance, and it appears to me to cover all the principal phenomena, and to be called in question by no known evidence, internal or external. As against Professor Parker's dates, it appears to offer an occasion wholly adequate to call into being the profound passions of the play; and it saves, and accounts for, those scarcely veiled allusions to

the lords of the Restoration and the leaders of the Puritan parties, which he would sacrifice. As against Masson's date [i.e. 1667–70], it avoids the difficulty of the wide interval between the doctrine, temper and tone of *Samson Agonistes* and *Paradise Regained*, and the startling contrast between the mood from which *Samson* takes its rise and the tranquillity, and even cheerfulness, which Milton, by universal testimony, manifested in his later years.[13]

Notes

TO INTRODUCTION

1. Based on *The Shorter Oxford English Dictionary*, 3rd ed., revised (Oxford, 1975), s.v.
2. Old Testament vocation is discussed in greater detail in Chapter 3: cf. below, pp. 82–6.
3. See, for example, the following: Romans 11: 29; Ephesians 1: 18, 4: 4; Philippians 3: 14; 2 Thessalonians 1: 11; 2 Timothy 1: 9; Hebrews 3: 1; 2 Peter 1: 10. Indeed, the only exception in the New Testament is 1 Corinthians 7: 20.
4. Quoted in Heinrich Heppe, *Reformed Dogmatics Set Out and Illustrated from the Sources*, trans. G. T. Thomson (London, 1950), p. 510.
5. Robert Greville, Lord Brooke, in *A Discourse opening the Nature of Episcopacie* (1641; 2nd ed., 1642) defines *recta ratio* or 'right reason' as being 'the candle of God, which he hath lighted in man, lest man groping in the darkness should stumble and fall' (p. 25). See also Douglas Bush, *'Paradise Lost' in Our Time* (Ithaca, N.Y., 1945), p. 37: 'Right reason is not merely reason in our sense of the word; it is not a dry light, a nonmoral instrument of inquiry. Neither is it simply the religious conscience. It is a kind of rational and philosophic conscience which distinguishes man from the beasts and which links man with man and with God. This faculty was implanted by God in all men, Christian and heathen alike, as a guide to truth and conduct. Though its effectual workings may be obscured by sin, it makes man, in his degree, like God; it enables him, within limits, to understand the purposes of a God who is perfect reason as well as perfect justice, goodness, and love.'
6. Quoted in Heppe, *Reformed Dogmatics*, pp. 510–11.
7. By the phrase 'so-called elect' Milton wishes to distinguish his own Arminian view of predestination from both Calvinistic supralapsarianism and infralapsarianism. (Cf. n 14 below.)
8. 'It is by MAN'S RENOVATION that he is BROUGHT TO A STATE OF GRACE AFTER BEING CURSED AND SUBJECT TO GOD'S ANGER' (*DDC*, I, xvii; *YP*, VI, p. 453).
9. 'But vocation, and the consequent change which occurs in the natural man, are parts only of a natural mode of renovation. As a result, if they fall short of regeneration they do not lead to salvation. Matt. xxii. 14: *many are called, few chosen*.' (*YP*, VI, p. 460)
10. Although Milton discusses natural renovation first (Chapter xvii) and then moves on to supernatural renovation in Chapter xviii, it would seem that in at least one sense supernatural must precede natural renovation, for free will must be restored before the sinner is in a position to respond to his

vocation. Cf. *DDC*, I, iv: 'when God determined to restore mankind, he also decided unquestionably (and what could be more just?) to restore some part at least of man's lost freedom of will.' (*YP*, VI, p. 187)

11. Cf. *Paradise Lost*, IX, 351–2: 'But God left free the will, for what obeys/ Reason, is free. . . .' Cf. also *Areopagitica* (*YP*, II, p. 527): 'when God gave [Adam] reason, he gave him freedom to choose, for reason is but choosing; he had bin else a meer artificiall *Adam*, such an *Adam* as he is in the motions.'

12. Calvin, *Institutes of the Christian Religion* (1559), III, xxi, 5; trans. Henry Beveridge, 2 vols (Grand Rapids, Mich., 1970), II, p. 206.

13. Quoted in Carl Bangs, *Arminius: A Study in the Dutch Reformation* (New York, 1971), pp. 66–7.

14. Supralapsarianism is 'the form of the Calvinistic doctrine of Predestination which maintains that God decreed the election and non-election of individual men before the Fall of Adam. Calvin himself regarded Divine Predestination as an inscrutable mystery . . . [and] did not presume to elaborate the whole subject. It was his followers who boldly asserted such doctrines as supralapsarianism. Though logical consistency may appear to favour the supralapsarian position, the milder sublapsarian doctrine has been generally dominant among Calvinists, esp. since the Synod of Dort (1618).' (*ODCC*, p. 1324) Sub- or infralapsarianism holds that the divine decree relative to election and non-election of individuals was enacted only after the Fall.

15. Bangs, *Arminius*, p. 208.

16. Ibid., p. 209. Bangs discusses the theology of Arminius's reply to Perkins on pp. 209–21, and my own summary is much indebted to his thorough examination of the issues. (The *Examination of Perkins' Pamphlet* was published posthumously in 1612.)

17. Ibid., p. 216.

18. Quoted in *SOED* (1975) s.v. Pelagian, and dated 1449; no source given. Not quoted in *OED*.

19. In the *Examination of Perkins' Pamphlet*, Arminius 'emphasises . . . that evangelical grace has to do with man as sinner. . . . [He argues] that "the predestination of which the Scriptures treat is of men as they are sinners". It includes the means by which those who are predestined will be "certainly and infallibly" saved, "but those means are the remission of sins and the renewing of the Holy Ghost and his perpetual assistance even to the end, which means are necessary and communicable to none but sinners". Predestination must then refer to sinners, and it has its ground only in Christ. "Since God can love to salvation (*ad salutem amate possit*) no one who is a sinner unless he be reconciled to himself in Christ, it follows that predestination cannot have had place except in Christ." But Christ was given for sinners, so that "it is certain that predestination and its opposite, reprobation, could not have had place before the sin of man,—I mean, foreseen by God—and before the appointment of Christ as Mediator, and moreover before his discharging, in the foreknowledge of God, the office of Mediator, which appertains to reconciliation".' (Bangs, *Arminius*, pp. 209–10)

20. Bangs, *Arminius*, p. 219.

21. *The Works of James Arminius*, trans. James Nichols and W. R. Bagnall, 3 vols

(Buffalo, N.Y., 1853), I, pp. 565, 568. For a similar statement, see Arminius's *Declaration of Sentiments* (1608), in ibid., I, pp. 247–8. See also Philip Schaff, *The Creeds of Christendom*, 3 vols (New York, 1919), III, pp. 545–9. There is a helpful bibliography in *YP*, VI, p. 80, n 30.

22. Cf. also the following statement: 'It is quite clear, then, that God has predestined from eternity all who would believe and persist in their belief. It follows, therefore, that there is no reprobation except for those who do not believe or do not persist, and that this is rather a matter of consequence than of an express decree by God. Thus there is no reprobation from eternity of particular men. For God has predestined to salvation all who use their free will, on one condition, which applies to all. None are predestined to destruction except through their own fault, and, in a sense, *per accidens.*' (*YP*, VI, p. 190)

23. While Arminius distinguishes between God's absolute and contingent decrees of predestination, Milton argues for a single decree which is a conflation of Arminius's two decrees: 'It seems, then, that predestination and election are not particular but only general: that is, they belong to all who believe in their hearts and persist in their belief. Peter is not predestined or elected as Peter, or John as John, but each only insofar as he believes and persists in his belief. Thus *the general decree of election is individually applicable to each believer*, and is firmly established for those who persevere.' (*YP*, VI p. 176; italics mine.) On Arminius's two decrees, see above, p. 11.

24. Cf. *YP*, VI, pp. 188–9.

25. Cf. above, n 9.

26. Arminius's doctrine of 'unequal grace' is set out in his public disputation *On the Vocation of Men to Salvation* (1609): 'Here Arminius proposes a doctrine of "unequal grace". In implied response to his enemies who had accused him of teaching that God's grace is given equally to all, Arminius turns the tables on them by denying the same. God reserves for himself, says Arminius, the "full and free power . . . of bestowing unequal grace on those who are equals, and equal grace on those who are unequal, nay, of employing greater grace on those who are more wicked".' (Bangs, *Arminius*, p. 323)

27. The *Thirty-Nine Articles* (Church of England), Article x, 'Of Free Will'.

28. On the Reformed doctrines of justification and sanctification, see Heppe, *Reformed Dogmatics*, pp. 543–80, and Philip E. Hughes, *Theology of the English Reformers* (Grand Rapids, Mich., 1965), pp. 47–118.

29. The doctrine is based on Romans 3: 28 ('Therefore we conclude that a man is justified by faith [δικαιοῦσθαι πίστει ἄνθρωπον] without the deeds of the law'), where Luther translates πίστει as *allein durch den Glauben* 'by faith alone'. Luther developed the doctrine of solifidianism, which is the cornerstone of Reformed theology as a whole, in his early tract on Christian liberty, *Von der Freiheit eines Christenmenschen* (1520).

30. 'By the justification of man Holy Scripture thinks not of an inpouring of God's righteousness into him (i.e. not of an *actus physicus*), but of a judicial declaratory act (*actus forensis*) by which God declares man righteous, i.e. to be an object of His good pleasure. Hence justification is an exterior but not an interior change in man.' (Heppe, *Reformed Dogmatics*, pp. 543–4)

31. See also *De Doctrina Christiana*, I, xxii (*YP*, VI, pp. 485–94), and *Paradise Lost*, XII, 293–6:

> Some blood more precious must be paid for man,
> Just for unjust, that in such righteousness
> To them by faith imputed, they may find
> Justification towards God. . . .

32. Heppe, *Reformed Dogmatics*, pp. 565–6.
33. Quoted in Hughes, *Theology of the English Reformers*, p. 81.
34. Heppe, *Reformed Dogmatics*, p. 695.
35. Quoted in ibid., p. 695.
36. Steele, *The Tradesman's Calling* (London, 1684), p. 1
37. Calvin, *Institutes*, III, x, 6; trans. Beveridge, II, p. 34.
38. See M. M. Knappen, *Tudor Puritanism: A Chapter in the History of Idealism* (Chicago, 1939; reprt. 1970), pp. 397–8. For examples of the idea in seventeenth -century Puritanism, see R. H. Tawney, *Religion and the Rise of Capitalism* (London, 1926; reprt. 1966), esp. pp. 239–44.
39. The literature on the topic is enormous. The first major treatment of it was Max Weber's *The Protestant Ethic and the Spirit of Capitalism* (1904–5), trans. Talcott Parsons (London, 1930; reprt. 1974); Weber's seminal study was followed by Tawney's *Religion and the Rise of Capitalism* (above, n 38) which examines the theme in relation to English Puritanism. The religious aspects of the subject are examined in Georgia Harkness, *John Calvin: The Man and His Ethics* (Nashville, 1963), pp. 178–220, and Ian Breward (ed.), *The Work of William Perkins* (Abingdon, Berks., 1970), pp. 72–6; there are select bibliographies both in Harkness (p. 178, n 2) and Breward (p. 125, nn 28–9).
40. Gustaf Wingren, *The Christian's Calling: Luther on Vocation*, trans. Carl C. Rasmussen (Edinburgh and London, 1958), p. 180.
41. Ibid., p. 10.
42. The treatise, probably written about the turn of the century, was first published at Cambridge in 1603. It subsequently appeared in the first volume of *The Workes of that Famovs and VVorthie Minister of Christ, in the Vniversitie of Cambridge, M[r]. W. Perkins*, 3 vols (London, 1608–9); page references for quotations used in my text are to volume one of this edition. An abbreviated and normalised version of *A Treatise of Vocatons* is available in *Work*, ed. Breward (above, n 39), pp. 446–76.
43. Certain occupations explicitly forbidden in Scripture or contrary to the spirit of God's Word are not lawful: 'we learn, that many perswading themselues of their callings, haue for all this, no calling at all. As for exaple, such as liue by usury, by carding and dicing, by maintaining houses of gaming, by plaies, and such like: for God is the authour of euery lawfull calling; but these and such miserable courses of liuing, are either against the word of God, or else they are not grounded thereupon. And therefore, are no callings or vocations, but auocations from God and his waies.' (p. 727)
44. Boccaccio, *Genealogia*, XV, x; in *Boccaccio on Poetry*, trans. C. G. Osgood, 2nd ed. (New York, 1956), pp. 131, 133.
45. It may be added that Milton frequently applied this view of vocation to other men. In *Of Education*, for example, he says that Samuel Hartlib's 'extraordinary pains and diligence' in educational reform had been occasioned 'either by the definite will of God so ruling, or the peculiar sway of

nature, which is also Gods working' (*YP*, II, p. 363); similarly, in *Pro Populo Anglicano Defensio*, he maintains that the regicides had acted 'according to the will of God whether manifest or innate' (*YP*, IV, i, p. 346).

TO CHAPTER 1

1. Fletcher, *The Intellectual Development of John Milton*, incomplete in 2 vols (Urbana, Illinois, 1956–61), II, p. 457; Woodhouse, *The Heavenly Muse: A Preface to Milton*, ed. H. R. MacCallum (Toronto, 1972), p. 18; Shawcross, 'Milton's Decision to Become a Poet', *MLQ*, 24 (1963), 21–30. See also William Haller, *The Rise of Puritanism* (New York, 1938; reprinted 1957), p. 313; Douglas Bush, *John Milton: A Sketch of His Life and Writings* (New York, 1964; reprinted 1967), p. 32; J. S. Diekhoff, ed., *Milton on Himself* (London, 1939; reprinted 1966), p. 13, n 10.

2. Haller, *The Rise of Puritanism*, pp. 288–322.

3. *The Stuart Constitution 1603–1688*, ed. J. P. Kenyon (Cambridge, 1969), pp. 138–9.

4. Bullock, *A History of Training for the Ministry of the Church of England* (London, 1955), p. 7.

5. The relative youth of students matriculating in the seventeenth century—at Cambridge about 1625 the average age was probably sixteen—meant that there was often time left 'for theological study after the taking of the M. A. degree' (Bullock, *History*, p. 6). In the *Apology for Smectymnuus* (1642) Milton fondly recalls the 'more then ordinary favour and respect' accorded him by the Fellows of Christ's who, on his departure from the university in 1632, 'signifi'd many wayes, how much better it would content them that I would stay' (*YP*, I, p. 884). Since it is almost certain that he could not have been offered a fellowship at Christ's (see n 12), it is reasonable to suppose that these men had encouraged him to remain at the university and read for one of the higher degrees, probably the Bachelor of Divinity. However, on the basis of Milton's harsh assessment of university curricula and teaching methods in the *Prolusions* and *Of Education*, it is not difficult to imagine the feelings that would have prompted him to decline such an offer of prolonged preparation.

6. Fletcher, *Intellectual Development*, II, p. 457.

7. Ibid., p. 549. Contradiction and indecision, however, seriously impair Fletcher's dating argument. After the uncompromising declaration that 'every scrap of evidence we possess for his having made this decision points to his junior year as the time as which he so decided' (p. 457), he repeatedly undermines his own position: 'He decided by the time of the M.A. in 1632 that he would not enter the church' (p. 530); 'Milton, perhaps during his undergraduate days, had decided against the priesthood as a career' (p. 549); 'sometime before 1630 he had evidently decided not to take orders' (p. 549); 'a decision [was] made about 1627 or 1628 and then strongly attested before proceeding B. A. in the early spring of 1629' (p. 549).

8. Ibid., pp. 549–50.

9. Tillyard, *Milton* (London, 1930; revised 1966), p. 16.

10. Haller, *The Rise of Puritanism*, p. 313.

11. There is no reason to doubt Milton's academic distinction. He graduated *cum laude* in 1632 (*YP*, IV, i, p. 613) and in the graduation-book of his college, his name appears first on the subscription list of those receiving the M. A.—a circumstance that suggests that he was 'the outstanding recipient of the M. A. from Christ's College' in that year: see *LM*, I, p. 258, and also Fletcher, *Intellectual Development*, II, pp. 542–3.

12. Chapter 26 of the statutes of Christ's College specifies that certain counties (London among them) cannot be represented by more than one fellow at any given time. Since Michael Honywood (a Fellow of Christ's since 1618) was, like Milton, a Londoner, Milton was ineligible for a fellowship. (See *MB*, I, p. 85 and II, pp. 760–1, n 45; also Fletcher, *Intellectual Development*, II, pp. 508–12.)

13. Woodhouse, *The Heavenly Muse*, p. 18. On a 1632 dating of this decision, see also *LM*, I, p. 323, and Bush, *Milton: A Sketch of His Life*, p. 32. Ernest Sirluck ('Milton's Idle Right Hand', *JEGP*, 60 [1961], 757–8) argues for 1629; however, he offers no evidence to support his suggestion.

14. Woodhouse's argument depends heavily on the dating of the Italian sonnets, which he confidently assigns to 1630 and treats as the most striking instances of Milton's reversion to secular verse after the resolution of 1629 to compose only religious poetry. The dating of these sonnets is more problematical than Woodhouse suggests. Much recent criticism assigns them either to mid-1629 or to 1638: see the summary of these arguments in *Milton's Sonnets*, ed. E. A. J. Honigmann (London, 1966), pp. 76–81. The 1630 dating is, however, defended by J. E. Shaw and A. B. Giamatti: see *CV*, I, p. 367. In any case Woodhouse's general argument is valid even without the Italian sonnets, for Milton wrote much non-religious verse in the years 1630–2.

15. Woodhouse, *The Heavenly Muse*, p. 38.

16. Woodhouse, 'Notes of Milton's Early Development', *UTQ*, 13 (1942–3), 67. Chapter 2 of *The Heavenly Muse* (pp. 15–54) is a revision of this early paper; although the exact sentences quoted here were dropped in revision, the ideas are retained unaltered: see *The Heavenly Muse*, p. 19.

17. This dating of *Sonnet 7*, first proposed by W. R. Parker (*RES*, 11 [1935], 276–83), is accepted by almost all scholars. E. Sirluck (*JEGP*, 60 [1961], 781–4) attempts to re-establish the traditional dating of December 1631, but Parker has vigorously and cogently defended his argument for December 1632 (*MB*, II, pp. 784–7, n 16).

18. The letter is preserved in the *Trinity Manuscript* in two heavily revised drafts, both in Milton's hand; the fair copy of the letter has not survived. W. R. Parker (*TLS*, 16 May 1936, p. 420, and *RES*, 11 [1935], 276–83) assigns the letter to 1633, a date now generally accepted by scholars, and suggests that it may have been written to Thomas Young.

19. Woodhouse, *The Heavenly Muse*, pp. 51–2; Sirluck, 'Milton's Idle Right Hand', 758; Bush, *Milton: A Sketch of His Life*, pp. 46–7.

20. Woodhouse, *The Heavenly Muse*, p. 51.

21. Hanford, *Studies in Shakespeare, Milton and Donne* (Ann Arbor, 1925), p. 130.

22. Parker (*MB*, II, p. 801, n 3) believes on the basis of handwriting and orthography that note-taking was begun in 'late 1634 or, at least, 1635'.

Ruth Mohl (*YP*, I, p. 344) suggests that some of the entries may date from as early as 1631. J. H. Hanford, however, argues that the compilation was probably not begun until 1636: see 'The Chronology of Milton's Private Studies', *PMLA*, 36 (1921), 286.

23. The *Commonplace Book* contains several references to an 'Index Theologicus' in which Milton recorded notes on religious topics. Unfortunately it is impossible to say when this notebook might have been begun or when its use was discontinued. (See *YP*, I, p. 365 and *MB*, II, p. 804, n 6).

24. For detailed accounts of Milton's reading programme in 1632–8, see Hanford, 'Private Studies', 251–314, and Parker, *MB*, II, pp. 803–4, n 5.

25. The metropolitan visitations of Archbishop Laud, begun in a modest way in 1633, had become particularly oppressive by 1637 when they resulted in the dismissal of a number of dissenting ministers from their charges. In January 1637 John Lilburne was imprisoned for his defiance of ecclesiastical authority and his complicity in the distribution of books attacking the bishops. More serious still were the harsh sentences passed on Henry Burton, John Bastwick and William Prynne for their antiprelatical writings: 'Burton was condemned on June 14 to be fined 5,000 pounds (a penalty never exacted), removed from the ministry, degraded from his degrees, to be set in the pillory and have his ears cut off, imprisoned for life at Lancaster Castle, prohibited access to wife or friends, and denied use of pen and ink. Prynne and Bastwick were condemned to similar punishments; Prynne suffered branding on each cheek (with the letters *SL* for "seditious libeller") and the loss of the remaining fragments of his ears. . . . When the sentences were carried out on June 30, Prynne's stumps were sawed instead of cut off, and Burton's ears were sheared so close to his head that his temporal artery was opened, and the blood gushed out upon the scaffold.' (*YP*, I, pp. 43–4)

26. Shawcross, 'Milton's Decision to Become a Poet', *MLQ*, 24 (1963), 30.

27. Barker, 'The Pattern of Milton's *Nativity Ode*', *UTQ*, 10 (1940–1), 171–2.

28. See for example Haller, *The Rise of Puritanism*, p. 321, and Malcolm Ross, *Poetry and Dogma* (New Brunswick, N. J., 1954), p. 202.

29. The 'grim wolf' (line 128) is the Roman Church, the epithet being a stock image of vituperation among Reformed writers. E. S. Le Comte (*SP*, 47 [1950], 606) argues that the allusion refers specifically to the Jesuits, in the escutcheon of whose founder, Ignatius Loyola, appear two grey wolves; however, the image applies equally well to the pope who was often depicted as a wolf or fox ravening the English sheep-fold: see *The Sermons of Edwin Sandys*, ed. John Ayre (Cambridge, 1841), pp. 56–72.

30. There was considerable excitement in London during the summer of 1637, the most sensational event being the public mutilations of Prynne, Burton and Bastwick (see n 25). D. M. Wolfe notes that, 'when Burton was taken from the Fleet to be imprisoned at Lancaster Castle, it was estimated that a hundred thousand people lined the streets to acclaim the earless hero' (*YP*, I, p. 44).

31. Many prominent Puritans and parliamentarians of the period—Hampden, Pym, Strode, Oliver St John, and Sir Henry Vane the younger—matriculated and proceeded to degrees at Oxford. And V. H. H. Green notes in a recent study that 'the Puritan movement . . ., contrary to what one might expect, seems to have been rooted almost as deeply at Oxford

as it was at Cambridge' (*Religion at Oxford and Cambridge* [London, 1964], p. 107). Moreover, Christ's College, Cambridge was not remarkable for its Puritan sympathies; if Milton had been a committed Puritan in 1625, he would presumably have chosen a college like Emmanuel or St John's, which would have reflected his convictions.

32. *The Early Lives of Milton*, ed. Helen Darbishire (London, 1932), pp. 37, 94. Translation: 'If your mind, form, grace, features, and manners were equalled by your creed, then, I swear, you would be no Angle but a very angel.' (*MB*, I, p. 176)

33. 'In Geneva I conversed daily with John Diodati, the learned professor of theology.' (*YP*, IV, i, p. 620) Although the two men undoubtedly discussed and lamented the death (1638) of Charles Diodati, most of these 'daily' conversations would have been about theological issues. The talks would have influenced Milton's growing Calvinist sentiments, and they would have watered, if indeed they did not sow, the seeds of his later Presbyterian convictions.

34. The 1640 *Canons* are reprinted (with some omissions) in *YP*, I, pp. 985–98; the 'Et Cetera' oath is on pp. 990–1. (See also *The Stuart Constitution*, ed. Kenyon, pp. 166–71.)

35. Since Milton had twice subscribed to the 1604 oath, S. B. Liljegren accuses him of intellectual dishonesty in this justification of his abandonment of holy orders in *The Reason of Church-Government*: 'his conscience was said to have prevented his entering the Church because he was unable truthfully to subscribe to the established creed, [and yet] it did not hinder him from doing this very thing in subscribing to the 39 articles, an act accompanying the obtaining of the M. A. degree.' (*Studies in Milton* [Lund, 1918], p. xxx) Such arguments evaporate, of course, if Milton's reference is to the 'Et Cetera' oath of 1640. However, for those critics who think that Milton was 'Church-outed' in 1628, 1632 or 1637 it still remains to answer Liljegren's charges, which cannot be ignored because they seriously impugn Milton's moral and ethical credibility.

36. In *Animadversions* he writes: 'As for Ordination what is it, but the laying on of hands, an outward signe or symbol of admission? it creates nothing, it conferres nothing; it is the inward calling of God that makes a Minister, and his own painfull study and diligence that manures and improves his ministeriall gifts' (*YP*, I, p. 715). See also *YP*, I, pp. 537, 843.

TO CHAPTER 2

1. For a full account of John Milton senior's reputation and extant works, see Ernest Brennecke, Jr., *John Milton the Elder and His Music* (New York, 1938).

2. *Early Lives*, ed. Darbishire, p.2.

3. In the two editions of the minor poems published in Milton's lifetime (1645, 1673), the headnote to these paraphrases announces that they 'were done by the Author at fifteen years old'. It may be that they were composed at the suggestion of Milton's father who had recently published three new musical settings in Ravenscroft's *Whole Book of Psalmes* (1621).

4. The Latin epigrams are *Carmina Elegiaca* ('Surge, age surge, leves') and 'Ignavus satrapum'—both of which were discovered in the 1870s by A. J. Horwood—and *Apologus De Rustico et Hero* which Milton published in 1673. The Greek epigram, *Philosophus ad regem*, first appeared in Milton's 1645 volume. It may be added that Parker (*MB*, I, p. 18) assigns many more poems to Milton's time at St Paul's than I am willing to.

5. Since Parker's discovery of the date of Anne Phillips' burial (*TLS*, 17 December 1938, p. 802), most scholars have accepted a date in early 1628 for the composition of *Fair Infant*. John Carey (*PM*, p. 14) argues for the older dating of winter 1625–6, but Bush concludes after examining his argument that 'what knowledge we have seems to favour Parker's date' (*CV*, II, i, p. 120).

6. 'I beg you, gentlemen, to accept this explanation: it is to give you pleasure that I have put off and for the moment laid aside my usual habit, and if anything I may say is loose or licentious, put it down to the suggestion, not of my real mind and character, but of the needs of the moment and the genius of the place.' (*YP*, I, p. 277)

7. The Cambridge statutes required that undergraduates speak Latin except during periods of relaxation in their own rooms.

8. The allusion in these lines has been the subject of much scholarly debate: see *CV*, II, i, p. 142 for a summary of the various arguments and suggestions. I do not think the lines are directed at any particular 'school' (e.g., the Metaphysical poets); rather, they refer to all poetry that is superficially elegant and image-ridden but morally vacuous.

9. Hanford, *Studies in Shakespeare, Milton and Donne* (Ann Arbor, 1925), p. 117.

10. For a similar reading see E. M. W. Tillyard, *The Miltonic Setting* (Cambridge, 1938), pp. 168–73.

11. See D. C. Allen, *Neo-Latin Poetry of the Sixteenth and Seventeenth Centuries* (Los Angeles, 1965), p. 47: *Elegy 5* 'is more a poem on the ecstasy of poetic insight in its apollonian manifestation than on the ancient topic of the annual renewal of earthly life. But the "advent of spring" is not to be read under, for the poem intends to remind us that the force of poetry is also renewed with each generation. Standing on the margin of promised poetic achievement, Milton recognized the eternal revival in himself.'

12. The *Nativity Ode* was still unfinished when Milton described it to Diodati in *Elegy 6*: 'I am writing [*canimus*] a poem about the king who was born of heavenly seed, and who brought peace to men.' (80)

13. See J. M. Steadman, 'Chaste Muse and "Casta Juventus": Milton Minturno, and Scaliger on Inspiration and the Poet's Character', *Italica*, 40 (1963), 28–34; also Z. S. Fink, 'Wine, Poetry, and Milton's *Elegia Sexta*', *ES*, 21 (1939), 164–5. See also *Prolusion 7*: 'I am well aware, gentlemen, that this contemplation, by which we strive to reach the highest goal, cannot partake of true happiness unless it is conjoined with integrity of life and character.' (*YP*, I, p. 292)

14. 'He was an early riser. Sc: at 4 a clock manè. yea, after he lost his sight. He had a man read to him: the first thing he read was the Hebrew bible, & yᵗ was at 4ʰ manè—½h+. then he contemplated. At 7 his man came to him again & read to him and wrote till dinner: the writing was as much as the reading.' *Early Lives*, ed. Darbishire, p. 6.

15. Woodhouse, *The Heavenly Muse*, p. 36.
16. In *The Statesman's Manual* (1816) Coleridge argues that a *symbol* is, above all, characterised 'by the translucence of the Eternal through and in the Temporal. It always partakes of the Reality which it renders intelligible; and while it enunciates the whole, abides itself as a living part in that Unity, of which it is the representative': see *The Collected Works of Samuel Taylor Coleridge*, ed. K. Coburn *et al.*, 16 vols (London, 1969–*), VI, p. 30.
17. Rajan, 'In Order Serviceable', *MLR*, 63 (1968), 22.
18. See D. C. Allen, *The Harmonious Vision: Studies in Milton's Poetry* (Baltimore, 1954), pp. 22–3.
19. Parker (*MB*, I, p. 142) is rationalising in saying that Lawes 'had to explain (using a familiar formula) that it was "not openly acknowledged by the Author"'. Formula or no formula, it was Lawes and not Milton who published the masque. That fact alone makes Milton's reticence an inescapable conclusion.
20. *Poetical Works*, ed. H. W. Garrod (Oxford, 1966), p. 54.
21. If it seems incredible that the poet who has just published *Comus* and who is engaged in composing *Lycidas* should complain that his 'Pegasus still raises himself on very tender wings', it is well to bear in mind that time and the critical tradition afford us an objectivity and distance denied to him. Milton hoped to be a great poet and he believed that he would eventually become one; but he can never have been quite as certain as we are.
22. There is, as Bush points out, 'no ground for the suggestion that he may possibly have written *Lycidas* "without knowledge of the proposed Cambridge volume"' (*CV*, II, ii, p. 545).
23. *Notes and Queries*, 198 (1953), 103.
24. For blue as the colour of hope, see R. C. Fox's note in *Explicator*, 9 (1950–1), Item 54. Given Milton's view of the poet's sacerdotal nature and role, 'mantle blue' probably also alludes to the divine instructions for Aaron's robe in Exodus 28: 31, 'And thou shalt make the robe of the ephod all of blue'. As Aaron's vestments are the symbols of his priestly vocation, so Milton's blue cloak symbolises his election as God's poet-priest. For blue as the traditional colour of the Druid bard's cloak, see J. F. Forrest, 'The Significance of Milton's "Mantle Blue"', *MQ*, 8 (1974), 41–8.
25. 'This subject was first designed a Tragedy, and in the Fourth Book of the Poem there are ten verses [lines 32–41], which several Years before the Poem was begun, were shewn to me, and some others, as designed for the very beginning of the said Tragedy.' *Early Lives*, ed. Darbishire, p. 72.
26. All scholars except Fletcher have accepted 1640 as the most probable date of this private printing: see *CV*, I, p. 283, n.

TO CHAPTER 3

1. E. M. W. Tillyard, *Milton* (London, 1930; rev. ed., 1966) p. 100.
2. William Kerrigan, *The Prophetic Milton* (Charlottesville, Virginia, 1974), p. 11.
3. Later in the same preface Milton makes it clear that the *conscience* is a mode

of divine prompting: 'But were it the meanest under-service, if God by his Secretary conscience injoyn it, it were sad for me if I should draw back. . . .' (*YP*, I, p. 822) As R. A. Haug observes in his note to this passage, 'The conscience was understood as a God-given sense which knew the right intuitively; hence it is privy to God's commands and secrets' (ibid).

4. This seminal insight is perhaps the guiding principle in A. S. P. Woodhouse's approach to Milton; and I suspect that I may have come perilously close to reproducing his very words, although I cannot now trace the exact source in his writings. While I often find myself at variance with Professor Woodhouse in the application of this principle to individual poems, I believe that the critical theory itself is sound and regret that many recent commentators insist on divorcing Milton's art from his biography.

5. '"Alcestis from the Grave": Image and Structure in *Sonnet XXIII*', *Milton Studies*, 10 (1977), pp. 127–39.

6. On the doctrine of the remnant, see E. W. Heaton, *The Old Testament Prophets* (London, 1958), pp. 143–6.

7. In the New Testament the situation is almost exactly reversed, for election is there pre-eminently personal and individual rather than outward and national. 'Whereas the personal aspect of election in the OT is throughout subordinate to the idea of service, in the NT, on the other hand, stress is laid on the personal election to eternal salvation; and the aspect of election as the means to an end beyond itself falls into the background, without, however, being at all intended to be lost sight of.' (*DB*, p. 239) Although private and public election are often distinct and unrelated concepts in the New Testament, the Old Testament emphasis on the interdependence of individual and national vocation does survive in a number of important cases—as, for example, in the experience of the Apostles at Pentecost (Acts 2) and in Paul's commission to serve as the apostle to the Gentiles (e.g. Romans 11: 13). In the New Testament the particular covenant with Israel is transferred from the nation at large to the body of elect believers comprising the church, which Peter addresses in metaphors drawn from the national covenant in Exodus 19: 'But ye are a chosen generation, a royal priesthood, an holy nation, a peculiar people; that ye should shew forth the praises of him who hath called you out of darkness into his marvellous light.' (1 Peter 2: 9) The doctrine of the remnant is also carried into the New Testament, but its context is likewise limited to the church. While the nation as a whole is called to honour the new covenant established in Christ, it is clear that the work must eventually be performed by the elect remnant alone; for, as St Paul trenchantly observes, 'they are not all Israel, which are of Israel' (Romans 9: 6).

8. Albright, *From the Stone Age to Christianity: Monotheism and the Historical Process* (Baltimore, 1940; 2nd ed., New York, 1957), p. 305.

9. Norman Cohn cites a number of instances in *The Pursuit of the Millennium* (New York, 1970). An interesting example is his account of an anonymous German chiliast (*fl. ca.* 1510) who believed that originally the Germans had been the chosen people: 'Behind this curious idea lay a whole philosophy of history. The Old Testament was dismissed as valueless; for from the time of the Creation onwards it was not the Jews but the Germans who were the Chosen People. Adam and all his descendants down to Japhet, including all

the Patriarchs, were Germans speaking German; other languages —Hebrew among them—came into existence only at the Tower of Babel. . . . This ancient German Empire was a vast one, for it covered the whole of Europe—Alexander the Great could be claimed as a German national hero. And it was the most perfect of empires, a true earthly Paradise, for it was governed according to a legal code, known as the Statutes of Trier, in which the principles of fraternity, equality and communal ownership were enshrined. It was in these Statutes, and not in the Decalogue invented by the charlatan Moses, that God had expressed his commandments to mankind.' (p. 123)

10. *Correspondence of Matthew Parker*, ed. John Bruce and T. T. Perowne (Cambridge: Parker Society, 1853), pp. 418–19.
11. The image, which is common in Protestant apologetics, owes its origin to Luther's *The Babylonian Captivity of the Church* (1520).
12. Haller, *Foxe's Book of Martyrs and the Elect Nation* (London, 1963), p. 134.
13. The Geneva Bible (1560), A2^r.
14. *Foxe's Book of Martyrs*, ed. and abr. G. A. Williamson (London, 1965), p. 458.
15. Ibid., p. 311.
16. Ibid., p. 191.
17. *The Sermons of Edwin Sandys*, ed. John Ayre (Cambridge: Parker Society, 1841), p. 60.
18. *XCVI. Sermons by the Right Honourable and Reverend Father in God, Lancelot Andrewes*, 5th edition (London, 1661), p. 583. (*XCVI. Sermons* was first published in 1629.)
19. Ibid., p. 584.
20. Ibid., p. 589.
21. Burges, *A Sermon Preached to the Honourable House of Commons Assembled in Parliament. At their Pvbliqve Fast, Novem. 17. 1640* (London, 1641), p. 42.
22. John F. Wilson, who discusses this programme of fasts and examines many of the sermons in detail, describes the routine observed by members of the Lower House on these occasions in this way: 'On the regular fast days [the last Wednesday of each month] business was usually omitted, and members of Commons were expected to attend the services at St Margaret's, Westminster. The basic program included two exhortations, one in the morning and one in the afternoon. Conventionally the preachers were "thanked" for their efforts, and motions "desiring them" to print their sermons were passed, often on the fast day itself but sometimes after a lapse of several days.' (*Pulpit in Parliament* [Princeton, 1969], p. 61)
23. Jeremiah Burroughs, *Sions Joy. A Sermon Preached to the Honourable House of Commons assembled in Parliament, At their publique Thanksgiving, September 7. 1641. For the Peace concluded between England and Scotland* (London, 1641), pp. 51–2.
24. Calamy, *Gods free Mercy to England: Presented as a Pretious, and Powerfull Motive to Humiliation* (London, 1642), p. 2.
25. Ibid., p. 8.
26. Ibid., p. 10.
27. Ibid., p. 13.
28. Ibid., p. 17.
29. Ibid., pp. 24–5.

30. Ibid., p. 41.
31. Ibid., p. 45.
32. Ibid., p. 47.
33. Ibid., p. 49. The image of the 'golden pipes' alludes to Zechariah 4: 12, where the context is the prophet Zechariah's divine commission to exhort Zerubbabel to complete the work of rebuilding the Temple. The parallel with God's prophet-preacher exhorting the Long Parliament to complete the reformation of the English church would have been clear enough to Calamy's audience.
34. The reference is to the English reformers from Wycliffe on. Milton believed that the Reformation had begun in England with 'our *Wicklefs* preaching', and not in Germany or Geneva as was commonly supposed. In *Of Reformation* (1641) Milton reminds his readers that England has 'had this *grace* and *honour* from God to bee the first that should set up a Standard for the recovery of *lost Truth*, and blow the first *Evangelick Trumpet* to the *Nations*, holding up, as from a Hill, the new Lampe of *saving light* to all Christendome' (*YP*, I, p. 525). This idea is not uncommon among English writers. In *An Harborowe for faithful and true subjectes* (1559), for example, John Aylmer has a personified England tell her children that 'God hath brought forth in me the greatest and excellentest treasure that He hath for your comfort and all the world's. He would that out of my womb should come that servant of Christ John Wyclif, who begat Huss, who begat Luther, who begat the truth.' See also Lucy Hutchinson, *Memoirs of the Life of Colonel Hutchinson*, ed. J. Hutchinson (London: Everyman, 1968), p. 5: 'Here it was that the first Christian emperor received his crown; here began the early dawn of Gospel light, by Wickliffe and other faithful witnesses, whom God raised up after the black and horrid midnight of antichristianism; and a more plentiful harvest of devout confessors, constant martyrs, and holy worshippers of God, hath not grown in any field of the church, throughout all ages, than those whom God hath here glorified his name and gospel by.'
35. See preceding note.
36. The quotations are from *Doctrine and Discipline* (*YP*, II, p. 232) and *On the New Forcers of Conscience*, lines 12 and 16 (*PM*, p. 297).
37. Donald A. Roberts, the editor of *Defensio Secunda* in *YP*, writes as follows: 'Milton's final sentence, brave and proud, is richly expressive of the abiding faith of genius. All great masters, in every medium, have known they were masters, and they have said so with sublime dignity.' (*YP*, IV, i, p. 686, n 546) Statements such as this, while they may satisfy the modern rationalist, do less than justice to Milton's own deep conviction of inspired utterance; and they attempt to transform a prophet into a mere exponent of the egotistical sublime.
38. Barker, *Milton and the Puritan Dilemma* (Toronto, 1942), p. 331.
39. Heaton, *The Old Testament Prophets* (London, 1958), p. 51. For other helpful accounts of prophetic inspiration in the Old Testament, see William Sandy, *Inspiration: Eight Lectures on the Early History and Origin of the Doctrine of Biblical Inspiration* (London, 1893), and H. Wheeler Robinson, *Inspiration and Revelation in the Old Testament* (Oxford, 1946).
40. Kerrigan, *The Prophetic Milton*, pp. 32–3.
41. After a detailed study of inspiration in the theological tradition, Kerrigan

applies his findings primarily to Milton's poetry. Kerrigan has a tendency, however, to overemphasise the rationalistic element in Milton's view of inspiration.

42. Barker, *Milton and the Puritan Dilemma*, p. 17.

43. *Elizabethan Critical Essays*, ed. G. G. Smith, 2 vols (Oxford, 1904), I, p. 195. For a similar statement in Ben Jonson's *Timber, or Discoveries*, see *Critical Essays of the Seventeenth Century*, ed. J. E. Spingarn, 3 vols (Oxford, 1907; reprt. London, 1968), I, p. 52.

44. Hobbes, 'Answer to Davenant's Preface to *Gondibert*', in *Critical Essays*, ed. Spingarn, II, p. 59.

45. John Skelton, *A Replication*, in *Complete Poems of John Skelton*, ed. Philip Henderson, 4th ed. (London, 1966), p. 427. For other examples of the *stylus Dei*, see Edward Benlowes' 'Author's Prayer' prefixed to *Theophilia, or Loves Sacrifice* (1652) and Robert Herrick's little lyric in *Hesperides* (1648) beginning "Tis not ev'ry day, that I/ Fitted am to prophesie'. The idea was popular among the Quakers in particular (cf. George Fox's *Journal*), and there is an interesting statement of it in the autobiography of Milton's Quaker friend, Thomas Ellwood:

> Against this practice of these false teachers the zeal of the Lord had flamed in my breast for some time; and now the burthen of the word of the Lord against them fell heavily upon me, with command to proclaim his controversy against them. Fain would I have been excused from this service, which I judged too heavy for me. . . . But the Lord would not be entreated but continued the burden upon me with greater weight; requiring obedience from me, and promising to assist me therein. Whereupon I arose from my bed, and in the fear and dread of the Lord committed to writing what He, in the motion of His divine Spirit, dictated to me to write. (*The History of Thomas Ellwood, Written by Himself*, ed. Henry Morley [London, 1885], pp. 81–2.)

46. Marshall, *A Sermon Preached . . . November 17, 1640*, as quoted in Wilson, *Pulpit in Parliament*, p. 38; Calamy, *Gods free Mercy to England* (London, 1642), p. 2; Goodwin, *Zerubbabels Encovragement to Finish the Temple. A Sermon Preached before the Honourable House of Commons, at their late Solemne Fast, Apr. 27. 1642* (London, 1642), A2ʳ.

47. John F. Huntley would not accept this statement: see his paper, 'The Images of Poet & Poetry in Milton's *The Reason of Church-Government*', in *Achievements of the Left Hand: Essays on the Prose of John Milton*, ed. M. Lieb and J. T. Shawcross (Amherst, Massachusetts, 1974), pp. 83–120.

48. For references to inspiration in the prose of 1655–60, see the following: *Pro Se Defensio* (1655), *YP*, IV, ii, p. 735; *Pro Populo Anglicano Defensio*, second edition (1658), ibid., IV, i, p. 536; and *The Likeliest Means to Remove Hirelings* (1659), ibid., VII, p. 277. As Arthur Barker points out, the late pamphlets (especially those of 1659) 'heavily emphasize Scripture and the Spirit as the only sources of faith because Milton himself had necessarily turned in the reconsideration of his thought to God's word illuminated by the celestial light' (*Milton and the Puritan Dilemma*, p. 234).

49. Gardner, *A Reading of Paradise Lost* (Oxford, 1965; rev. ed. 1967), p. 19. It is

well worth putting the phrase I have quoted in its context:

> The Heavenly Muse has no status within the epic itself. She is inseparable from the poet, and is no part of the universe he presents to us. She has another kind of reality. In his invocation to her Milton has summed up all his feeling about the sacredness of his vocation, the reality of his calling, and the truth of his subject, all his awe at his own temerity and his sense that through him great things are to be said. In invoking her aid he expresses also his sense that although he goes forward alone 'in darkness, and with dangers compast round', he is not alone; he has great allies, others before him and others who will come after him 'smit with the love of sacred song'. Through his invocation of her he declares that inspiration is a reality, not a subjective fancy. She is the poetic embodiment of Milton's belief in his vocation.

50. Milton's critics have made heavy weather of this phrase. 'Unattempted even in the Bible?' asks David Daiches; 'unattempted in English literature ...?' ('The Opening of *Paradise Lost*', in *The Living Milton*, ed. Frank Kermode [London, 1960], p. 63) If the identification of the Muse as Milton's own poetic talent is accepted, then the phrase must mean things unattempted yet by Milton's own Muse; and he extends his talent from 'poetic' to 'literary' in order to include his work in prose as God's spokesman.

51. See Geoffrey Nuttall, *The Holy Spirit in Puritan Faith and Experience* (Oxford, 1947).

52. Pierre de Ronsard, *Oeuvres Complètes*, ed. Paul Laumonier, 18 vols (Paris, 1914–67), XIV, p. 6.

53. Kerrigan, *The Prophetic Milton*, p. 138.

TO CHAPTER 4

1. Aubrey says that *Paradise Lost* was begun about two years before the Restoration, that is, about May 1658. Milton's anonymous biographer, however, says that composition was begun shortly after the publication of *Pro Se Defensio* in August 1655. (See Darbishire, *Early Lives*, pp. 13, 29.) Tillyard (*Milton*, 1966 edition, pp. 165–6) argues persuasively that 'the serious beginnings of *Paradise Lost* are to be found in the state of mind that prompted the *Defensio Secunda* [1654]'. There is no chance of certainty on the question of when composition actually began; however, the poem's emphasis on individual vocation and regeneration—themes central to the prose works of 1659–60—incline me toward a 1658 dating.

2. Tillyard, *Milton*, p.250.

3. The quotations are from *Areopagitica* (*YP*, II, p. 554), *Eikonoklastes* (ibid., III, p. 601), and the second edition of *The Readie and Easie Way to Establish a Free Commonwealth* (ibid., VII, p.463).

4. Although the idea of a 'fit audience, though few' can be traced as far back in Milton's writings as *Prolusion I* (cf. *YP*, I, pp. 218–20), it does not become a

central aspect of his thought until it is connected with the doctrine of the regenerate remnant in the prose works of 1644–60. The mature theory takes its point of departure from the statement in the preface added to the revised edition of the *Doctrine and Discipline of Divorce* (February 1644) where Milton, having experienced the slings and arrows of the Westminster Assembly for daring to publicise his views on divorce, declares to the Long Parliament that 'I seek not to seduce the simple and illiterat; my errand is to find out the choisest and the learnedest, who have this high gift of wisdom to answer solidly, or to be convinc't' (*YP*, II, p. 233). The theme is further developed in *Areopagitica* in terms of the fitness of individuals to discriminate for themselves between good and evil: 'To the pure all things are pure, not only meats and drinks, but all kinde of knowledge whether of good or evill; the knowledge cannot defile,.... if the will and conscience be not defil'd.' (Ibid., p. 512). After 1644, the 'fit audience' theme is almost a common-place; Milton addresses his remarks only to the regenerate, only to those who possess the spiritual credentials to understand and accept the truth when it is presented to them. In *Eikonoklastes*, for example, he tells his reader that truth must not be smothered, 'but sent abroad, in the native confidence of her single self, to earn, how she can, her entertainment in the world, and to finde out her own readers; few perhaps, but those few, such of value and substantial worth, as truth and wisdom, not respecting numbers and bigg names, have bin ever wont in all ages to be contented with' (*YP*, III, pp. 339–40).

5. *De Doctrina Christiana* was begun about 1655 and, although Milton seems to have continued revising it until the end of his life, the original manuscript was probably completed in 1660. *Paradise Lost*, which was begun in 1658 or perhaps earlier in the 1650s (cf. n 1 above), was finished sometime between 1663 (Aubrey's date) and the autumn of 1665 when Milton gave the completed copy to Thomas Ellwood to read. Since the composition of the two works overlaps, it is reasonable to suppose that his doctrinal position is the same in both—although, of course, certain of Milton's more heterodox beliefs (e.g. his view of the Son) may be played down in the poem to make it more universally acceptable. There is, however, nothing particularly heterodox about Milton's doctrines of vocation and regeneration in *De Doctrina Christiana*, and, consequently, there is no reason to think that they have been attenuated in *Paradise Lost*.

6. The 'template' approach, first advocated by Maurice Kelley in *This Great Argument* (Princeton, 1941), has been adopted by a number of recent critics. See, for example, George M. Muldrow's *Milton and the Drama of the Soul* (Paris and The Hague, 1970), where Milton's soteriology in *De Doctrina Christiana* is used as a thematic gloss and structural guide for the last poems. However, since the technique is less easily applied to *Paradise Lost* than to *Samson Agonistes* or *Paradise Regained*, Muldrow finds it necessary to confine his analysis of the former to Adam's postlapsarian regeneration in Books X–XII and largely to ignore the first nine books of the epic.

7. Barker, 'Structural and Doctrinal Pattern in Milton's Later Poems', in *Essays in English Literature from the Renaissance to the Victorian Age, Presented to A. S. P. Woodhouse*, ed. M. MacLure and F. W. Watt (Toronto, 1964), p. 171.

8. Ibid., pp. 172–3. See also Barker's later paper '*Paradise Lost*: The Relevance

of Regeneration', in *Paradise Lost: A Tercentenary Tribute*, ed. B. Rajan (Toronto, 1969), pp. 48–78.

9. Barker, 'Structural and Doctrinal Pattern', p. 174.

10. See Milton's discussion of the postlapsarian situation in *Areopagitica*, where he suggests that 'perhaps this is that doom which *Adam* fell into of knowing good and evill, that is to say of knowing good by evill' (*YP*, II, p. 514). In the fallen world, where 'Good and evill . . . grow up together almost inseparably', the good is potential rather than actual until it has been consciously chosen over evil, and therefore Milton 'cannot praise a fugitive and cloister'd virtue, unexercis'd & unbreath'd, that never sallies out and sees her adversary' (ibid., p. 515). In Eden, on the other hand, goodness *per se* is not won by trial (though it may be reconfirmed by trial), for it is the natural state of prelapsarian existence.

11. For a theological statement of this idea, see Ralph Cudworth's 'Sermon Preached before the House of Commons. March 31, 1647':

> Happinesse is nothing but that inward sweet delight, that will arise from the Harmonious agreement between our wills and Gods will. There is nothing contrary to God in the whole world, nothing that fights against him but *Self will*. This is the strong Castle, that we all keep garrison'd against heaven in every one of our hearts, which God continually layeth siege unto: and it must be conquered and demolished before we can conquer heaven. It was by reason of this *Self-will*, that Adam fell in Paradise; that those glorious Angels, those *Morning-starres*, kept not their first station, but dropt down from heaven like Falling Starres, and sunk into this condition of bitternesse, anxiety, and wretchednesse in which now they are. They all intangled themselves with the length of their own wings, they would needs will more and otherwise then God would will in them: and going about to make their wills wider, and to enlarge them into greater amplitude; the more they strugled [*sic*], they found themselves the faster pinioned, & crowded up into narrownesse and servility; insomuch that now they are not able to use any wings at all, but inheriting the *serpents* curse, can onely creep with their *bellies* upon the earth. Now our onely way to recover God & happiness again, is not to soar up with our Understandings, but to destroy this *Self-will* of ours: and then we shall find our wings to grow again, our plumes fairly spread, & our selves raised aloft into the free Aire of perfect Liberty, which is perfect Happinesse. . . . God will not hurt us, and Hell cannot hurt us, if we vvill nothing but vvhat God wills. Nay, then we are acted by God himself, and the whole Divinity floweth in upon us; and when we have cashiered this *Self-will* of ours, which did but shackle and confine our soules, our will shall then become truly free, being widened and enlarged to the extent of Gods own will. (*The Cambridge Platonists*, ed. C. A. Patrides [London, 1969], pp. 98–9.)

12. Barker, 'Structural and Doctrinal Pattern', p. 172.

13. Fish, *Surprised by Sin: The Reader in Paradise Lost* (London, 1967; London, Berkeley and Los Angeles, 1971), p. 184.

14. 'Raphael learns much in his effort to respond adequately to his call. His

effort fails ... because he does not yet understand the meaning implied by the Son's willing response to the call to sacrifice and so (blushingly) cannot quite explain the implications of angelic and human love. Yet he learns much, both from his own rehearsal of the War and Creation, about justice and mercy and the Son, and from Adam's responsive relations and doubtful or wondering questions and his own answers.' (Barker, 'Structural and Doctrinal Pattern', p. 187).

15. For an excellent analysis of the Son's mutability and deepening vocational awareness, see Stella P. Revard, 'The Dramatic Function of the Son in *Paradise Lost*: A Commentary on Milton's "Trinitarianism"', *JEGP*, 66 (1967), 45–58.

16. The theme of the reader's vocation and education has been thoroughly and sensitively investigated by Stanley Fish in *Surprised by Sin* (1967). I have little to add to his account, and such points as I do wish to add may best be incorporated in the discussion as it proceeds, since they could hardly justify their existence in a separate section.

17. Lewalski, 'Innocence and Experience in Milton's Eden', in *New Essays on Paradise Lost*, ed. Thomas Kranidas (London, Berkeley and Los Angeles, 1969; reprt. 1971), p. 88.

18. Ibid., p. 94.

19. Ibid., pp. 116–17.

20. Lewalski, who develops this point with the aid of a number of examples from the poem, concludes: 'Each new situation in Milton's Eden is an opportunity to grow in wisdom, virtue, and perfection, and normally Adam and Eve must take the initiative in interpreting what happens to them and in seeking new knowledge and experience. Normally, too, they respond to a new situation by one or two false starts or false guesses before they find or are led to the proper stance. But this human growth by trial and error, like the excessive growth of the Garden, is wholly without prejudice, so long as they prune and direct and reform what grows amiss.' (Ibid., pp. 99–100)

21. Barker, 'Structural and Doctrinal Pattern', p. 189.

22. Browne, *Religion Medici* (Everyman ed.; London, 1962), p. 39.

23. Baldassare Castiglione, *The Book of the Courtier*, trans. Sir Thomas Hoby (Everyman ed.; London, 1959), p. 304.

24. A growing number of Milton's readers in recent years have argued forcefully that anticipations of the Fall are proleptic only for the fallen reader; for Adam and Eve, yet sinless, such incidents as Eve's dream or Adam's dangerous stabs at forbidden knowledge are completely without prejudice and function as corrective guides to right action rather than indications of sullied innocence and anticipations of the Fall. Arthur Barker puts the case cogently and succinctly when he writes that 'Every prelapsarian action in *Paradise Lost* is so far from foreboding the Fall that it stands in the sharpest continous contrast with it, to underline the fact that the Fall is, as to right action, a parodic obliquity and anomaly' ('Structural and Doctrinal Pattern', p. 190). I endorse this position unreservedly, in its application to Adam and Eve; however, since Milton is addressing the fallen reader in the poem, it is equally true that he provides numerous incidents which, for the reader, prefigure the 'inevitable'. Moreover, as a conscious and careful artist, Milton must prepare for his climax by using controlled proleptic

themes and images.

25. Satan had prepared the ground for this approach much earlier, in Eve's dream-temptation:

> he drew nigh, and to me held,
> Even to my mouth of that same fruit held part
> Which he had plucked; the pleasant savoury smell
> So quickened appetite, that I, methought,
> Could not but taste.
>
> (V, 82–6)

26. The word 'appetite' is used only twice in the poem after this passage. In Book X it is connected with gluttony and delusion and is applied (in ironic reversal) to Satan and his minions:

> greedily they plucked
> The fruitage fair to sight, like that which grew
> Near that bituminous lake where Sodom flamed;
> This more delusive, not the touch, but taste
> Deceived; they fondly thinking to allay
> Their appetite with gust, instead of fruit
> Chewed bitter ashes. . . .
>
> (560–6)

In Book XI it is applied to the victims of excess confined to the lazar-house: 'Their maker's image . . ./ Forsook them, when themselves they vilified/ To serve ungoverned appetite' (515–17). Adam is shown this vision of the lazar-house's 'monstrous crew'—men deformed and diseased through gluttony—in order that 'thou mayst know/ What misery the inabstinence of Eve/ Shall bring on men' (475–7).

27. Rajan, *Paradise Lost and the Seventeenth-Century Reader* (London, 1947; reprt. Ann Arbor, Michigan, 1967), p. 76.

28. For a more detailed examination of Milton's position in *De Doctrina Christiana*, see Introduction, esp. pp. 4–5.

29. In *De Doctrina Christiana*, I, xiv Milton explains the reason for this veiled prophecy: 'For in pronouncing punishment upon the serpent, at a time when man had only grudgingly confessed his guilt, God promised that he would raise up from the seed of the woman a man who would bruise the serpent's head, Gen. iii. 15. This was before he got as far as passing sentence on the man. Thus he prefaced man's condemnation with a free redemption.' (*YP*, VI, p. 416) For the tradition treating Genesis 3: 15 as a messianic prophecy and its relevance to *Paradise Lost*, see John M. Steadman, 'Adam and the Prophesied Redeemer', *SP*, 56 (1959), 214–25; and C. A. Patrides, 'The "Protevangelium" in Renaissance Theology and *Paradise Lost*', *SEL*, 3 (1963), 19–30.

30. Svendsen, 'Adam's Soliloquy in Book X of *Paradise Lost*' (1949), in *Milton: Modern Essays in Criticism*, ed. Arthur E. Barker (New York, 1965), p. 329.

31. Ibid.

32. Addison, *The Spectator*, no. 369; Lewis, *A Preface to Paradise Lost* (Oxford,

1942; reprt. New York, 1961), p. 125.

33. Prince, 'On the Last Two Books of *Paradise Lost*' *Essays and Studies*, n.s., 11 (1958), 38–52; Summers, *The Muse's Method* (London, 1962; reprt. 1970), pp. 186–224; Sasek, 'The Drama of *Paradise Lost*, Books XI and XII' (1962), in *Milton: Modern Essays*, ed. Barker, pp. 342–56; MacCallum, 'Milton and Sacred History: Books XI and XII of *Paradise Lost*', in Woodhouse *Festschrift* (above, n 7), pp. 149–68.

34. MacCallum, 'Milton and Sacred History', pp. 159–60.

35. Giles Fletcher, *Christs Victorie, and Triumph* (1610), Pt. ii, St. 7, in *The Poetical Works of Giles Fletcher and Phineas Fletcher*, ed. F. S. Boas, 2 vols (Cambridge, 1908), I, p. 59.

36. The theme of the 'one just man alive' serves, of course, as a *leitmotiv* through the last two books of *Paradise Lost*, but it is nowhere as fully developed as in the case of Noah. Although implied in the cases of Abel, Enoch, Moses, Joshua and David, it is made explicit only in connection with Abraham (XII, 113) and Noah (XI, 719–26, 808–18, 874–8, and 890).

37. MacCallum, 'Milton and Sacred History', p. 155.

38. Similar figural triads—each involving a figure in Graeco-Roman mythology, a type under the Old Dispensation, and the antitype in the New Dispensation—occur relatively frequently in Milton's later poetry. See, for example, the Proserpine-Eve-Mary triad in *Paradise Lost* (IV, 268–72 and V, 386–7). Often these figures are of great structural importance, as in the case of *Sonnet 23*: cf. my paper '"Alcestis from the Grave": Image and Structure in *Sonnet XXIII*' in *Milton Studies*, 10 (1977), pp. 127–39. Undoubtedly the most complex example is the Hercules-Samson-Christ figure in *Samson Agonistes* where the triad is implicit but never explicitly set out and where the allusive triptych is mirrored in the play's structure—a Greek form, a Hebrew hero and story, and a Christian theme.

39. The phrase used here to describe Noah had earlier been applied to Christ: 'all men . . . in thee/ As from a second root shall be restored' (III, 287–8). Deucalion is likewise linked with global restoration in the phrase 'to restore/ The race of mankind drowned' (XI, 12–13).

TO CHAPTER 5

1. There is little in the pre-Miltonic literary treatments of the story to support or parallel the spiritual and psychological complexity of Milton's Samson. In Judges 13–16 he is presented as no more than a boisterous Israelite *shôphet* of vast and primitive energy. Although Josephus attempted to ennoble this Hebrew ruffian to make him more acceptable to Roman readers, the Samson of the *Jewish Antiquities* (V, viii) is still a hero of strength, a hero of action. In the medieval analogues of Chaucer, Lydgate and Gower, and also in the anonymous fourteenth-century *Cursor Mundi*, he continues to be remarkable for his strength of body rather than his strength of mind. Indeed, it is not until one comes, in the Renaissance, to Marcus Andreas Wunstius's *Simson, Tragœdia Sacra* and Joost van den Vondel's dramatisation of the subject in *Samson, of Heilige Wraeck, Treurspel* that one

finds a conscious attempt to depict the spiritual growth of the protagonist; yet neither Wunstius nor Vondel can be said to explore in any depth the dramatic potential inherent in Samson's inner development. [For information on the literary analogues to *Samson Agonistes*, see Watson Kirkconnell, *That Invincible Samson* (Toronto, 1964) or my own rudimentary analysis in 'Sophistication of Samson: Milton's *Samson Agonistes* and the Literary Samson Tradition from Judges to 1670' (unpub. Master's thesis, Queen's University, Kingston, Canada, 1968).]

2. Barker, 'Structural and Doctrinal Pattern', p. 176.
3. Low, *The Blaze of Noon: A Reading of Samson Agonistes* (New York and London, 1974), pp. 107–3. An early—and still important—analysis of the poem in terms of Milton's doctrines of vocation and renovation is John M. Steadman's essay '"Faithful Champion": The Theological Basis of Milton's Hero of Faith', *Anglia*, 77 (1959), 12–28; reprt. in *Milton: Modern Essays*, ed. Barker, pp. 467–83.
4. Low, *The Blaze of Noon*, p. 99.
5. Woodhouse, 'Tragic Effect in *Samson Agonistes*', *UTQ*, 28 (1958–9), 208.
6. Stein, *Heroic Knowledge: An Interpretation of Paradise Regained and Samson Agonistes* (Minneapolis, 1957; London, 1965), p. 146.
7. Krouse, *Milton's Samson and the Christian Tradition* (Princeton, 1949), p. 127.
8. I am not concerned here with Dalila's motivation or characterisation, but only with Samson's response to her arguments. Dalila is, in her own right, a complex figure: her object in coming at all is difficult to determine and, as Anthony Low says, 'one is never quite sure just how much she is telling the truth, or where she is lying; how much she is the conscious temptress and how much the victim of her own passions' (*The Blaze of Noon*, p. 157). For a summary of recent critical attitudes to Dalila, see John B. Mason, 'Multiple Perspectives in *Samson Agonistes*: Critical Attitudes Toward Dalila', *Milton Studies*, 10 (1977), 23–33.
9. Samson's willingness to transgress ceremonial law because a higher authority demands it—a stance which Kierkegaard, in *Fear and Trembling*, designates 'the teleological suspension of the ethical'—may be compared with the case of Abraham. In a flagrant breach of God's law, Abraham is prepared to sacrifice his only son, Isaac, because God commands him to do so. Genesis 22: 1 explicitly refers to the divine command as a trial to 'tempt' Abraham, and the Lord personally commends him for his unquestioning obedience: 'for now I know that thou fearest God, seeing that thou hast not withheld thy son, thine only son from me' (Gen. 22: 12). The whole episode is, in Miltonic terms, a 'good temptation' to exercise and demonstrate Abraham's faith—and it is interesting to note that, according to the *Trinity MS*, Milton had once contemplated (at least momentarily) composing a drama on the Abraham and Isaac theme.
10. 'God does not consider everyone worthy of equal grace, and the cause of this is his supreme will. But he considers all worthy of sufficient grace, and the cause is his justice' (*DCC*, I, iv; *YP*, VI, p. 193). On Milton's use of the terms 'unequal grace' and 'sufficient grace', see above, pp. 14–15, where they are discussed in relation to the doctrine of vocation.
11. Allen, *The Harmonious Vision: Studies in Milton's Poetry* (Baltimore, 1954), pp. 85–7.

12. Wilkenfeld, 'Act and Emblem: The Conclusion of *Samson Agonistes*', *ELH*, 32 (1965), 165.
13. Summers, 'The Movements of the Drama', in *The Lyric and Dramatic Milton*, ed. J. H. Summers (New York, 1965), pp. 161–2.

TO CHAPTER 6

1. The depth of my indebtedness to Barbara Lewalski's *Milton's Brief Epic: The Genre, Meaning, and Art of Paradise Regained* (London and Providence, 1966) will become apparent as this chapter progresses.
2. I am concerned primarily with the Son's *vocatio specialis* as Messiah; however, the Son's 'general vocation' and his renovation are also important themes in the poem: 'What illuminates the significance of the ministry is [the Son's] developing response to the call as it comes to him from his meditation on the recorded experience of his own people; and each of the poem's four books will be found to centre on and conclude with some significant aspect of the process of natural and supernatural renovation as *De Doctrina* attempts to define these.' (Barker, 'Structural and Doctrinal Pattern', p. 181)
3. Stein, *Heroic Knowledge*, p. 91.
4. Frye, 'The Typology of *Paradise Regained*' (1956), in *Milton's Epic Poetry: Essays on Paradise Lost and Paradise Regained*, ed. C. A. Patrides (Harmondsworth, 1967), pp. 314–15.
5. In fact, however, as Michael Fixler has shown, Satan's banquet is knowingly designed to tempt Christ into violating Jewish dietary law: see Fixler, 'The Unclean Meats of the Mosaic Law and the Banquet Scene in *Paradise Regained*', *MLN*, 70 (1955), 573–7.
6. Milton discusses the 'triple function of [Christ's] mediatorial office'—his roles as prophet, priest, and king—in *DDC*, I, xv: cf. *YP*, VI, pp. 432–5.

TO APPENDIX

1. *Early Lives*, ed. Darbishire, p. 275.
2. Gilbert, 'Is *Samson Agonistes* Unfinished?', *PQ*, 28 (1949), 106. Gilbert speculates that, in 1671, Milton's publisher may have asked the poet to supply him with something to flesh out the *Paradise Regained* volume and that Milton 'thought of his old tragedy, had it found, and turned it over to the bookseller. I incline to think that he did no further work on it...' (ibid.).
3. Parker has written the following: (1) 'The Date of *Samson Agonistes*', *PQ*, 28 (1949), 145–66; (2) 'The Date of "Samson Agonistes": A Postscript', *Notes & Queries*, 203 (1958), 201–2; (3) *MB*, I, 313–22 *passim*, and II, 903–17; and (4) 'The Date of *Samson Agonistes* Again', in *Calm of Mind: Tercentenary Essays on Paradise Regained and Samson Agonistes*, ed. J. A. Wittreich, Jr (Cleveland and London, 1971), pp. 163–74. Parker's position is endorsed by J. T. Shawcross (below, n 7) and by John Carey (*PM*, pp. 330–2) who prints *Samson Agonistes*—dated '1647–53?'—before *Paradise Lost*.

4. The traditional date is maintained by the following: (1) Ants Oras (below, n 7); (2) Ernest Sirluck, 'Milton's Idle Right Hand', *JEGP*, 60 (1961), 749–85—for *SA*, see pp. 773–81; George M. Muldrow, *Milton and the Drama of the Soul* (The Hague and Paris, 1970), pp. 240–62; and (4) Low, *The Blaze of Noon* (1974), pp. 223–9.

5. Woodhouse, '*Samson Agonistes* and Milton's Experience', *Transactions of the Royal Society of Canada*, 3rd ser., 13 (1949), 170–1. Before Woodhouse, the 1660–1 dating had been suggested by William Hayley, *Life of Milton* (1796), and by Charles Dunster (1809) and A. J. Church (1872) in their respective editions of *Samson Agonistes*.

6. *Early Lives*, ed. Darbishire, p. 75. The fact that Edward Phillips, who followed his uncle's career intimately, does not know when *Samson Agonistes* was written implies that it was composed at a time when Phillips was not in close contact with Milton. This information is not, however, very helpful; for, as Sirluck (above, n 4) points out, they were separated on a number of occasions: 'for example, Edward Phillips was living away from London in 1664–65 (also in 1650–51, and he may well have been away at other times). And of course Milton was in hiding in 1660, and in Chalfont in 1665.' (p. 778) Even Parker, who clings to the importance of an alleged separation in 1647–8, now grudgingly admits that 'There were, of course, later periods about which Phillips seems equally uninformed, and part or all of the composition of *Samson Agonistes* may belong to one of them' (*MB*, II, p. 906).

7. For a statistical analysis used to support the traditional dating of *Samson Agonistes*, see Ants Oras, 'Milton's Blank Verse and the Chronology of His Major Poems', in *SAMLA Studies in Milton*, ed. J. Max Patrick (Gainesville, Fla., 1953), pp. 128–97; see also Oras's book *Blank Verse and Chronology in Milton* (Gainesville, 1966). Oras's findings are disputed by John T. Shawcross, who uses statistical analysis to support Parker's dating of *Samson Agonistes*: cf. Shawcross, 'The Chronology of Milton's Major Poems', *PMLA*, 76 (1961), 345–58.

8. Parker (*MB*, II pp. 911–17) offers a long list, in parallel columns, of the 'surprising number of words and phrases' shared by *Samson Agonistes* and the prose works of 1641–9. But this critical procedure is a double-edged sword—as may be seen, for example, by comparing the imagery of Samson's initial soliloquy—

>   I seek
> This unfrequented place to find some ease,
> Ease to the body some, none to the mind,
> From restless thoughts, that like a deadly swarm
> Of hornets armed, no sooner found alone,
> But rush upon me thronging, and present
> Times past, what once I was, and what am now—
> (16–22)

with Christ's opening soliloquy in *Paradise Regained*:

> O what a multitude of thoughts at once
> Awkened in me swarm, while I consider

> What from within I feel myself, and hear
> What from without comes often to my ears,
> Ill sorting with my present state compared.
> (I, 196–200)

9. Cf. *MB*, II, p. 904.
10. Hanford, *John Milton, Englishman* (New York, 1949), p. 213. See also Hanford's seminal paper '*Samson Agonistes* and Milton in Old Age', in *Studies in Shakespeare, Milton and Donne* (New York, 1925), pp. 167–89.
11. Low, *The Blaze of Noon*, pp. 38–9.
12. *Early Lives*, ed. Darbishire, p. 74.
13. Woodhouse, '*Samson Agonistes* and Milton's Experience', 159–60.

Index

An asterisk indicates that the author or work is quoted. Footnotes which merely supply bibliographical information for works cited in the text are normally not included in the Index.

Addison, Joseph, 147*

Albright, W. F., 85–6*

Allen, D. C., 170, 213 (n 11)*, 214 (n 18)

Ames, William, 19*

Andrewes, Lancelot, 89*

appetite (images of), 132–9

Ariosto, Ludovico, 38, 69

Aristotle, 103

Arminius, Jacobus, 9–13*, 14, 206–7 (nn 15–21)*, 207 (nn 23, 26)*

Ash, Simeon, 90

Aubrey, John, 51–2*, 59, 196, 213 (n 14)*, 219 (n 1), 220 (n 5)

Augustine (Bp of Hippo), 7, 8, 12, 14

Aylmer, John, 217 (n 34)*

Ayre, John, 211 (n 29), 216 (n 17)

Bagnall, W. R., 206 (n 21)

Baillie, Robert, 97

Bangs, Carl, 10*, 206 (nn 15–20)*, 207 (n 26)*

Barker, Arthur E., 41*, 77, 101*, 102*, 119*, 121*, 127*, 151*, 218 (n 48)*, 220–1 (nn 7–9), 221–2 (n 14)*, 222 (n 24)*, 223 (n 30), 224 (n 33), 225 (nn 2–3), 226 (n 2)*

Bastwick, John, 211 (nn 25, 30)

Bede, the Venerable, 71

Benlowes, Edward, 218 (n 45)

Beveridge, Henry, 206 (n 12), 208 (n 37)

Beza, Theodore, 8*, 9, 10

Bible (Authorised Version)

OLD TESTAMENT: Genesis, 82, 223 (n 29), 225 (n 9)*; Exodus, 1*, 82*, 214 (n 24)*; Judges, 91, 153*, 224 (n 1); Psalms, 82*, 88, 89, 98–9*; Isaiah, 60*, 61, 75, 77, 83–4*, 85*, 108, 118; Jeremiah, 77, 79–80*, 85, 101*, 105, 106, 107*, 108; Hosea, 83; Amos, 83, 84*, 118; Micah, 84,

85; Zephaniah, 85*; Zechariah, 87*, 217 (n 33)

NEW TESTAMENT: Matthew, 2*, 36 (n), 58, 177*, 205 (n 9)*; Luke, 174*; John, 3, 144*; Acts, 3, 215 (n 7); Romans, 3, 5*, 7, 9, 10, 13, 97*, 205 (n 3), 207 (n 28), 215 (n 7)*; 1 Corinthians, 19*, 22*, 123, 131*, 205 (n 3); Ephesians, 7, 205 (n 3); Philippians, 205 (n 3); 1 Thessalonians, 18*; 2 Timothy, 2*, 205 (n 3); Hebrews, 205 (n 3); 1 Peter, 18*, 215 (n 7)*; 2 Peter; 205 (n 3)

Bible (Geneva), 87*

Blake, William, 126

Boas, F. S., 224 (n 35)

Boccaccio, Giovanni, 25–6*

Brennecke, E., Jr, 212 (n 1)

Breward, Ian, 208 (nn 39, 42)

Browne, Thomas, 129*

Bruce, John, 216 (n 10)

Bucer, Martin, 106, 107

Buchanan, George, 54

Bullock, F. W. B., 28*, 209 (n 5)*

Bunyan, John, 63

Burges, Cornelius, 89*

Burroughs, Jeremiah, 90*

Burton, Henry, 211* (nn 25, 30)

Bush, Douglas, 205 (n 5)*, 209 (n 1), 210 (n 13), 213 (n 5)*, 214 (n 22)*

Byrd, William, 51

Calamy, Edmund, 90, 91–3*, 94, 105*

Calvin, John, 8*, 14, 19*, 95, 206 (n 14), 208 (n 39)

Carey, John, 196*, 213 (n 5), 226 (n 3)

Carlyle, Thomas, 20

Castiglione, Baldassare, 136*

Charles I (King of England), 46–7, 99

Charles II (King of England), 101, 197, 198, 199
Chaucer, Geoffrey, 224 (n 1)
Chrysostom, John, 39
Church, A. J., 227 (n 5)
Cicero, 100
Coburn, K., 214 (n 16)
Cohn, Norman, 215–16 (n 9)*
Coleridge, Samuel Taylor, 61, 214 (n 16)*
Cromwell, Oliver, 100–1, 116
Cudworth, Ralph, 221 (n 11)*
Cursor Mundi, 224 (n 1)

Daiches, David, 219 (n 50)*
Dante, 38
Darbishire, Helen, 212 (n 32), 212 (n 2), 213 (n 14), 214 (n 25), 219 (n 1), 226 (n 1), 227 (n 6), 228 (n 12)
Diekhoff, J. S., 209 (n 1)
Diodati, Charles, 45, 56, 58, 65, 212 (n 33)
Diodati, Giovanni, 45, 212 (n 33)
Donne, John, 28, 30
Du Bartas, Guillaume, 54
Dunster, Charles, 227 (n 5)
Durye, John, 90

Edward VI (King of England), 88*
Elizabeth I (Queen of England), 86–7, 88
Ellwood, Thomas, 218 (n 45)*, 220 (n 5)
Essex, Robert Devereux, second earl of, 93
Euripides, 68
Eusebius, 38

Fink, Z. S., 213 (n 13)
Fish, Stanley, 121–2*, 222 (n 16)
'fit audience, though few', 118, 219–20 (n 4)
Fixler, Michael, 77, 226 (n 5)
Fletcher, Giles, 28, 149*
Fletcher, H. F., 27*, 30–1*, 209 (n 7)*, 210 (nn 11–12), 214 (n 26)
Fletcher, Phineas, 28
foreknowledge (doctrine of), 5–7, 9, 11, 123–4
Forrest, J. F., 214 (n 24)
Fowler, Alastair, 131
Fox, George, 218 (n 45)
Fox, R. C., 214 (n 24)
Foxe, John, 88*
free will: Arminius on, 10–11; in Calvinist doctrine, 9; Milton on, 5–7, 12–13, 120–5, 126–50 *passim,* 151–2, 168–9, 172
Frye, Northrop, 180*

Gardner, Helen, 110*, 218–19 (n 49)*
Giamatti, A. B., 210 (n 14)
Gilbert, A. H., 195*, 226 (n 2)*
Gildas, 71
Gill, Alexander, 31
glorification (doctrine of), 18–19
Golding, Arthur, 8
Gomarus, Franciscus, 11
'good temptations', 124, 128, 130, 153, 159, 225 (n 9)
Goodwin, Thomas, 90, 105*
Gower, John, 224 (n 1)
Green, V. H. H., 211–12 (n 31)*
Greville, Robert, 205 (n 5)*

Hall, Joseph, 94
Haller, William, 27, 32–3*, 87*, 209 (n 1), 211 (n 28)
Hanford, J. H., 37*, 53*, 198*, 211 (nn 22, 24), 228 (n 10)
Harkness, Georgia, 208 (n 39)
Hartlib, Samuel, 208 (n 45)
Haug, R. A., 215 (n 3)*
Hayley, William, 227 (n 5)
Heaton, E. W., 102*, 215 (n 6)
Henderson, Philip, 218 (n 45)
Heppe, Heinrich, 18*, 205 (nn 4, 6), 207 (nn 28, 30)*
Herbert, George, 28, 30, 38
Herrick, Robert, 30, 218 (n 45)
Hesiod, 54
Hill, John S., 215 (n 5), 224 (n 38), 225 (n 1)
Hobbes, Thomas, 104*
Hoby, Thomas, 222 (n 23)
Holinshed, Raphael, 71
Homer, 54, 68
Honigmann, E. A. J., 34, 210 (n 14)
Honywood, Michael, 210 (n 12)
Horwood, A. J., 213 (n 4)
Hughes, Philip E., 207 (n 28)
Huntley, J. F., 218 (n 47)
Hutchinson, John, 99
Hutchinson, Julius, 217 (n 34)
Hutchinson, Lucy, 217 (n 34)*

James I (King of England), 89
Johnson, Samuel, 151
Jonson, Ben, 218 (n 43)
Josephus, Flavius, 224 (n 1)
justification (doctrine of), 16–18, 20, 24, 25, 124, 143, 207 (nn 29–30)

Keats, John, 65*
Kelley, Maurice, 220 (n 6)

Kenyon, J. P., 209 (n 3), 212 (n 34)
Kermode, Frank, 219 (n 50)
Kerrigan, William, 77*, 102*, 112*, 217–18 (nn 40–1)
Kierkegaard, Søren, 225 (n 9)
King, Edward, 38, 41, 67
Kirkconnell, Watson, 225 (n 1)
Knappen, M. M., 208 (n 38)
Kranidas, Thomas, 222 (n 17)
Krouse, F. Michael, 163*

Latimer, Hugh, 88*
Laud, William, 39, 45, 46–7, 48, 49, 72, 211 (n 25)
Laumonier, Paul, 219 (n 52)
Lawes, Henry, 51, 64–5*
Le Comte, E. S., 211 (n 29)
Leiden *Synopsis*, 3*, 14
Lewalski, Barbara, 126*, 222 (n 20)*, 226 (n 1)
Lewis, C. S., 147*
Lieb, M., 218 (n 47)
Lilburne, John, 211 (n 25)
Liljegren, S. B., 212 (n 35)*
Low, Anthony, 151–2*, 153*, 198*, 225 (n 8)*, 227 (n 4)
Loyola, Ignatius, 211 (n 29)
Luther, Martin, 17, 20, 21, 95, 207 (n 29), 216 (n 11), 217 (n 34)
Lydgate, John, 224 (n 1)

MacCallum, H. R., 147*, 149, 209 (n 1)
MacLure, M., 220 (n 7)
Malmesbury, William of, 71
Manso, Giovanni Battista, 44–5*; *see also Mansus, under* Milton: Poetical Works
Maresius, Samuel, 2*
Marshall, Stephen, 90, 105*
Mason, John B., 225 (n 8)
Masson, David, 197–9*, 203, 210 (nn 11–13)
merit (doctrine of), 17, 131–2, 140
Milton, John (poet's father), 51, 212 (nn 1, 3)
Milton, John:
  POETICAL WORKS: *Ad Patrem*, 31*, 51, 54, 64; *Apologus De Rustico et Hero*, 213 (n 4); *Arcades*; 51, 66*; 'Arthuriad' 71–2; *At a Solemn Music*, 63–4*, 65, 74; *Carmina Elegiaca*, 213 (n 4); *Comus*, 42, 51, 57, 64–5, 66, 67, 72, 214 (n 21); *Elegy 5*, 33, 54, 55–6*, 59, 104, 213 (n 11); *Elegy 6*, 30, 31, 33, 35, 44, 49, 54–9*, 74, 76, 104, 201, 213 (n 12)*; *Epitaphium*

Damonis, 70–2*; *Ignavus Satrapum*, 213 (n 4); *Il Penseroso*, 62–3*, 66, 73, 104; Italian sonnets, 54, 210 (n 14); *Lycidas*, 28, 39–42*, 49, 64, 66–8*, 72, 81, 104, 109, 199, 214 (nn 21–4); *Mansus*, 71*; *Nativity Ode*, 33, 34, 44, 56, 58–62*, 65, 75, 81, 102, 104, 199, 201, 213 (n 12); *On the Death of a Fair Infant*, 52, 54, 213 (n 5); *On the New Forcers of Conscience*, 97*; *On Shakespeare*, 61*, 67, 72; *Paradise Lost*, 3–4*, 6–7*, 12–13*, 16, 17*, 43*, 55*, 58*, 60*, 61, 72, 73, 78, 81–2, 108–12* (Invocations), 115–50*, 155, 156–7, 169*, 175, 188*, 196–7, 198, 201–2, 206 (n 11)*, 207–8 (n 31)*, 223 (nn 25–6)*, 224 (nn 36, 38–9), 226 (n 3); *Paradise Regained*, 16, 103, 108, 112–13*, 122, 125, 175–93*, 195, 198, 201, 202, 203, 220 (n 6), 227–8 (n 8)*; *Philosophus ad regem*, 213 (n 4); Psalm paraphrases and translations, 52, 54, 64, 98–9*, 212 (n 3); *Samson Agonistes*, 15*, 16, 23, 72, 81, 151–74*, 178–9, 220 (n 6), 224 (n 38), 227 (n 8)* — date of, 81, 82, 195–203*; *Sonnet 7*, 33, 34–6*, 38, 44, 49, 63, 66, 81, 199; *Sonnet 16*, 100*; *Sonnet 19*, 26*, 107, 199; *Sonnet 23*, 81, 199, 215 (n 5), 224 (n 38); *Vacation Exercise*, 27, 52–5*, 56, 59, 65, 104, 115, 199
  PROSE WORKS: *Animadversions upon the Remonstrant's Defence*, 74*, 93*, 212 (n 36)*; *Apology for Smectymnuus*, 32*, 57–8*, 93–4*, 209 (n 5)*; *Areopagitica*, 94–5*, 96*, 97–8*, 99, 118*, 200, 206 (n 11)*, 220 (n 4)*, 221 (n 10)*; *Character of the Long Parliament*, 98; *Commonplace Book*, 25*, 38, 71, 211 (n 23); *De Doctrina Christiana*, 2–19*, 49, 118–20*, 124*, 129, 140, 142*, 145*, 151–2, 153*, 155*, 156, 157*, 161*, 169*, 201, 205–6 (nn 8–10)*, 207 (nn 22–3)*, 207 (n 31), 220 (nn 5–6), 223 (nn 28–9)*, 225 (n 10)*, 226 (n 6); *Defensio Secunda*, 45–6*, 99–100*, 107–8*, 219 (n 1); *Doctrine and Discipline of Divorce*, 95*, 96, 97*, 106*, 220 (n 4)*; *Eikonoklastes*, 99*, 118*, 220 (no 4)*; 'Index Theologicus', 38, 211 (n 23); *Judgement of Martin Bucer*, 96,

Milton: Prose Works *(contd.)*
106–7*; Letter to Alexander Gill, 31–2*; 'Letter to a Friend', 34, 36–8*, 49; *Likeliest Means to Remove Hirelings*, 49, 218 (n 48); *Of Education*, 208–9 (n 45)*, 209 (n 5); *Of Reformation*, 73–4*, 78, 217 (n 34)*; *A Postscript*, 48, 73; *Prolusion 1*, 219 (n 4); *Prolusion 3*, 32; *Prolusion 6*, 24, 52*, 213 (n 6)*; *Prolusion 7*, 30, 31, 35, 58*, 75, 213 (n 13)*; *Pro Populo Anglicano Defensio*, 99*, 209 (n 45), 218 (n 48); *Pro Se Defensio*, 218 (n 48), 219 (n 1); *Readie and Easie Way*, 80*, 118*; *Reason of Church-Government*, 25*, 29–30*, 31, 39, 48*, 58*, 60*, 68–70*, 74–5*, 79–80*, 94*, 102, 105–6*, 110, 115–16*, 212 (n 35); *Trinity Manuscript*, 72*, 195, 225 (n 9)
Mohl, Ruth, 211 (n 22)
Morley, Henry, 218 (n 45)
Muldrow, George M., 220 (n 6), 227 (n 4)

Newton, Thomas, 197
Nichols, James, 206 (n 21)
Nuttall, Geoffrey, 219 (n 51)

Oras, Ants, 227 (nn 4, 7)
Origen, 102
Osgood, C. G., 208 (n 44)
Ovid, 28, 149*

Parker, Matthew, 86*
Parker, W. R., 38*, 39*, 195, 196*, 201*, 202, 210 (nn 12, 17, 18, 22)*, 211 (nn 23–4), 212 (n 32)*, 213 (nn 4–5), 214 (n 19)*, 226 (n 3), 227 (nn 6–8)*
Patrick, J. Max, 227 (n 7)
Patrides, C. A., 221 (n 11), 223 (n 29), 226 (n 4)
Pelagianism, 7, 9, 10, 14
Perkins, William, 9, 10, 20, 21–5*, 208 (nn 42–3)*
Perowne, T. T., 216 (n 10)
Philaras, Leonard, 26
Phillips, Anne, 213 (n 5)
Phillips, Edward, 46, 72, 73, 196*, 199*, 202, 214 (n 25)*, 227 (n 6)
Phillips, John, 46, 73, 196
Plato, 60, 66, 68, 103, 135
poet: and divinely-implanted talent, 58–61, 103, 110; and inspiration, 54, 55–6, 59–61, 102–13, 115–16; and morality, 57–8, 115; Milton's exalted view of, 54–5, 57–8, 64, 65–6, 74–6, 115–16

Powell, Mary, 96
predestination (doctrine of), 7–13, 206 (nn 14, 19), 207 (nn 22–3)
Prince, F. T., 147
Prynne, William, 211 (nn 25, 30)
Pym, John, 47, 93, 211 (n 31)

Rajan, B., 62*, 139*, 221 (n 8)
Rasmussen, Carl C., 208 (n 40)
remnant (doctrine of), 84–5, 97, 100, 118, 215 (n 6)
Revard, S.P., 222 (n 15)
Richardson, Jonathan, 195*
Riissenius, Leonardus, 2*
Rinehart, K., 67
Roberts, D. A., 217 (n 37)
Robinson, H. W., 217 (n 39)
Ronsard, Pierre de, 111*
Ross, Malcolm, 211 (n 28)
Salmasius, 70, 107
sanctification (doctrine of), 17–18, 20–1, 24, 25
Sandy, William, 217 (n 39)
Sandys, Edwin, 18*, 88*, 211 (n 29)
Sasek, L., 147
Schaff, Philip, 207 (n 21)
Sedgwick, William, 90
Shakespeare, William, 20*, 61, 128*, 136*, 163*; *see also On Shakespeare, under* Milton: Poetical Works
Shaw, J. E., 210 (n 14)
Shawcross, John T., 27, 40*, 218 (n 47), 226 (n 3), 227 (n 7)
Sidney, Philip, 54, 103*, 104
Sirluck, Ernest, 97*, 210 (nn 13, 17, 19), 227 (nn 4, 6)*
Skelton, John, 104*, 218 (n 45)
Smectymnuus, 48, 90–1, 93, 96, 104–5; *see also Apology for Smectymnuus under* Milton: Prose Works
Smith, G. G., 218 (n 43)
Socrates Scholasticus, 38
solifidianism, *see* justification (doctrine of)
Sophocles, 79
Spenser, Edmund, 54
Spingarn, J. E., 218 (nn 43–4)
Steadman, John M., 213 (n 13), 223 (n 29), 225 (n 3)
Steele, Richard, 19*
Stein, Arnold, 158, 179*
St John, Oliver, 211 (n 31)
Stow, John, 71
Strafford, Thomas Wentworth, earl of, 46, 47
Strickland, John, 90